The Catholic
Theological Union
LIBRARY
Chicago, Ill.

WITHDRAWN

D1590976

9/28/74

The Church
Theological Library
Perkins
Crawdon

# THE ANGLICAN ORDINAL

ALCUIN CLUB COLLECTIONS
No. 53

# The Anglican Ordinal

## ITS HISTORY AND DEVELOPMENT FROM THE REFORMATION TO THE PRESENT DAY

Paul F. Bradshaw

Published for the Alcuin Club

The Catholic
Theological Union
LIBRARY
Chicago, Ill.

LONDON
S · P · C · K
1971

*First published in 1971*
*by S.P.C.K.*
*Holy Trinity Church*
*Marylebone Road*
*London NW1 4DU*

*Printed in Great Britain by*
*William Clowes & Sons, Limited*
*London, Beccles and Colchester*

© Paul F. Bradshaw, 1971

The Catholic
Theological Union
LIBRARY
Chicago, Ill.

SBN 281 02653 X

TO
RONALD C. D. JASPER

The Catholic
Theological Union
LIBRARY
Chicago, Ill.

# Contents

Quotations from *The Plan of Church Union in North India and Pakistan* are used by permission of the Christian Literature Society of Madras.

# Preface

Some apology might seem to be needed for adding yet another book to the already lengthy list of publications on the Anglican Ordinal and Anglican Orders, for there can be few subjects which have had as much written about them as this. Yet in spite of all that has already been written, it does not seem difficult to justify this study.

Firstly, almost all other works on this subject have been of a polemical nature. Anglicans have generally been concerned to stress the continuity between the medieval rites and their own Ordinal, and to deny that any changes in doctrine were intended by the changes in liturgy. Roman Catholics, on the other hand, have sought to show that the Anglican Ordinal was defective in form, matter, or intention, and they have emphasized the similarities between it and the ordination rites of the reformed Churches. Thus there has been so far no really objective historical survey of the Ordinal, all other authors being from the outset committed to a particular attitude. This present study, although by an Anglican, is not an attempt to defend the validity of Anglican Orders. It is concerned solely to describe the various rites used and proposed for use in the Anglican Communion the reasons for, and the sources of, the changes made in them, and the objections which have been raised to them. The question of the validity of these rites, as will be seen, depends upon the principles upon which they are judged, and since various criteria can be adopted, various answers are possible.

Secondly, the strange fact about the majority of previous studies of the Ordinal is that they have entirely neglected to take into account the beliefs of the man chiefly responsible for its original composition and the effects of those beliefs upon the rites he produced. There is very strong evidence that Thomas Cranmer, Archbishop of Canterbury, was the real author of the Ordinal, and yet more often than not the text has been studied in isolation from his own understanding of ordination. Even where Cranmer's influence has been considered there has been only a superficial judgement of his doctrine based on one or two of his writings. The complexities, and sometimes apparent contradictions, of his theology of Order warrant a more careful study than they have so far received and all his statements on the subject need to be considered.

Thirdly, in spite of the numerous publications on the Ordinal, only those aspects which affect the question of Anglican Orders have received detailed treatment. Hardly anything has been written on the many alternatives proposed, nor has there been a comprehensive study of the ordination rites and of the methods of uniting Anglican and non-episcopal ministries proposed in the various schemes of reunion. Although not part of the history of the Anglican Ordinal in its narrow sense, the Ordinals and rites of unification in reunion schemes have in many cases been closely derived from the Anglican Ordinal. Moreover, since the ordination rites are intended to be used by ex-Anglicans in the united Churches and since many have interpreted the rites of unification as the equivalent of ordination, or rejected them as failing to fulfil the requirements of ordination, they seem to deserve a place in the history of Anglican rites of ordination.

On the other hand, this study does not pretend to be a complete history of the Anglican Orders controversy, although such a history is badly needed. Apart from books which are themselves part of the controversy, only one historical study has so far appeared, and that is concerned exclusively with the events which led up to the papal condemnation of Anglican Orders in 1896.[1] There has been no critical and detailed account of all the aspects of the controversy and of the many important historical and theological problems raised by it. Unfortunately it lies outside the scope of this present work to attempt to cover this enormous subject, and it has been necessary to limit it to the liturgical aspects of the controversy. Similarly, it has not been possible to deal with the attitude of the Orthodox and Old Catholic Churches towards Anglican Orders, interesting though these are, but they have been omitted since they have not exercised a direct influence upon the history and development of the Anglican rites in the way that Roman Catholic criticism has. Nor does this study claim to be a definitive history of the doctrines of Ordination, Apostolic Succession, Episcopacy, or other related subjects in the Church of England. It is essentially a liturgical study and questions of doctrine have been included only in so far as they influenced liturgical proposals made concerning the Ordinal.

Finally, I would like to express my gratitude to the very many people who in different ways have assisted in the preparation of this

[1] John Jay Hughes, *Absolutely Null and Utterly Void* (1968).

book, especially to all those, too numerous to mention, who have offered helpful comments and suggestions and supplied valuable information. My thanks are particularly due to the Reverend Canon R. C. D. Jasper for his careful supervision of my work and his help in other ways, and to him this book is dedicated as a token of my gratitude. I would also like to thank the Reverend J. B. Chalklen for making available to me his unpublished thesis "The Political Thought of Thomas Cranmer", Dr T. J. Fawcett for guiding me through the labyrinth of eighteenth-century liturgical publications, Dr E. C. John of the United Theological College, Bangalore, for supplying material from the College Archives, the Reverend D. McEwan for obtaining for me photocopies of the rare periodical *Le Canoniste Contemporain*, Dr A. M. Ward for the loan of papers of the Church of South India Synod Liturgy Committee, and the Reverend R. W. Wood for reading the first draft of this work and making many useful suggestions. I am indebted to the Trustees of Doctor Williams's Library for permission to quote from the manuscript, "The Seconde Parte of a Register", to the Cleaver Trust for financial assistance towards the expenses of research, to the Alcuin Club for publishing the results of my labours, and to the Reverend A. K. W. Wright for accepting me as his curate and allowing me so much time to complete this work. Last, but by no means least, I am grateful to Mrs M. H. Broadhurst and Mrs F. A. Street for undertaking the typing of the final draft of the book.

# Abbreviations

ACC   Alcuin Club Collections
CDCP  Council for the Defence of Church Principles
CHS   Church Historical Society
*CQR*   *Church Quarterly Review*
HBS   Henry Bradshaw Society
LACT  Library of Anglo-Catholic Theology
PS    Parker Society
*RAR*   *Revue Anglo-Romaine*. 3 vols. Paris 1895–96
*RB*    Matthew Sylvester, *Reliquiae Baxterianae* (1696), cited by book and
      paragraph.

Place of publication is not given for books published in the United Kingdom.
Where the place or date of publication is not stated in a book, this is indicated
by "n.p." and "n.d." respectively.

# 1. The Beginning of the Reformation

The New Testament provides very little evidence for the practice of ordination in the primitive Church. There were undoubtedly a variety of offices and functions of ministry in the first century, at least some of which were conferred by prayer and the imposition of hands, and it would appear that in some cases the candidates were selected by the people.[1] Beyond this, however, it is impossible to go. The oldest extant ordination rites date from the beginning of the third century and are contained in a document known as the *Apostolic Tradition*, believed to have been written by St Hippolytus at Rome. By this time the three orders of bishops, priests, and deacons had emerged as the universal ministry of the Church. A candidate for the episcopate was to be chosen and approved by the people, and then ordained on a Sunday. All the bishops present laid their hands on his head while the congregation prayed in silence for the descent of the Holy Spirit. One of the bishops then recited the ordination prayer while laying his hands on the candidate, and the rite ended with the new bishop receiving the kiss of peace and celebrating the Eucharist. The ordination of priests and deacons was very similar. Several other offices—widows, virgins, readers, subdeacons, and healers—are also mentioned, but appointment to these was without any ceremony, except for the office of reader which was conferred by the bishop handing to the candidate the book from which he would read.[2]

Because this document was originally written in Greek it had greater influence in the East than in the West, and most of the early Eastern ordination rites are directly or indirectly descended from it.[3] The later Western rites follow the same basic structure, but the prayers are entirely new compositions. They fall into two main groups, the Roman, and the non-Roman or Gallican. According to the former,

[1] Acts 6.2–6 and 13.1–3; 1 Tim. 4.14; 2 Tim. 1.6.

[2] *The Treatise on the Apostolic Tradition of St Hippolytus of Rome*, ed. Gregory Dix, revised H. Chadwick (1968), pp. 2–22.

[3] See W. H. Frere, "Early Forms of Ordination", in *Essays on the Early History of the Church and the Ministry*, ed. H. B. Swete (1918), pp. 263–312. For the later Eastern rites see W. K. Firminger, "The Ordinal", in *Liturgy and Worship*, ed. W. K. Lowther Clarke and Charles Harris (1932), pp. 636–41.

when a candidate had been elected to the episcopate by his province, he came to Rome where he was examined and approved by the Pope. The ordination itself took place on a Sunday after the Epistle in the Eucharist. The Pope called upon the congregation to pray for the candidate and then all prostrated themselves in silent prayer while the litany was sung. This contained a special suffrage for the candidate. At the end the Pope rose and recited a collect summing up the petitions of the people and then the ordination prayer itself, while laying his hands on the candidate. The rite ended with the kiss of peace and the Eucharist continued. The ordinations of priests and deacons were similar, except that they always took place in one of the four Ember weeks, at first the December one being preferred. The candidates, chosen by the Pope, were presented to the people at the Eucharist on the Wednesday and Friday in order to allow anyone to make objections to them, and then they were ordained on the Saturday at the Eucharist of the Vigil, celebrated originally at night but from the eighth century onwards in the afternoon. The candidates for the diaconate were presented to the Pope by the archdeacon after the Epistle. He then pronounced a bidding inviting the congregation to pray for them, the litany was sung, concluded by a collect, and the ordination prayer followed, accompanied by the imposition of hands. The rite ended with the kiss of peace. The candidates for the priesthood were then presented and ordained in exactly the same way. Later the ordination prayers in all three rites had the Salutation, *Sursum corda*, and a eucharistic preface added at the beginning. Five minor orders were also established in the West, but the Roman rites make no provision for any ceremony for appointment to three of these, exorcist, lector, and doorkeeper, and for the other two, acolyte and subdeacon, there is merely the *porrectio instrumentorum*, the symbolic ceremony of handing to the candidate some instrument representative of his function, as an authorization to exercise that function, following the practice of conferring office in civil life. The acolyte received a linen bag, the receptacle then used to carry the consecrated hosts, and the subdeacon an empty chalice. These orders could be conferred at any time of the year at the time of Communion in any Eucharist by the Pope, or by another bishop if he were not present. Later a simple blessing was added to the rites.[1]

---

[1] M. Andrieu, *Les Ordines Romani du Haut Moyen Age* III, pp. 601–13; IV, pp. 1–308 (Louvain 1951, 1956); H. B. Porter Jr, *The Ordination Prayers of the Ancient Western Churches*, ACC XLIX (1967), pp. 12–35.

The Gallican rites, though basically similar, differed in several ways from the Roman usage. Since the Ember seasons were unknown in countries where the Gallican rite was used, the rites for all three sacred orders began with a presentation of the candidate to the people by the bishop, to which the people replied, *Dignus est*. The ordination itself consisted simply of a bidding and an ordination prayer accompanied by the imposition of hands. In the rite for the priesthood this was followed by an anointing of the hands, and in the rite for the episcopate the imposition of hands was accompanied by two bishops holding the book of the Gospels over the head of the candidate. There was also a *porrectio instrumentorum* for all five minor orders accompanied by a solemn charge to the candidate and followed by a bidding and a solemn blessing.[1]

It will be clear that all ancient rites for the three sacred orders have three elements in common: the election of the candidates by the people, or at least opportunity to object to them; the prayer of the people, either in silence or in the shape of the litany; and the ordination prayer itself said while hands are laid upon the candidate. In addition, the rites all take place within the context of the Eucharist, in which the candidates fulfil the liturgical function of their new order. Apart from the Roman usage, where the Pope alone performed the imposition of hands for all the orders, it was the universal practice for the imposition of hands to be performed by all the bishops present in the case of the episcopate (three being regarded as a minimum); by the bishop together with the priests in the case of the priesthood, as a sign of their acceptance of their new colleague; and by the bishop alone in the case of the diaconate.

During the course of the Middle Ages in the Western Church the simple Roman and Gallican rites became fused into one composite rite, with the result that in the case of the minor orders the Gallican rite entirely superseded the meagre Roman one and in the case of the sacred orders the Gallican bidding and ordination prayer were added after the Roman ordination prayer. The rites also appear in the medieval Pontifical service-books in the reverse order to that of the early rites: the minor orders first, followed by the rites for the diaconate and priesthood, with the episcopate now coming last. Gradually they were enriched by many additional ceremonies, although the same additions do not occur in all the Pontificals and those which do occur in several

[1] Porter, pp. 36–57; L. Duchesne, *Christian Worship, its origin and evolution* (1903), pp. 363–75.

do not always occur in the same place. Table 1 shows the structure of the Sarum rites of ordination at their most fully developed stage. These are typical of the rites in the English Pontificals. Those portions drawn from the Gallican rite are in capital letters and all later additions are enclosed within brackets, leaving only the Roman rite.[1] The presentation and examination of a candidate for the episcopate has now become part of the rite itself instead of a preliminary to it, as has the final inquiry of the people concerning the candidates for the other orders. It will also be seen that in the ordination of deacons and priests the litany has become detached from the bidding and collect which originally began and ended it. This seems to have occurred because the bidding, litany, and collect were not regarded as a unity—the prayer of the people—but simply as three separate elements, and so the litany was transferred to the beginning of the rite for the diaconate in order that it need be said only once for both diaconate and priesthood. Moreover, in all three rites the imposition of hands has become detached from the ordination prayers. This seems to have happened because, owing to the large number of candidates for ordination as deacons or priests at any one time, it was impractical to repeat the prayers for each one. Thus an imposition of hands on each candidate in silence was introduced before the prayers were said collectively while hands were extended over them all. Although the problem of numerous candidates did not arise in the case of the episcopate, the alteration was also made here, presumably to bring it into line with the other rites. In the course of time it was felt desirable to enrich this silent imposition of hands with some formula similar to those accompanying other actions in the rites, and by the end of the medieval period many Pontificals included such formulas. Most adopted *Accipe Spiritum Sanctum* in the rite for the diaconate and the episcopate, although in England only the Exeter Pontifical had the latter: the other English Pontificals either had silence or the singing of the hymn *Veni Creator* at this point.[2] In the rite for the priesthood the imposition of hands

---

[1] For the full text of the rites see W. Maskell, *Monumenta Ritualia Ecclesiae Anglicanae* (2nd edn, 1882) II, pp. 164–297. For the sake of clarity in this table the first ordination prayer in the rite for the episcopate has been shown as Roman and the second as Gallican, whereas in fact the two are really one prayer, broken in the middle by the unction of the head. This prayer was the original Roman ordination prayer with the Gallican interpolated into the middle of it. The Gallican bidding has entirely disappeared from this rite, as it did also from the other two rites in the course of the Middle Ages, although it has been retained in this table in those rites in the position in which it is found in the earlier Pontificals. For the origin of the third ordination prayer in the rite for the episcopate see Porter, pp. 72ff.

[2] Maskell, II, p. 273.

Table 1: The Development of the Medieval Ordination Rites

| *Celebratio Ordinum* | *Consecratio Electi In Episcopum* |
|---|---|
| 1. Eucharist as far as collect | 1. (Presentation to consecrating bishop) |
| 2. Presentation of candidates (and Question as to suitability) | 2. (Examination and oath of canonical obedience) |
| 3. (Final inquiry of the people) | 3. Eucharist as far as Epistle |
| 4. ADMISSION TO MINOR ORDERS | 4. (Instruction in duties) |
| 5. Epistle of the day | 5. Bidding |
| 6. Litany with special suffrages | 6. Litany with special suffrages |
| 7. (Instructions of deacons in duties) | 7. Imposition of hands BY ALL BISHOPS WITH IMPOSITION OF GOSPEL BOOK (and hymn *Veni Creator*) |
| 8. Imposition of hands on deacons by bishop (with formula *Accipe Spiritum Sanctum*) | 8. Collect |
| 9. Bidding, Collect, and Ordination Prayer for deacons | 9. Ordination Prayer |
| 10. (Vesting with stole and delivery of Gospel book to deacons) | 10. (Unction of head) |
| 11. BIDDING AND ORDINATION PRAYER FOR DEACONS | 11. ORDINATION PRAYER |
| 12. (Vesting of deacons in dalmatics) | 12. (Ordination Prayer) |
| 13. Gospel of the day read by one of the deacons | 13. (Sevenfold blessing) |
| 14. (Instruction of priests in duties) | 14. (Unction of head and hands) |
| 15. Imposition of hands on priests by bishop AND PRIESTS in silence | 15. (Putting on of gloves) |
| 16. Bidding, Collect, and Ordination Prayer for priests | 16. (Delivery of pastoral staff) |
| 17. (Vesting of priests with stole and chasuble) | 17. (Delivery of ring) |
| 18. BIDDING AND ORDINATION PRAYER FOR PRIESTS | 18. (Delivery of mitre) |
| 19. (Hymn *Veni Creator*) | 19. (Delivery of Gospel Book) |
| 20. (Blessing and) UNCTION OF HANDS OF PRIESTS | 20. Eucharist continues |
| 21. (Delivery of paten and chalice to priests) | 21. (Final Collect) |
| 22. Eucharist continues | |
| 23. (Imposition of hands on priests with formula, *Accipe Spiritum Sanctum quorum peccata*, etc.) | |
| 24. (Kiss of peace, special blessing, Exhortation, Post-communion, etc.) | |

usually remained in silence and an additional imposition of hands after

6          THE ANGLICAN ORDINAL

usually remained in silence and an additional imposition of hands after the Eucharist, accompanied by the words, *Accipe Spiritum Sanctum, quorum peccata*, etc. (Christ's commission to the Apostles in John 20.22–3), appeared in many Pontificals, although a few, including the English Magdalen College Pontifical, inserted this formula at the first imposition of hands instead.[1] Finally, it must be noted that a *porrectio instrumentorum* has been added to the sacred orders as well as the minor orders.

The medieval theologians did not have the advantage of knowing the history of the Christian ministry or of the rites of ordination which they found in the Pontificals. They were therefore compelled to make their theological statements simply on abstract principles and on current usage. This inevitably produced considerable difference of opinion. They were unanimously agreed that Order was a sacrament and that, at least in the ordination to the sacred orders, grace was conferred. In normal practice only a bishop could confer the sacred orders, although it was not unknown for abbots, and even priests, to be given permission by the Pope to confer the minor orders. Some theologians thought that he could extend this permission to cover the sacred orders also, and instances of Popes actually doing this have been discovered.[2] There were various opinions as to how many different orders there were: seven was the most commonly accepted number, but some thought that there were eight, or even nine. These differing views were occasioned partly by some uncertainty as to whether the episcopate formed a separate order, distinct from the priesthood, or was simply a different degree in the same order, and partly by a doubt as to whether the giving of the tonsure was to be accounted as another order. There was also a considerable diversity of opinion as to what the essential "matter" and "form" of Order were.[3] Some believed that the matter and form for all the orders had been instituted by Christ himself, others that it had been left to the Church to determine the specific matter and form in each case. Thus Pope Innocent IV said that, if the Church had not instituted the different rites, it would have been

[1] *The Pontifical of Magdalen College*, ed. H. A. Wilson, HBS xxxix (1910), p. 66, n. 4; see also *Liturgy and Worship*, pp. 652–3.
[2] See H. Denzinger, *Enchiridion Symbolorum Definitionum et Declarationum de rebus fidei et morum*, 33rd edn (Barcinone 1965), nos. 1145, 1146, 1290, and 1435; L. N. Crumb, "Presbyteral Ordination and the See of Rome", *CQR* clxiv (1963), pp. 19–31.
[3] "Matter" and "form" were used by medieval theologians to describe the essential action and formula of words which constituted the rite of ordination and it is in this sense that they will be used throughout, except in quotations.

sufficient for the bishop to have said *Sis Sacerdos* or *Sis Episcopus* in each case. Some scholars thought that the matter and form were the imposition of hands and the accompanying formula, others that these were only part of the matter and form. Many believed that the matter and form for the sacred orders as well as for the minor orders were the *porrectio instrumentorum* and the imperative formula which accompanied this.[1] This theory was upheld by Pope Eugenius IV.[2] Others thought that the unctions were at least part of the matter.[3] William Tyndale, the English Reformer, well illustrates the confusion which existed: "Last of all, one singular doubt they have; what maketh the priest; the anointing, or putting on of the hands, or what other ceremony, or what words? About which they brawl and scold, one ready to tear out another's throat. One saith this, and another that; but they cannot agree."[4]

These ideas were all thrown into question by the Reformation. The continental reformers believed that the hierarchical structure of the ministry of the medieval Church was not warranted by the Scriptures and must therefore be replaced by the ministry which, they believed, was clearly prescribed in the New Testament. They substituted a ministry of the word for the sacrificial priesthood, and attempted to restore to the diaconate what they regarded as its scriptural function, the care of the needy. They insisted on a stringent examination of the candidates, publicly in the ordination services, to attempt to ensure that they were truly called by God and to prevent unsuitable men from being ordained, as they had so often been in the medieval Church. They rejected the idea that ordination conferred grace, although a few of them were prepared to retain the name sacrament for it as it was a rite instituted by Christ, and they replaced the complex ceremonies of the Pontificals by simple rites of ordination, which usually consisted of the examination of the candidates and an imposition of hands accompanied by prayer for the Holy Spirit, and sometimes by the Lord's Prayer also.[5]

---

[1] Thomas Aquinas, *Summa Theologica*, Pt. III (Supplement), questions xxxiv–xxxviii; Maskell, II, pp. lxxxviii–xcviii; E. C. Messenger, *The Reformation, The Mass and the Priesthood* (1936–37) I, pp. 73–94.

[2] In the Bull *Exultate Deo*; see Denzinger, no. 1326.

[3] That this theory was still current in the sixteenth century is shown by *Encheridion Christianae Institutionis* (Cologne 1537), fol. cxcviii.

[4] *Doctrinal Treatises and Introductions to Different Portions of the Holy Scriptures by William Tyndale*, ed. Henry Walter (PS, 1848), p. 258.

[5] See, for example, *Luther's Works* LIII (Philadelphia 1965), pp. 122–6, and the ordination rite of Bugenhagen in *Documents Illustrative of the Continental Reformation*, ed. B. J.

The first signs of the influence of the ideas of the continental reformers at an official level in England appear in *The Institution of a Christian Man*, or *The Bishops' Book* as it was popularly called, published in 1537.[1] This work continued to teach that Order was a sacrament:

> The sacrament of orders may worthily be called a sacrament, because it is a holy rite or ceremony instituted by Christ and his apostles in the New Testament, and doth consist of two parts, like as the other sacraments of the church do, that is to say, of a spiritual and an invisible grace, and also of an outward and a visible sign. The invisible gift or grace conferred in this sacrament is nothing else but the power, the office, and the authority before mentioned.

It rejected, however, the medieval theories concerning the matter and form, and turned to the evidence of the New Testament: "The visible and outward sign is the prayer and imposition of the bishop's hands upon the person which receiveth the said gift or grace." All other ceremonies were devised by the early Church, for in the New Testament there was not "any word spoken of any other ceremony used in the conferring of this sacrament; but only of prayer, and the imposition of the bishop's hands". It also rejected the idea that there were of necessity seven or more orders. The institution of the minor orders by the early Church had no foundation in the New Testament where "there is no mention made of any degrees or distinctions in orders but only of deacons or ministers, and of priests or bishops".[2] It retained, however, the same powers and functions of the clergy as the Pontificals had assigned to them. They were

> to preach and teach the word of God unto his people; to dispense and administer the sacraments of God unto them, and by the same to confer and give the graces of the Holy Ghost; to consecrate the blessed body of Christ in the sacrament of the altar; to loose and absoyle from sin all persons which be duly penitent and sorry for the same; to bind and excommunicate such as be guilty in manifest crimes and sins and will not amend their defaults; to order and consecrate others in the same room, order and office.[3]

---

Kidd (1911), pp. 330–4. The latter was contained in a *Pia Ordinatio* presented to Henry VIII in 1537, and so was possibly well known in England, particularly to Thomas Cranmer; see *Cranmer's Liturgical Projects*, ed. J. Wickham Legg, HBS L (1915), p. xxxiv.

[1] Text in *Formularies of Faith put forth by authority during the reign of Henry VIII*, ed. Charles Lloyd (1825), pp. 21–211.

[2] Ibid., pp. 104–5.

[3] Ibid., p. 101. Cf. the Sarum Pontifical: "Sacerdotem oportet offerre, benedicere, praesse, praedicare, conficere, et baptizare." "Episcopum oportet iudicare, interpretari, consecrare, confirmare, ordinare, offerre, et baptizare" (Maskell, II, pp. 214, 270). *The Bishops' Book* does not mention the powers or functions of deacons.

Several years later a more radical questioning of the traditional beliefs by some of the English bishops and divines, and in particular by Thomas Cranmer, can be seen. Seventeen questions concerning the sacraments and the appointment and power of bishops and priests were put to a number of bishops and divines in 1540, and their answers reveal a considerable diversity of opinion on a number of points.[1] There was still almost unanimous agreement that there was clear evidence in Scripture for Order to be considered as a sacrament. Only Thomas Cranmer denied this and maintained that "there is no more promise of God that grace be given in the committing of ecclesiastical office, than in the committing of civil office". Similarly, they all seem to have been agreed that the matter and form were imposition of hands and prayer. Once again Cranmer was the only exception: "In the admission of many of these officers be divers comely ceremonies and solemnities used which be not of necessity but only for a good order and seemly fashion; for if such offices and ministrations were committed without such solemnity, they were nevertheless truly committed"; and in answer to question 12, "whether in the New Testament be required any Consecration of a Bishop and Priest, or only appointing to the office be sufficient?", Cranmer said, "In the New Testament he that is appointed to be a bishop or a priest, needeth no consecration by the Scripture, for election and appointing thereto is sufficient."[2] These statements would seem to suggest that he did not believe that any matter and form were essential.

When asked whether the power of ordaining belonged to bishops by authority from God or by permission of the king, some expressed the former view, others claimed that the authority was from God but was exercised by the licence and permission of the king. Two, Dr Redmayn and Dr Edgeworth, drew a distinction between the power of ordaining, which necessarily belonged only to bishops, and the right of election, which could be exercised by kings and princes.[3] Henry VIII, from his annotations on one copy of the answers, seems to have been dissatisfied with this distinction: "Since you confess that the Apostles did occupate the one part, which now you confess belongeth to princes, how can you prove that ordering is only committed to you bishops?"[4] A variety of answers was also given to the question, "Whether Bishops

[1] Printed in G. Burnet, *History of the Reformation of the Church of England* (1841) II, pp. lxxxviii–cv.

[2] Ibid. II, pp. xcvi, xcix.    [3] Ibid. II, pp. xcvi–xcvii.

[4] British Museum Cotton Ms. Cleo. E.V., fol. 42.

or Priests were first? and if the Priests were first, then the Priest made
the Bishop". Some, like Cranmer, believed that "the bishops and
priests were at one time, and were not two things, but both one office
in the beginning of Christ's religion". Others allowed that the Apostles
were ordained as priests and bishops at the same time, but maintained
that the two orders were still distinct from the first.[1]

The majority inclined to the view that according to the Scriptures
only bishops could ordain, although a few were prepared to admit
exceptions in cases of necessity. Dr Redmayn and Dr Edgeworth cited
the examples of Moses, who was not a priest, making Aaron a priest as
a scriptural precedent for laymen ordaining "by a special commission
or revelation from God". Cranmer himself was much more radical:

> A bishop may make a priest by the Scripture, and so may princes and
> governors also, and that by the authority of God committed to them, and
> the people also by their election; for as we read that bishops have done it, so
> Christian emperors and princes usually have done it, and the people before
> Christian princes were, commonly did elect their bishops and priests.

He was supported by William Barlow, Bishop of St David's, who said,
"Laymen have other whiles made priests." When pressed by further
questions as to who might ordain in cases of necessity, some were unwilling to be more specific, believing that *Necessitas non habet legem*,
while others said that where it was impossible to obtain a bishop, the
king might do it. Only one, Edward Lee, the Archbishop of York,
denied this power to the king in unambiguous terms. Another, Dr
Symmons, said that, "if the King be also a bishop, as it is possible, he
may appoint bishops and priests to minister to his people: but hitherto
I have not read that ever any Christian king made bishop or priest."[2]

In 1543 a revised version of *The Bishops' Book* was produced under
the title, *A Necessary Doctrine and Erudition for any Christian Man*, which
was commonly known as *The King's Book*.[3] Although Henry VIII
appears to have been very dissatisfied with the section on Order in *The
Bishops' Book*,[4] the corresponding section in *The King's Book* contains
substantially the same teaching. The section is still entitled "The
Sacrament of Orders" and it states that "order is a gift or grace of
ministration in Christ's Church, given of God to Christian men, by the
consecration and imposition of the bishop's hands upon them".[5] It also

---

[1] Burnet, II, pp. xcvii–xcviii.      [2] Ibid. II, pp. xcviii–cii.
[3] Also in *Formularies of Faith*, pp. 213–377.
[4] *The Works of Thomas Cranmer*, ed. John Edmund Cox (PS, 1844, 1846), II, pp. 96ff.
[5] *Formularies of Faith*, p. 277.

maintained the view that in the New Testament there were only two orders, bishops or priests, and deacons, and that these were conferred by prayer and the imposition of hands. It assigned to bishops and priests the same duties as *The Bishops' Book*, but to this it added the duties of deacons: "Their office in the primitive church was partly in ministering meat and drink and other necessities to poor people found of the church, partly also in ministering to the bishops and priests, and in doing their duty in the church."[1]

Nevertheless, although prayer and the imposition of hands were regarded as the only essentials of ordination, the other ceremonies of the Pontificals were by no means considered wrongful additions. *The Rationale of Ceremonial*, written at about this time, stated that "the ceremonies, observances and prayers said and done in the consecration of Bishops, and giving orders to priests, deacons, subdeacons and other inferior ministers, as heretofore hath been accustomed, and as it is devised in the books called pontificals ... be very laudable and expedient to be used".[2]

After this date there were no further official statements in England on ordination until the publication of the Ordinal some seven years later. It is, therefore, no easy task to determine what were the common beliefs about Order in the intervening period. *The King's Book* would seem to mark a return to a more conservative position than some had expressed in 1540, but it is questionable whether the majority continued to hold this view seven years later, or indeed whether *The King's Book* does mark a real change of opinion; it may well be that Cranmer and others who held somewhat unorthodox views found it expedient to assent to the more traditional teaching of this book out of obedience to the king, while at the same time maintaining their own personal opinions.

However, although there are no further official pronouncements or any other writings on the subject of ordination by other bishops or divines, there are a number of other writings by Cranmer which throw some more light on his own views. In 1547 he published a Catechism which included statements on ordination. This must be treated with some caution as it was not his own composition but a translation he had made of a Latin work by the German Reformer, Justus Jonas. Nevertheless, it may be argued that Cranmer would not have translated anything with which he was not in substantial agreement and,

---

[1] Ibid., p. 281.
[2] *The Rationale of Ceremonial 1540–1543*, ed. C. S. Cobb, ACC xviii (1910), p. 13.

since it is not a literal translation but he freely omits sections of the Latin and inserts new material in places, it may fairly be said to represent his own views at the time, or at least the views which he thought people in England should hold. This work makes no mention of Order as a sacrament, calling it instead an office and a commission, but although it does not use the word "grace", it does say that,

> the ministration of Gods worde (which our Lorde Jesus Christ hymselfe dyd first institute) was deryved from the apostles unto other after theim, by imposition of handes, and gyvynge of the Holy Ghost, from the apostles tyme to our dayes. And this was the consecration, ordres and unction of the apostles, wherby they, at the begynnynge, made byshopes and pryestes, and this shall continewe in the churche, even to the worldes ende. And what soever rite or ceremonye hath ben added more than this commeth of mannes ordinaunce and policye, and is not commaunded by Goddes worde.[1]

Thus it would seem that in 1547 Cranmer held substantially the same beliefs as *The King's Book* had expressed. On the other hand, this Catechism too could simply be a deferring to traditional ideas while his personal beliefs remained the same as in 1540. His other writings on Order are unfortunately not able to settle decisively which of these is the case. There is a short manuscript work entitled *De Sacramentis*, which contains a brief section on Order,[2] and also the manuscript usually referred to as Cranmer's Commonplace Book, which has a long section (pp. 417–79) on this subject,[3] but it is not possible to date either of these accurately, and so both may belong to the earlier period and throw no light at all on Cranmer's views after 1543.[4] Furthermore, the latter must in any case be treated with some caution as evidence for Cranmer's own beliefs. It is mainly a collection of quotations from the Bible and from patristic and other sources, and he may not have agreed with every, or even any, view which he reproduced. There is another manuscript work on Order attributed to Cranmer, *De Ordine et Ministerio Sacerdotum et Episcoporum*, but its status is in considerable doubt and so it cannot be treated as a reliable source for Cranmer's own thought. It forms part of a collection of papers belonging apparently

[1] *A Short Instruction into Christian Religion being a Catechism set forth by Archbishop Cranmer in MDXLVIII together with the same in Latin translated from the German By Justus Jonas in MDXXXIX*, ed. E. Burton (1829), p. 196.
[2] Fols. 84–93 of Lambeth Palace Library Ms. 1107.
[3] British Museum Royal Ms. 7. B. xi.
[4] Peter Brooks in *Thomas Cranmer's Doctrine of the Eucharist* (1965), p. 22, n. 2, suggests that the collection of extracts in the latter was probably made over a long period, from about the mid 1530s until the early 1540s, but not later.

to the conference held with the Lutherans in 1538. On the other hand, it contains some portions of the chapter on Order from *The Bishops' Book* and other portions which appear in *The King's Book*. Its reliability is the more questionable as it is not in Cranmer's own handwriting, nor is it annotated or signed by him.[1] As it contains nothing which is not also stated in other writings with which Cranmer was associated, no use will be made of it here as a source for his beliefs.

It is possible, however, that the conflict between Cranmer's views as expressed in 1540 and the other writings on the subject of Order with which he was associated is not as great as would appear at first sight. It would seem that at least for a time Cranmer did share the traditional view that grace was conferred in ordination. His Commonplace Book includes a long extract from King Henry VIII's book, *Assertio septem sacramentorum contra M. Lutherum*, which sets out to refute Luther's view that grace is not conferred in ordination.[2] There are also extracts from Ambrose, Augustine, and Theophilactus which speak of grace being conferred by the imposition of hands.[3] Finally, under the heading "Quod ordo sit sacramentum", Cranmer quotes 1 Tim. 4.14 and 2 Tim. 1.6, and opposite these quotations in the margin he notes, "gratia data ordinatis per manuum impositionem". Under the same heading he has other quotations from the Gospels with notes opposite them of the various powers he believed were conferred on those occasions—consecrating, binding and loosing, preaching, baptizing, etc.[4]

The point at issue, therefore, is whether he continued to hold this position after 1540. His statements in the seventeen questions and answers may not be so radical as they appear at first sight. It has been assumed so far that they mean that Cranmer thought that no grace at all was conferred in ordination, but that is not the only possible interpretation of them. All that he said was that God had no more promised that grace was conferred in admission to one office than in admission to another. If "grace" is understood as power to perform certain functions, which would seem to be Cranmer's view, then this could mean that ecclesiastical power is not superior to civil power, but that both are derived equally from God. Thus the statement implies not so much a low doctrine of ordination as a high doctrine of civil power. That Cranmer held such a view of civil power is clear both from the questions and answers and from his other writings:

---

[1] Messenger, I, pp. 269–70, Text in Cranmer, *Works* II, pp. 484–9.
[2] Pp. 441–4.    [3] Pp. 434, 437–8, 453.    [4] Pp. 477–8.

All christian princes have committed unto them immediately of God the
whole cure of all their subjects ... the civil ministers under the king's
majesty in this realm of England be those whom it shall please his highness
for the time to put in authority under him ... the ministers of God's word
under his majesty be the bishops, parsons, vicars and such other priests as be
appointed by his highness to that ministration.[1]

Nor does the fact that he believed that Scripture had no concept of
Order as a sacrament necessarily mean that he thought that nothing
was conferred in ordination: his Catechism talks of only three sacraments, baptism, absolution, and communion, but it still claims that the
Holy Ghost is given in ordination;[2] and it is clear from *De Sacramentis*
that he preferred to reserve the name "sacrament" for rites which
signified the remission of sins rather than use it in a more general sense.[3]
If this is the correct interpretation of his replies, then they are consistent
with what he says elsewhere about the nature of ordination.

It is also possible that his opinions on the matter and form of Order
in his replies are not so radical and out of line with his other statements
as would appear at first, although in this case it must be admitted that
some passages in his Commonplace Book do seem to support the interpretation of his replies that no matter and form were essential. On page
476 there is the heading "Multi sacerdotalem dignitatem constituti
sunt sine episcoporum consecratione", and under this Cranmer claims
that nowhere do we read that Christ consecrated the Apostles or the
seventy disciples, or that St Paul was ever consecrated. He then quotes
extracts from Eusebius' *Ecclesiastical History* which state that Thomas
sent a certain Tatthaeus, one of the seventy disciples, to Edessa, that
Philip was the first to preach to the Samaritans, and the eunuch the first
to preach to the Ethiopians. He adds extracts from Rufinus who says
that a king of Iberia became an apostle to his people "non initiatus
sacris", as did Frumentius in India. Finally, he says that Joseph of
Arimathea was the first to fulfil the apostolic function in Britain.
Presumably he believed that in each case the people concerned had not
received episcopal consecration. Moreover, on the two previous pages

---

[1] Answer to Question 9. See Burnet, II, p. xcvi. Similar statements appear in *The
Bishop's Book* and *The King's Book*: "God constituted and ordained the authority of
Christian kings and princes to be most high and supreme above all other powers and
offices in the regiment and governance of his people...." *Formularies of Faith*, p. 120,
repeated almost verbatim p. 286. See also Cranmer's speech at the coronation of Edward
VI (*Works* II, p. 127): "Your majesty is God's vice-gerent and Christ's vicar within your
own dominions...."
[2] Pp. 183, 196.   [3] Fol. 85.

he lists a large number of actions which, he says, Christ and the Apostles did but which we do not do, ranging from shaking dust off their feet to daily Communion. The purpose of this list would appear to be to prove that he was not bound to do all that the apostolic Church did in appointing ministers. These pages imply that Cranmer's opinions in 1540 were no sudden aberration but the result of some careful study.

On the other hand, both his replies in 1540 and the statements in the Commonplace Book do not necessarily contradict his views as expressed elsewhere. In the questions and answers he says that there are "divers comely ceremonies and solemnities used which be not of necessity". It must be noted that he does not say that no ceremony at all is necessary, but only that there are many which are not, and even his answer to Question 12 need not mean that imposition of hands and prayer are not required. What Cranmer is actually contrasting here is "consecration" with "election and appointing", believing that only the latter is required. It has been assumed so far that by "consecration" he meant ordination by imposition of hands, but it is clear from their replies to the same question that at least two others did not understand the word to mean this:

> By Scripture there is no consecration of bishops and priests required, but only the appointing to the office of a priest, cum impositione manuum—Dr Cox.

> Consecration of bishops and priests I read not in the New Testament, but ordinatio per manuum impositionem cum oratione is read there—Dr Day.[1]

It is therefore possible that by consecration Cranmer too may have meant unction and similar ceremonies, and he may have understood "appointing" to mean ordination by prayer and imposition of hands. Some support is lent to this view by the Commonplace Book. On pages 469–72 under the headings "Constitutio", "Consecratio", "Ordinatio", and "De impositione manuum", Cranmer lists biblical examples of these actions and, although he has examples from the New Testament under three of the headings, most of them coming under the last, he has only examples from the Old Testament under "Consecratio". This suggests that he saw a distinction between "consecration" and "ordination by imposition of hands", and did not regard the former as applicable to the New Testament practice. It is also to be noted that the examples he quotes on page 476 of the Commonplace Book were of men appointed "sine episcoporum consecratione" and not "sine

<hr/>

[1] Burnet, II, p. xcix.

manuum impositione". Moreover, in his manuscript *De Sacramentis* he clearly regards ordination by imposition of hands as the normal New Testament practice, if not an absolute necessity: "Satis constat ex actis apostolorum et epistola Pauli ad Timothiam, ministros ecclesiae ordinandos esse per impositionem manuum sacerdotis."[1] Thus his writings seem to point to the conclusion that, if he thought any ceremonies at all were essential, they were prayer and the imposition of hands.

His view that bishops and priests were one order was in line with the teaching of the other writings of the period, and with the opinions of many medieval theologians. It would also appear from his Commonplace Book that he believed that in affirming the identity of the two offices he was making no innovation but simply returning to the teaching of the Fathers, for under the heading, "Quod idem sit episcopus et presbyter", he refers to and quotes various patristic writers on this subject—Ambrose, Augustine, Basil, Chrysostom, and Jerome.[2]

The views expressed by Cranmer and others in the questions and answers concerning the power of ordaining do not contradict the opinions to which they elsewhere assented. For *The Bishops' Book* and *The King's Book* deal with the normal practice of the Church and therefore regard the bishop as the minister of ordination, whereas the questions and answers deal with the extraordinary situations where this is not possible. From his manuscript *De Sacramentis* it appears that Cranmer held an orthodox view of who should ordain in normal circumstances. He there says that it is clear from the Acts of the Apostles and from Paul's Epistle to Timothy that ministers of the Church were to be ordained "per impositionem manuum sacerdotis" and that it was the Church which afterwards gave this power to the bishops. He also refers to works by Cyprian and Origen which, he says, "declarant quomodo in ordinandis omnibus ecclesiae ministris requirantur electio et responsio populi, adhuc Paulus aperte dicit per impositionem manuum et authoritatem sacerdotii dari donum dei".[3] These works by Cyprian and Origen are also quoted in his Commonplace Book in the section on Order, but without any indication as to whether he agreed or disagreed with them.[4]

The theory put forward by Cranmer and others, that in cases of necessity the king or the people might ordain, sounds most unorthodox, and it certainly has no precedent in patristic or medieval theology. Yet it is perhaps not as unorthodox as it appears, since it is not very

---

[1] Fol. 91b.  [2] Pp. 430–6.  [3] Fols. 91b, 92a.  [4] Pp. 423, 452.

different from the commonly accepted belief that in cases of necessity a layman, and even a non-Christian, could administer baptism.[1] It certainly does not mean that those who put forward the idea did not think that grace was conferred in ordination. It must be admitted that it was usually held that only those who themselves had the powers could confer them, but if this was not required for baptism in cases of necessity, it could be argued that lay ordination too might be valid in cases of necessity. Power could be conferred by God through one who did not have the power himself. Thus those who put forward this view were only extending a principle which was already accepted in the Church. It would seem, however, that Cranmer based his argument that princes and governors might make priests not on this sacramental principle but on biblical precedents, as did Dr Redmayn and Dr Edgeworth. For his Commonplace Book devotes three pages to a discussion of the Old Testament passages which describe Moses as a priest and appears to come to the conclusion that Scripture frequently calls the leaders of the people *sacerdotes* because, although they were not really priests, they themselves consecrated priests and fulfilled other priestly functions.[2] On the other hand, it should be recognized that these statements about the power of the king made by Cranmer were more likely the result of political desire, to set the authority of the king against that of the Pope, than the products of deep theological reflection.

Thus it can be seen that it is possible to trace a consistent doctrine of Order in the writings of Cranmer and to reconcile his apparently conflicting views. It would seem likely, therefore, that he continued to hold this attitude towards ordination at the time when he was involved in compiling the Ordinal.

[1] "In causa autem necessitatis non solum sacerdos vel diaconus, sed etiam laicus vel mulier, immo etiam paganus et haereticus baptizare potest" (Eugenius IV in the Bull *Exultate Deo*). See also Aquinas, *Summa Theologica* III, Q. LXVII, Articles 3–5.
[2] Pp. 461–3.

# 2. The First Anglican Ordinal

A Bill authorizing "such form and manner of making and consecrating of Archbishops, Bishops, Priests, deacons and other ministers of the Church, as by six prelates and six other men of this realm, learned in God's law, by the King's Majesty to be appointed and assigned, or by the most of them, shall be devised for that purpose and set forth under the Great Seal of England before the first day of April next coming" was passed by the House of Lords on 1 February 1549/50, with nine bishops voting in favour and five against.[1] The Acts of the Privy Council record the appointment of the commission to devise the Ordinal on 2 February, but no names are given in the book, although a space was left for that purpose. On 8 February, just six days after its appointment, Nicholas Heath, Bishop of Worcester, was called before the Privy Council "for that he wolde not assent to the boke made by the reste of the bishops and clergy appointed". He was again brought before the Council on 28 February and for his obstinate refusal was committed to the Fleet Prison on 4 March.[2] The short interval of time between the appointment of the commission and Heath's refusal to subscribe is hardly sufficient for the commission to have drawn up new rites of ordination, and it is much more probable that they simply approved ones already compiled, perhaps making minor modifications. If this was so, then it seems assured that the draft rites before them were the work of Thomas Cranmer.

According to John Strype, Cranmer, assisted by Nicholas Ridley, Bishop of Rochester and later Bishop of London, used the new Ordinal at an ordination in 1549 before it was approved by the commission.[3] If this is true, it lends support to the view that the Ordinal was Cranmer's composition. Strype, however, may well have mistaken the year in which this ordination took place, since one of those said by him to have been ordained then is known to have been ordained deacon

[1] Statute 3 and 4 Edw. VI. c. 12; *Journal of the House of Lords* I, p. 387.
[2] *Acts of the Privy Council*, ed. J. R. Dasent, New Series, II (1890), pp. 379, 388, 403, 405.
[3] John Strype, *Memorials of Thomas Cranmer* (1812) I, p. 273.

by Ridley on 10 August 1550.[1] The consecration of Robert Ferrar as Bishop of St David's in September 1548 has also been suggested as an occasion on which the new Ordinal was used, but the account of the ceremony in Cranmer's register is too ambiguous to prove this. It would appear that the new English litany was used on this occasion and that a special Epistle and Gospel were used at the English Communion service which followed, instead of those of the day which would have been the normal practice. On the other hand, the Gospel was taken from St Matthew's Gospel, and was therefore not one which later appeared in the rite in the Ordinal, and the register does not give any clear indication that any changes were made in the actual ceremony of ordination; the absence of any explicit mention of the unctions and of the giving of the episcopal insignia does not necessarily mean that they were omitted.[2]

The Ordinal was published at the beginning of March 1550, under the title, *The forme and maner of makyng and consecratyng of Archebishoppes, Bishoppes, Priestes and Deacons.*[3] Although the Act of Parliament had provided for rites of ordination for the minor orders as well, it is hardly surprising, in view of Cranmer's belief that the minor orders had no scriptural foundation, that he made no use of this provision in drawing up the Ordinal, particularly as the minor orders had fallen into disuse in England.[4] He provided rites for the diaconate, priesthood, and episcopate, the last to be used also for consecrating archbishops. These were preceded by a Preface setting out the principles underlying their construction and the requirements of candidates for ordination. It also stated that the diaconate was to be conferred on a Sunday or holyday, and it was to be done "in the face of the church". Both these requirements were features of all reformed rites of ordination. Presumably they were also to apply to the conferring of the priesthood, as the final rubric in the rite for that order expects that

[1] W. H. Frere, *The Marian Reaction in its relation to the English Clergy*, CHS XVIII (1896), p. 88n.
[2] Text in E. E. Estcourt, *The Question of Anglican Ordinations Discussed* (1873), Appendix VIII, p. xxvii.
[3] Text in F. E. Brightman, *The English Rite* (2nd edn, 1921) II, pp. 928–1017.
[4] *Liturgy and Worship*, pp. 664–5. One of the articles to which Stephen Gardiner, Bishop of Winchester, was required to subscribe in 1550 by the Privy Council was that "Th'ordres of Sub-deacons, Benet and Colet, and such others as were commonly called *minores ordines*, be not necessarie by the Worde of God to be reteigned in the Churche, and be justly lefte out in the said Boke of Ordres" (*Acts of the Privy Council* III (1891), p. 76). Benet was an exorcist, Colet an acolyte. Gardiner had been imprisoned in the Tower for his resistance to innovations in doctrine.

both orders may be conferred on the same day, but no explicit directions were given as to when the episcopate was to be conferred, possibly because the Pontificals had directed that this order was always to be conferred on a Sunday and this practice was expected to be continued.

It has been generally accepted that in compiling the Ordinal Cranmer was to some extent dependent upon a draft ordination rite prepared by Martin Bucer, the German Reformer who came to England in 1549, ever since the close similarity between the two was first noticed by Richard Travers Smith in 1872.[1] A few scholars have claimed that the dependence is the other way round: W. K. Firminger, for example, has suggested that Bucer's draft was a revision of the first Ordinal, intended as an appendix to his Censura, and therefore the passages which exhibit similarities to the Ordinal are actually Latin translations of it and not the original text which lay before the compilers of the Ordinal.[2] A close study of Bucer's document, however, will show that this view is incorrect: Bucer is describing a rite which was in actual use and not a revision proposed for the Anglican Ordinal. Nevertheless, even the majority of scholars, who have agreed that Cranmer made use of Bucer's rite, with one exception have not recognized or admitted the full extent of the dependence, but instead have generally emphasized the points of similarity between the Ordinal and the rites in the Pontificals, perhaps fearing that unless they could do this the Ordinal would appear invalid to Roman Catholics.[3] The exception is E. C. Messenger, a Roman Catholic, who has been the only one to recognize the important fact that Cranmer did not use the Pontifical as the foundation for the Ordinal and insert into its framework material drawn from Bucer's rite, as the others have supposed, but rather used Bucer's rite as the foundation and main source for the three services he drew up, and supplemented this with material from the Pontificals and with other material composed by himself.[4] Yet even Messenger has assumed uncritically that therefore Cranmer shared Bucer's doctrinal standpoint, and has not observed the significance of the

---

[1] Martin Bucer, De ordinatione legitima ministrorum ecclesiae revocanda, printed in his Scripta Anglicana (Basle 1577), pp. 238–59; Richard Travers Smith, We ought not to alter the Ordinal (Dublin 1872), pp. 113–52.

[2] Liturgy and Worship, p. 672; see also Edward Denny, The English Church and the Ministry of the Reformed Churches, CHS LVII (1900), p. 22.

[3] F. Procter and W. H. Frere, A New History of the Book of Common Prayer (1901), pp. 62, 662ff; C. H. Smyth, Cranmer and the Reformation under Edward VI (1926), pp. 229–31; C. Hopf, Martin Bucer and the English Reformation (1946), pp. 88–93; G. J. Cuming, A History of Anglican Liturgy (1969), pp. 92–5.

[4] E. C. Messenger, The Lutheran Origin of the Anglican Ordinal (1934).

alterations, omissions, and additions which Cranmer felt it necessary to make in Bucer's rite. In view of his heavy dependence on Bucer, these divergences are very significant in indicating where he did not share Bucer's beliefs about ordination, or at least where he felt that the English Church would not be satisfied with a Lutheran rite. The method he adopted in dividing the one service of Bucer's draft into the three of the Ordinal also throws considerable light on his understanding of the nature and functions of the three offices.

Table 2 indicates the way in which Cranmer used Bucer's rite as the foundation for his three services. The features in capital letters are those which are clearly based upon similar features in the rites in the Pontificals. It will immediately be apparent that very little is drawn directly from this source, and it should also be noted that none of these elements has been copied verbatim, as has happened with almost all the parts drawn from Bucer, but all have been altered and adapted. The inclusion of the ceremony of the presentation of the candidates to the bishop, and a question by him as to their suitability in the case of the diaconate and priesthood, followed the practice of the medieval Church but the precise wording is Cranmer's, as is the wording of the oath of canonical obedience in the rite for the episcopate. Similarly, the litany is not the litany of the Pontificals but the new English litany from the Prayer Book, and the *porrectio instrumentorum* has been altered; none of the formulas is copied exactly from those found in the Pontificals, and the actual ceremonies have been slightly changed.[1] Finally, the idea of the inclusion of a special final collect in the rites followed the practice of the Pontificals, but again the wording of the prayers is Cranmer's own, except for that for deacons, which is based on the Roman ordination prayer in the medieval rite for the diaconate. Unlike the prayers in the Pontificals these are not true post-Communion collects as they do not pray for grace derived from the sacrament which has just been received. However, all this is not to say that the Ordinal bears scarcely any resemblance to the rites in the Pontificals; many of the features drawn from Bucer are in turn derived from elements in the Pontificals, and the parts composed by Cranmer himself use language obviously influenced by the medieval

[1] Deacons receive the New Testament instead of the Book of Gospels, priests receive the Bible as well as the chalice and bread, and bishops are given only the pastoral staff and no other symbol of their office, and they have the Bible laid on their necks by the presiding bishop after the imposition of hands and not the Gospel Book laid on their necks and shoulders by two other bishops during it.

Table 2: The Relationship between Bucer's rite and the first Anglican Ordinal

| Bucer | Deacons | Priests | Bishops |
| --- | --- | --- | --- |
| Sermon | Sermon | Sermon | |
| *Veni sancte spiritus* | | (see below) | (see below) |
| Introit: Pss. 40; 132 or 135 | | Introit: Pss. 40; 132 or 135 | Introit: Pss. 40; 132 or 135 |
| | | Communion service as far as collect of the day. | Communion service as far as collect of the day. |
| Epistle: Acts 20.17–35; 1 Tim. 3; Eph. 4.1–16 or Titus 1.5–9. | | Epistle: Acts 20.17–35 or 1 Tim. 3. | Epistle: 1 Tim. 3.1–7. |
| Psalm 67. | | | |
| Gospel: Matt. 28.18–20; John 10.1–16; 20.19–23 or 21.15–17. | | Gospel: Matt. 28.18–20; John 10.1–16 or 20.19–23. | Gospel: John 21.15–17 or 10.1–16. |
| | | "Come Holy Ghost" | Creed |
| | PRESENTATION AND QUESTION AS TO SUITABILITY | PRESENTATION AND QUESTION AS TO SUITABILITY | PRESENTATION |
| Final Inquiry of the people | Shorter Final Inquiry of the people | Final Inquiry of the people | Reading of the King's Mandate for the consecration |
| | | | Oath of Supremacy |
| | | | OATH OF OBEDIENCE TO ARCHBISHOP |
| | | | Bidding |
| LITANY WITH SPECIAL SUFFRAGE | LITANY WITH SPECIAL SUFFRAGE | LITANY WITH SPECIAL SUFFRAGE | LITANY WITH SPECIAL SUFFRAGE |

| | | | |
|---|---|---|---|
| | collect of the day. | | |
| | Epistle: 1 Tim. 3.8–13 or Acts 6.2–7. | | |
| | Oath of Supremacy | Oath of Supremacy | Oath of Supremacy |
| Exhortation to candidates | | Exhortation to candidates | ADDRESS TO ELECT |
| Examination and concluding prayer | Examination | Examination and concluding prayer | Examination and concluding prayer |
| Space for silent prayer | | Space for silent prayer | "Come Holy Ghost" |
| Salutation | | Salutation | Salutation |
| Prayer | | Prayer | Similar Prayer |
| Imposition of hands by ministers and blessing | Imposition of hands BY BISHOP ALONE and special formula | Imposition of hands BY BISHOP & PRIESTS and special formula | Imposition of hands BY BISHOPS and special formula |
| | DELIVERY OF NEW TESTAMENT WITH FORMULA | DELIVERY OF BIBLE, CHALICE, AND BREAD, WITH FORMULA | IMPOSITION OF BIBLE with formula |
| | | | DELIVERY OF STAFF WITH FORMULA |
| | GOSPEL OF THE DAY | | |
| Creed | | Creed | |
| Communion Service | Communion Service | Communion Service | Communion Service |
| | SPECIAL FINAL COLLECT | SPECIAL FINAL COLLECT | SPECIAL FINAL COLLECT |

rites.[1] The reason for Cranmer's close dependence on Bucer and almost total rejection of the wording of the medieval rites, in contrast to his usual use of sources in compiling the Prayer Book, is almost certainly to be found in his denial of the popular view of the sacrifice of the Mass and of the sacrificial priesthood. The medieval ordination rites were so full of sacrificial language that there was little which he could have adopted as it stood without implying ideas about the ordained ministry which he no longer held.

The rite for the priesthood is copied very closely from Bucer; hardly anything which is in his rite is omitted, although a number of additions are made, the significance of which will be discussed later. The rite for the episcopate also uses Bucer's rite as its foundation, but Cranmer has varied it from the rite for the priesthood in a number of ways, and in particular by the inclusion of several features from the Pontificals. The placing of the rite after the Creed would seem to be his own idea, as it came before the Gospel in the Pontificals. On the other hand, the placing of the hymn "Come Holy Ghost" in closer proximity to the imposition of hands would appear to be due to its position in the medieval rites, whereas its position near the beginning of the rite for the priesthood is obviously influenced by the position of the version in Bucer's rite. In this rite the hymn occupies the space left for silent prayer in the rite for the priesthood. Cranmer has also replaced the long exhortation to the candidates in the rite for the priesthood by a short address to the elect based on the one found in the examination in the Pontificals, and he has varied the prayer before the imposition of hands by the inclusion of part of one of the Pontifical prayers: the prayer begins in the same way as that in the rite for the priesthood but the rest is a very free translation of part of the Gallican interpolation in the second ordination prayer of the medieval rites. The other differences from the rite for the priesthood will be noted later. The rite for the diaconate also is based much more freely on Bucer than the rite for the priesthood, although it still follows the same basic outline. Cranmer has varied this mainly by omitting and abbreviating parts of Bucer's rite, and he has added a choice of suitable epistles, 1 Tim. 3.8–13, describing the qualities required in a deacon, or Acts 6.2–7, describing the appointment of the first deacons. The result is an extremely simple rite, which probably indicates most clearly what

[1] So similar was it to the medieval rites in outward appearance that it was described as identical by one contemporary observer, Daniele Barbaro, the Venetian envoy (Procter and Frere, p. 62, n. 2).

he regarded as the essential minimum of an ordination rite. The idea of varying the one rite to create three in this way, by enriching it for the episcopate and simplifying it for the diaconate, had been suggested by Bucer himself at the end of his rite:

> Cum autem tres ordines sint presbyterorum et curatorum Ecclesiae, ordo Episcoporum: deinde presbyterorum, quos veteres Cardinales vocabant, qui primariam Ecclesiae gubernationem administrant in locis, ubi non sunt Episcopi: et eorum presbyterorum, qui his adiutorio sunt, et vocantur apud nos Diaconi, vel adiutores. Ita ordinatio quoque attemperatur: ut cum ordinatur aliquis Superintendens, id est Episcopus, omnia aliquanto pluribus et gravius gerantur et perficiantur quam cum ordinatur presbyter secundi ordinis, vel tertii. Ita enim sit nonnullum discrimen inter ordinationem presbyterorum secundi et tertii ordinis.[1]

It has frequently been assumed that the compilers of the Ordinal regarded the imperative formulas which they included at the imposition of hands as the essential sacramental form,[2] but it seems certain that Cranmer at any rate did not think of them in this way. As has already been said, he regarded prayer and the imposition of hands as the normal means of ordination, and he repeated this view in his Preface to the Ordinal, where he said that no man might execute any office in the Church "except he were first called, tried, examined, and knowen, to have suche qualities, as were requisite for the same. And also by publique prayer with imposicion of handes, approved, and admitted thereunto." It is really not possible to describe these imperative formulas as prayers in the ordinary sense of the word; they are without doubt addressed to the candidates, and not to God. Why then were these formulas included and what in the Ordinal is the "publique prayer" which Cranmer believed should accompany the imposition of hands?

---

[1] *Scripta Anglicana*, p. 259.

[2] *Liturgy and Worship*, p. 666; Procter and Frere, p. 661. The formulas were: (for the diaconate) "Take thou aucthoritie to execute the office of a Deacon in the Church of God committed unto thee: in the name of the father, the sonne, and the holy ghost. Amen." (for the priesthood) "Receive the holy goste, whose synnes thou doest forgeve, they are forgeven: and whose sinnes thou doest retaine, thei are retained: and be thou a faithful despensor of the word of god, and of his holy Sacramentes. In the name of the father, and of the sonne, and of the holy gost. Amen." (for the episcopate) "Take the holy gost, and remember that thou stirre up the grace of god, which is in thee, by imposicion of handes: for god hath not geven us the spirite of feare, but of power, and love, and of sobernesse." The first part of the formula for the priesthood is a quotation from John 20.22–3, and the words after "Take the holy gost" in the formula for the episcopate are from 2 Tim. 1.6–7.

In Bucer's rite the ordination prayer is the one which immediately precedes the imposition of hands, and it would seem natural that the corresponding prayer in the Ordinal should also be this. Unfortunately there is no such prayer in the rite for the diaconate. Furthermore, there is one important difference between the prayer in Bucer's rite and the version in the rite for the priesthood: it is almost a verbatim translation, except that Cranmer has entirely omitted the central section of the prayer, which was a petition that the Holy Spirit might be poured out on the candidates,[1] and has thus completely altered the sense of it, turning it from a prayer for the candidates into one for the congregation in general. It would, therefore, seem very unlikely that Cranmer intended this as the essential prayer, nor can it be the short prayer which concludes the examination, nor the hymn "Come Holy Ghost", as neither appears in the rite for the diaconate.

One therefore turns to consider whether any of the additions which Cranmer made to Bucer's rite was intended as the essential prayer. Three of them are prayers, they are for the candidates, and they occur in all three rites. They are the litany with its special suffrage, the collect which follows this, and the special collect at the end of each rite. Unfortunately all are widely separated from the imposition of hands, whereas one would have expected the prayer and the imposition of hands to be closely associated. However, before the litany in the rite for the episcopate Cranmer has included a bidding, presumably composed by himself, perhaps in imitation of the bidding which preceded the litany in the Pontificals, and this indicates his views on the relation of prayer and imposition of hands. It would seem that he thought that the prayer should come first, before the act of ordaining, and not as part of it:

> Brethren, it is written in the gospel of saincte Luke, that our savioure Christe continued the whole night in praier, or ever that he did chose and sende furth his xii Apostles. It is written also in the Actes of the Apostles, that the disciples whiche were at Antioche did fast and pray, or ever they layed handes upon, or sent furth Paul and Barnabas. Let us therefore, folowyng the example of oure savioure Christ and his Apostles, first fal to prayer, or that we admit and send furth thys person presented unto us, to the worke wherunto we truste the holy goste hath called hym.

---

[1] "Precamur ut spiritum sanctum tuum, in nomine filii tui, opulente in hos ipsos tuos ministros effundas: eosque semper eos doceas et gubernes, quo tuo populo, gregi boni pastoris nostri filii tui, ministerium suum et fideliter et utiliter praestent: ac eo quamplurimos gloriae tuae quotidie adducant: eosque quod adduxerint, ad omnem tuam

Since the litany follows immediately, it would appear that Cranmer intended this, and also the collect which follows it (since according to the rubric which precedes it in the rite for the episcopate the latter is meant as the conclusion of the litany and not as a separate entity) as the essential "publique prayer" to precede the imposition of hands, in spite of the fact that the two are separated by the examination and, in two of the rites, by a further prayer. In the other two rites, although there is not such a full bidding, the bishop begins the litany, according to the rubric, by "commending suche as shal be found mete to be ordered to the prayers of the congregacion".

A similar understanding of the relation of prayer and imposition of hands is revealed in the *Paraphrase* of Erasmus, which had been translated into English and ordered to be set up in every church in England in 1548, and so can be regarded as the officially accepted interpretation of the New Testament at the time. His paraphrase of the appointment of the Seven in Acts 6 reads:

> These seven, whan they wer chosen, wer set before thapostles, to thentent that what was done, they shulde allow the same by their authoritie. Thapostles whan they had made their prayers to god, as they were accustomed, layde their handes upon them.[1]

Similarly, his account of the setting aside of Paul and Barnabas in Acts 13 reads:

> At this commaundement of the holy ghost, Barnabas, and Saule, wer separated and set apart from the reste, that it myght appere to every man, who were chosen. And after that they with one consente, by fastynge, and prayer had made peticion to God that he would turne the offyce that they toke on theim, to the profit of the congregacion: those that wer highest of authorytie emonge theim, layed their handes on theim. . . .[2]

It is more than likely that Cranmer was influenced by Erasmus, particularly as the collect which concludes the litany in all three rites prays for gifts for the candidates so that they may serve in the office "to the profyte of the congregacion", the same expression as Erasmus had used.

It is not being suggested that Cranmer thought that the litany and its

---

sanctam voluntatem in dies perfectius instituant et conforment. Da quoque illis omnibus, quorum saluti vis istos ministrare, animos verbi tui capaces" (*Scripta Anglicana*, p. 259).
[1] "The Actes of the Apostles", fol. xxiiiia, in *The first tome or volume of the Paraphrase of Erasmus upon the newe testamente* (1548).
[2] Ibid., fol. xlvib.

collect were essential to any rite. Other rites could have other types of prayer, but the particular prayer in these rites intended as the one to precede the imposition of hands was the litany with its special suffrage and concluding collect. His choice of this as the essential prayer was perhaps partly influenced by the presence of a litany in the Pontifical rites, but it is more probable that his main reason for choosing this particular type of prayer was that it was the corporate prayer of the Church, and both his bidding and the *Paraphrase* of Erasmus describe the act of prayer as by the whole group and not by a single consecrator. It was impossible for him to have known that this was a very primitive feature in ordination rites. He was simply reverting to what he believed to have been the New Testament practice, but in so doing he was accidently restoring part of the structure of the ancient Roman rites with a bidding, litany, and collect, while at the same time he was departing from the universal practice of the Church, which had always included a prayer said while hands were laid on or held over the candidate.

It should not be thought that Cranmer, or anyone else at the time, regarded the imposition of hands as conferring what had been sought for the candidates in the prayers; there is no indication in any writings of the period that this relationship between the two elements of the rite was envisaged. It would appear instead that the two elements were thought of as distinct, both essential but both fulfilling different functions. None of the prayers in the rites asks for the bestowal of the office, or of its powers, as many of the early rites of ordination did, but they pray that the candidates may be endued with the necessary personal qualities to perform their functions well. The imposition of hands, therefore, conferred the office itself and its powers on the candidate. No words were necessary, the action alone was sufficient to signify this, as Bucer himself said in his rite.[1] If then the words were not important, why did Cranmer reject those proposed in Bucer's rite to accompany the imposition of hands,[2] and substitute for them the imperative formulas? It is most probable that he did this because he

---

[1] "Significat enim et repraesentat illa manuum impositio, directionem, corroborationem, et protectionem manus Dei omnipotentis, quo possit is qui ordinatur, suum praestare et perficere ministerium, ad gloriam nominis Dei, et salutem Ecclesiae. Significat etiam tradi ei potestatem, ut vice Christi Ecclesiam doceat et gubernet: Seque etiam, quod est boni pastoris, hostiam, ei opus sit, per fidem et salutem Ecclesiae, libenter impendat" (*Scripta Anglicana*, p. 255).

[2] "Manus Dei omnipotentis, Patris, Filii, et Spiritus sancti sit super vos, protegat et gubernet vos, ut eatis, et fructum vestro ministerio quamplurimum afferatis, isque maneat in vitam aeternam. Amen" (Ibid., p. 259).

wanted a different formula for each rite which would express more clearly the office being bestowed in each case. This was not because he thought that it was in any way essential for the validity of the rite that appropriate words should be said, but simply so that those involved in the ceremony should be reminded of what was happening. It is also possible that he included them to satisfy any who did attach importance to ordination being conferred by an imperative formula. E. C. Messenger has suggested that Cranmer may have derived the formula he adopted in the rite for the priesthood from the rite of the Church at Hesse, perhaps through Bucer himself who is thought to have been involved in compiling that rite, but this seems unlikely, particularly as Cranmer appears to have composed his own formula for the rite for the episcopate rather than use one of the alternative formulas used at Hesse.[1] It is much more probable that he was influenced by the late medieval tendency to introduce the first part of this formula at the silent imposition of hands in the ordination of priests.[2] For reasons which will be apparent later he preferred to compose his own formulas for the other two rites rather than copy ones found in the medieval Pontificals.

Thus, for Cranmer, the essential parts of the three rites of the Ordinal were the litany, with its suffrage and collect, and the imposition of hands. In addition he probably attached considerable importance to the question as to the candidates' suitability, the final inquiry of the people, and the examination, as the final stages of the process of ensuring that the candidates had "suche qualities, as were requisite", on which he had laid stress in his Preface. It is clear, however, from his other writings that he cannot have regarded the *porrectio instrumentorum* as anything other than one of the "divers comely ceremonies" of ordination. At the most it was a symbolic conferring of jurisdiction, but it was not the essential matter and form as far as he was concerned, although again he may have retained it to satisfy any who did attach significance to this ceremony.

Roman Catholic writers have frequently claimed that what is bestowed in this Ordinal by the imposition of hands is simply the authority of the Church to minister publicly; there is a Lutheran concept of ordination with no bestowal of powers but only the public recognition and admission of a person to an office. The Preface, for

---

[1] Messenger, *The Lutheran Origin of the Anglican Ordinal*, p. 51; cf. A. L. Richter, *Die Evangelischen Kirchenordnungen des sechszehnten Jahrhunderts* (Weimer 1846) I, pp. 65–6.

[2] See above, pp. 4–6.

example, states that calling, trial, examination, approval, and admission are required so that a man may have public authority to execute the office in question. It does not state that the office confers a sacred character or is a sacrament, or even that ordination is absolutely necessary for the exercise of functions. Throughout the Ordinal "admitted" is used rather than "consecrated", and "authority" rather than "power".[1]

However, one may question whether this wording positively rules out any other interpretation of the Ordinal. It is hardly surprising, when one considers that Bucer was its main source, that the language should appear so Lutheran, but this does not necessarily mean that Cranmer or the other members of the commission shared a Lutheran understanding of these words. Indeed, the other members of the commission may have been unaware of Bucer's part in its composition and may have thought that the draft Ordinal was entirely an original piece of work by Cranmer. In any case, the word "admitted" is not exclusively Lutheran: *Admittatur*, referring to ordination, is found in Canon VI of the Council of Lambeth, A.D. 1330,[2] and *ad sacrum ministerium admitti* also appears in the *Admonitio ad diaconos* of the Sarum Pontifical.[3] Moreover, it is extremely doubtful if Cranmer himself would have seen the distinction between "power" and "authority" which these writers try to make. If the king admitted a man to civil office, he would confer upon him not only the authority to do certain things, but also the power to perform them. The man may previously have had the natural powers to give orders, make decisions, fulfil certain functions, but without the authority of the king all these actions would have been ineffectual. Thus in this case power was derived from authority and could not exist independently of it. As has already been said, Cranmer appears to have thought of civil and ecclesiastical offices in the same way.[4] Therefore it is most unlikely that he could have conceived of the idea of all Christians individually having the power to perform the functions of the ministry, but only some having authority to do so. There is certainly no indication elsewhere in his writings of such an understanding: the only interpretation of *regale sacerdotium* and similar New Testament expressions which appears in his Commonplace Book is by Bede, who takes it to mean that all Christians are to

[1] Messenger, *The Reformation, the Mass and the Priesthood* I, p. 457.
[2] *Liturgy and Worship*, p. 671.    [3] Maskell, II, p. 244.
[4] See above, pp. 13–14. In practice there was very little difference between the two. For example, Thomas More was the first layman to be Chancellor of England; previously this office had always been held by a cleric.

offer spiritual sacrifices.[1] This is not to say, however, that other members of the commission did not understand the language of the Ordinal in a different way, or that Cranmer did not so phrase the Preface and other parts of the Ordinal so that it should also be acceptable to those with a different understanding of ordination from his own.

Nevertheless, it would appear that Cranmer, while not distinguishing between "power" and "authority" in this way, did differentiate between different sources of power in the three rites of the Ordinal. He undoubtedly believed that the source of the power bestowed on priests in their ordination was not the Church but the Holy Spirit; in his other writings he had affirmed that grace was bestowed on priests, he believed that the priesthood had been instituted by Christ, and he adopted at the bestowing of the office the words used by Christ in commissioning the Apostles, words which had already been used in ordaining priests in medieval rites, and which clearly implied that the Holy Spirit was being bestowed in this action. However, this would not seem to be the case with regard to the episcopate. Certain features of the rite suggest that he retained his earlier view that the priesthood and the episcopate were the same in New Testament times and that he did not believe that a new order or new powers of the Holy Spirit were conferred upon men who became bishops, but that he regarded them as priests on whom the commission of the Church for a particular function was conferred. It is sometimes argued that the provision of the three different rites as well as the wording of the Preface shows a return to the belief that the New Testament teaches a threefold order of ministry,[2] but a close look at the precise wording of the Preface will show that this is not necessarily so; it states that "from the Apostles tyme, there hathe bene these orders of Ministers in Christes church, Bisshoppes, Priestes, and Deacons"; it does not specifically claim that these are three separate orders, and the rite itself confirms that Cranmer did not think of the episcopate as a separate order.

Firstly, the rites for the diaconate and priesthood begin with "an exhortacion, declaring the duetie and office, of suche as come to be admitted Ministers, howe necessarie suche Orders are in the Churche of Christe, and also howe the people oughte to esteme them in theyr vocacion", but no such sermon is prescribed in the rite for the episcopate, presumably because this was not regarded as one of the

[1] Pp. 439–40. [2] *Liturgy and Worship*, p. 661.

necessary orders of the Church of Christ. Secondly, the word "ordering" is used in the Ordinal of deacons and priests, but not of bishops. Instead the word "consecrating" is used, implying that the rite is a setting aside for a holy purpose rather than an appointing to a new order. For example, the title of the rite for the diaconate is "The Fourme and Maner of Orderinge of Deacons"; for the priesthood it is "The Fourme of Ordering Priestes", but for the episcopate, "The Fourme of Consecrating of an Archebisshoppe or Bisshoppe". Furthermore, in the bidding which precedes the litany in the rite for the episcopate, as a precedent for what they are about to do, the congregation is reminded that "the disciples whiche were at Antioche did fast and pray, or ever they layed handes upon, or sent furth Paul and Barnabas".[1] There is firm evidence that Cranmer held the view that the imposition of hands on Paul and Barnabas mentioned here was not to appoint them to a higher order, but to commission them for particular work. On page 478 of his Commonplace Book he quotes the account of the sending forth of Paul and Barnabas from Acts 13, and notes in the margin, "Segregatio Barnabae et Sauli in ministerium missu Spiritus sancti". This passage is also quoted on page 472 in a list of the various uses of the imposition of hands in the New Testament, with the marginal note "ad conferendam functionem". Cranmer even preferred to avoid calling the episcopate an office as far as possible; the bidding describes this rite as admitting and sending forth the candidate "to the worke wherunto we truste the holy goste hath called hym", and the collect after the litany, although otherwise more or less identical with that in the rite for the priesthood, describes the candidate as "thy servaunt, now called to the worke and ministerie of a Bisshoppe", whereas in the rite for the priesthood the candidates are described as "thy servantes, now called to the Office of Priesthode". The identity of bishops and priests in New Testament times is further emphasized by the use of part of 1 Tim. 3, describing the qualities required in a bishop, as the Epistle in both services, and by the use of part of Acts 20 as the Epistle in the rite for the priesthood, as the passage mentions that the elders of the congregation at Ephesus are "overseers" who are to rule the congregation of God.

Nevertheless, the imperative formula at the imposition of hands[2] might seem to suggest that the compilers of the Ordinal did believe that at their consecration bishops received grace, further power which they had not had as priests, and not simply the commission of the

[1] See above, p. 26.    [2] See above, p. 25, n. 2.

Church to exercise powers which they received when they were ordained priests. It is possible that this formula was added under pressure from members of the commission who did not share Cranmer's beliefs about the identity of bishops and priests, or more probably the choice of the word "Take" instead of "Receive", as in the rite for the priesthood, is meant to indicate some difference between the two; "receive" involves the idea of "accept from someone else", whereas "take" can mean this, but can also mean "take up from within oneself". The latter certainly requires initiative on the part of the person addressed, which "receive" does not, and is therefore less suitable if something is being given to the candidate at this service; one speaks of "receiving a sacrament" or of "receiving a gift", but it is hardly fitting to substitute "taking" in such cases. It is also to be noted that Cranmer has not merely translated the formula *Accipe Spiritum Sanctum* which appeared in many medieval Pontificals at the imposition of hands on bishops, but has added to it a phrase from 2 Timothy, thus implying that the position held by Timothy is being conferred on the candidate. This phrase, however, is so worded that it does not necessarily mean that grace is being given by this particular imposition of hands; it could refer to the grace given when the candidate was ordained priest. This would seem to be another case where Cranmer may have deliberately chosen words with ambiguous meaning which would satisfy those with a different understanding from his own, while at the same time would not exclude his own interpretation.

It would seem from the wording of the prayers, formulas, and questions in the examination, as well as from the choice of Gospels, that the function for which bishops were commissioned was thought of as the pastoral oversight of the Church, as it had been in the medieval rites. Most of the questions in the examination follow the lines of those in the rite for the priesthood, with minor verbal differences, but additional questions are included and others modified so as to emphasize the bishop's particular functions of governing the Church, caring for the needy, maintaining purity of doctrine, and being an example of Christian living to others. There is no mention of any other function being committed to the candidate, not even that of ordination, although it is obvious from the provisions of the Ordinal that this was to be restricted to bishops.[1] There is nothing to suggest that

---

[1] There is one reported instance of a priest ordaining in the time of Cranmer; both John Foxe, *Acts and Monuments* (1841) VIII, p. 106, and Strype, *Cranmer* I, p. 273, say that a certain Robert Drakes was ordained by Dr Taylor of Hadley, at the commandment of

the priests who joined in the imposition of hands in the rite for the priesthood were thought of as co-consecrators.

The Ordinal also shows that Cranmer did not think of the diaconate and the priesthood in the traditional way as two consecutive orders, but as two completely different sorts of ministry. It is true that the final collect and final rubric in the rite for the diaconate expect the candidates to pass from "thys inferior offyce" to "the higher ministeries" of the Church after a minimum period of one year in which they are to become "perfecte, and wel expert in the thinges apperteyning to the Ecclesiasticall administracion". Nevertheless, differences between the two ordination rites demonstrate that the diaconate was thought of as something rather different from a mere stepping-stone to the priesthood. First of all, in the collects which conclude the litany the origin of the two orders is ascribed to different sources: in the rite for the diaconate the collect begins, "Almyghtie God, whiche by thy devyne providence, haste appoynted dyverse Orders of ministers . . .", but in the rite for the priesthood it begins, "Almyghtie God, gever of all good thinges, which by thy holy spirit has appoynted dyverse orders of ministers . . .". The collect in the rite for the episcopate begins in the same way as that for priests. Taken on its own, this variation might not seem significant, even though otherwise the collects are almost identical, except for the mention of the particular order and the inclusion of a clause in the collect for the diaconate recalling the appointment of Stephen and others as deacons, but it assumes significance in view of the fact that there is no reference anywhere in the rite for the diaconate to the bestowing of the Holy Spirit on the candidates. Cranmer did not adopt the formula *Accipe Spiritum Sanctum* found in many Pontificals at the imposition of hands on deacons but composed his own, which made no reference to the Holy Spirit.[1] The Holy Spirit is mentioned only once in the whole rite, and that is in an additional question at the beginning of the examination which does not appear in the other two rites or in Bucer's rite:

> Do you trust that you are inwardly moved by the holy Ghoste, to take upon you thys offyce and ministracion, to serve God, for the promotinge of hys glorye, and the edyfyinge of hys people?

This requirement, that the candidates should be moved by the Holy

Cranmer, but the accuracy of this account is open to question; see Frere, *Marian Reaction,* pp. 116–17.

[1] See above, p. 25, n. 2.

Spirit, is almost certainly derived from the account of the appointment of the Seven in Acts 6, where the Apostles direct the people to choose men "full of the Holy Ghost". These differences between the rites suggest that Cranmer saw a distinction between the rite for the diaconate, in which candidates are expected to have the gift of the Holy Spirit before hands are laid on them, and the rite for the priesthood where the Spirit is conferred at the imposition of hands. Thus it would seem that Cranmer distinguished between two different sources of power in ordination. The power or authority given to deacons at the imposition of hands was the permission of the Church to exercise certain functions for which they were fitted. This power originated in the Church, which by divine providence working through the Apostles had created the office of deacons. On the other hand, the power bestowed on priests came from the Holy Spirit, which had been given by Christ to the Apostles and their successors. It is perhaps significant that in the discussion in his Commonplace Book on the question "Quod ordo sit sacramentum" Cranmer mentioned only the powers of the priesthood. The question of grace being conferred on deacons did not seem to occur to him in this context.[1] Nor in any other of his writings is there any mention of the Holy Spirit being given by the Apostles to deacons, but only to bishops and priests.

The differences between the examination in the rite for the diaconate and that in the rite for the priesthood reveal a further difference in the nature of the diaconate from the office in the medieval Church. Of the eight questions in the rite for the priesthood, only four appear in the rite for the diaconate, and of these the one on their belief in the Scriptures is a briefer version of that in the priests' rite which omits all reference to teaching from the Scriptures, and instead a further question is included which asks whether they will diligently read the Scriptures to the people. In place of the other questions in the rite for the priesthood, which are concerned with duties applicable only to priests and bishops, there is a single long question which describes the functions of a deacon and asks if the candidates will fulfil them gladly and willingly. This reveals that the diaconate is no longer simply to provide assistance to the priest during services. All the duties which the Pontificals had assigned to it are still included,[2] but to them has been added the duty of searching out the needy, which had disappeared

[1] Pp. 477–8.
[2] Cf. the Sarum Pontifical: "Diaconum oportet ministrare ad altare, evangelium legere, baptizare, et praedicare" (Maskell, II, p. 202).

from the office in medieval times, and which *The King's Book* had noted was part of its function in the primitive Church.[1]

It is possible that Cranmer may have derived these two differences from the medieval diaconate—the absence of bestowal of the Holy Spirit and the addition of the duty of caring for the needy—from Bucer, who in the preface to his rite of ordination stated,

> Ministeria ecclesiae sunt duplicis generis, iuxta spiritus sancti institutionem. Uno continetur procuratio verbi, sacramentorum et disciplinae Christi, quae pertinet proprie ad Episcopos et presbyteros. Altero curatio egentium quae committebatur iis, quos vacabant Diaconos. . . .[2]

Or he may have been influenced by other continental Reformers who were trying to restore to the diaconate what they regarded as its scriptural functions, or perhaps by the *Paraphrase* of Erasmus, whose account of the appointment of the Seven in Acts 6 makes no mention of grace being conferred on them: "These seven, whan they wer chosen, wer set before thapostles, to thentent that what was done, they shulde allow the same by their authoritie."[3] It is equally possible that he developed the ideas by independent study of the New Testament.

[1] See above, p. 11.    [2] *Scripta Anglicana*, p. 238.    [3] See above, p. 27.

The "Liturgy of Compromise" adopted there provides for the four offices of the reformed ministry—pastors, teachers, elders, and deacons—and it states that, "as concerning the order and form of electing, the same form is to be observed which hath already been practised and is hereunto annexed", but no such rite is actually annexed.[1] The same provisions and statement occur in what is described as the "Old Discipline" but again no rite is included.[2] This was reformed in 1557 and the "New Discipline" provided that seniors, deacons, and all other ministers, except teachers and ministers of the word, should be appointed for one year only; that public prayer and fast be made before and at the election of all ministers; that before the election of the ministers, seniors, and deacons, "the places off the Scriptures for that purpos most fit be openlye redd, and a Sermon to be made uppon the same, As for the present purpose shall be most convenient"; that the elections were to be by ballot; and that "imposition off handes with praier be used at the institution off the saied ministers, seniors, and Deacons, according to the doctrine and examples off the Scriptures".[3]

A similar practice was followed by those exiles who were expelled from Frankfort and who sought refuge in Geneva. Their service book contained, not a complete Ordinal, but, like most of the reformed rites of ordination, simply a series of instructions as to what was to be done, based on Calvin's practice in ordaining, leaving the ministers involved to use their own words.[4] When a minister was required, the congregation were to be assembled and, if there was a choice of candidates, they were to appoint two or three to be examined by the elders and other ministers. The examination was to cover the doctrine and life of the candidates and to discover whether they had sufficient ability in preaching. After this, the examiners were to signify who in their opinion was the most suitable candidate, and allow a period of at least eight days for the people to make inquiries about the life and manners of the candidate and make objections to him. During this period the people were to "humble themselves to God, by fasting, and prayer, that bothe their election may be agreable to his will, and also profitable to the churche". If no objections were made to the candidate, one of the ministers was to present him again to the church at the morning

---

[1] *The Liturgy of Compromise*, ed. G. W. Sprott (1905), pp. 251–2.
[2] *A Brieff discours off the troubles begonne at Franckford in Germany Anno Domini 1554* (1846 edn), pp. cxiii–cxv.
[3] Ibid., pp. cxxv–cxxvi.
[4] Text in W. D. Maxwell, *The Liturgical Portions of the Genevan Service Book* (1931), pp. 165–8.

service, "framying his sermon, or some parte therof, to the settyng forthe of his dewtie". Then in the afternoon the ordination, or election as it was called, took place. There was no imposition of hands, but the minister who had preached prayed "as God shal move his herte" prior to the election, and afterwards he "geveth thankes to God with request of suche thinges as shalbe necessarie for his office". The service concluded with the singing of a psalm. The service book also described the offices of doctors, elders, and deacons, but gave no instructions for their election.[1]

When Elizabeth came to the throne in 1558, the exiles returned to England and many desired to continue the ministry to which they had become accustomed. To their dismay, the Ordinal of 1552 was restored with only small alterations: the Oath of the King's Supremacy was now styled, "The Oath of the Queen's sovereignty", and was directed against the power and authority of all foreign potentates, instead of against the usurped power and authority of the Bishop of Rome; and the special suffrage in the litany in the rites for deacons and priests was omitted, no doubt simply by accident.[2] The Puritan party found the Ordinal objectionable and throughout Elizabeth's reign they maintained a constant pressure for its reform. They regarded it as identical with the medieval rites[3] and thought that those ordained by it were not duly ordained according to the requirements of the New Testament. Their ideal was the structure of ministry and ordination found in the continental reformed Churches, and many refused to subscribe to the Thirty-nine Articles of Religion until that should be established in England.

One of their main objections to the ministry of the Church of England was that insufficient care was taken to ensure that only suitable candidates were ordained. They insisted that ministers of the gospel must have lives worthy of that gospel and be endowed with the ability to preach. The provisions for examining candidates for ordination were inadequate for that to be ascertained, and the provisions made for objections to be raised against unsuitable men were insufficient. Thomas

---

[1] These are not reproduced by Maxwell.

[2] Text in *Liturgical Services of the Reign of Queen Elizabeth*, ed. W. K. Clay (PS, 1847), pp. 272–98.

[3] "Their pontificall (which is annexed to the boke of common prayer, and whereunto subscribing to the Articles, we must subscribe also) whereby they consecrate Bishoppes, make ministers and deacons, is nothing else but a thing worde for worde drawne out of the Popes pontifical" (*Puritan Manifestoes*, ed. W. H. Frere and C. E. Douglas (1907), p. 30).

Cartwright, the leading Puritan divine, in a controversy with John Whitgift, who was later to become Archbishop of Canterbury, objected to the fact that the examination was entrusted to the archdeacon alone. He asked why the bishop did not ascertain the candidate's fitness himself, and he complained that the congregation which was to have the candidate as its pastor, and which would therefore be particularly concerned about his suitability, was not asked for its objections. The congregation at the ordination, whose objections were sought, did not usually know the candidate at all, nor were they given any time to make inquiries about him or experience his ability.[1]

The bishops were not indifferent to the importance of ensuring that candidates for the ministry were suitable, although they did not lay the same stress on the ability to preach. They disagreed with the Puritans, however, over the question of who was to examine them, believing that they were quite capable of doing this themselves and seeing no reason to permit the people to have any more share in it than they already had. Whitgift replied to Cartwright's criticism by denying that the examination was committed to one man; it was committed both to the bishop and to the archdeacon, who were the most suitable people for this purpose, and more were not necessary. The bishop did not admit men to the ministry only on the report of the archdeacon, but he did ascertain their fitness himself. It was totally impracticable for a number of reasons for the church of which he was to be pastor to make trial of the candidate, and the provisions for objections were quite adequate.[2] This Cartwright denied; the difficulties over the parish examining, which Whitgift had brought forward, were not insuperable, and the present provisions were not sufficient to prevent unsuitable men from obtaining ordination.[3]

The Puritans wanted the congregation to have not only opportunity to examine the candidates and to object to them, but also the right of electing them, as they believed was the practice of the primitive Church.[4] Whitgift denied that there was any scriptural evidence for this practice and he disputed with Cartwright that the Greek verb

[1] *The Works of John Whitgift*, ed. John Ayre (PS, 1851–53), I, pp. 300–10; see also John Udall, *A Demonstration of the trueth of that Discipline which Christ hath prescribed in his worde for the government of his Church, in all times and places, untill the end of the world* (1588), pp. 35ff.

[2] Whitgift, *Works* I, pp. 300–10.

[3] *The Second Replie of Thomas Cartwright agaynst Maister Doctor Whitgiftes second answer touching the Churche Discipline* (1575), pp. cxlvff.

[4] *Puritan Manifestoes*, p. 10; Udall, pp. 29ff.

χειροτόνειν meant "to elect", translating it instead "to ordain". He admitted that in some places in the Apostles' time and even up to Cyprian's time the people did elect their ministers, but he denied that this was always necessary and claimed that "now in this state of the church it were most pernicious and hurtful".[1]

The nature of the diaconate too came in for criticism from the Puritans: "Touchyng Deacons, though their names be remaining, yet is the office fowlie perverted and turned upside downe, for their dutie in the primitive church was to gather the almes diligently, and to distribute it faithfully, also for the sicke and impotent persones to provide painefully, having ever a diligent care, that the charitie of godly men wer not wasted upon loiterers and idle vagabounds. Now it is the first step to the ministrie, nay, rather a mere order of priesthode."[2] Whitgift admitted that collecting and providing for the poor was part of their office in the primitive Church, but claimed that they also preached and baptized, citing Stephen and Philip as examples. Cartwright denied this, maintaining that Philip preached and baptized not in his capacity as a deacon but as an evangelist, and that Stephen did not preach but merely defended himself against his accusers, which it was lawful for any Christian to do.[3]

The Puritans complained about the absence of lay elders, whom they believed were demanded by the New Testament, and they strongly criticized the distinction between bishops and priests, believing that the New Testament required the equality of ministers.[4] Therefore they resented some powers of the ministry being given to one man, the bishop, and not being shared by all ministers and elders. In particular they thought it wrong for the bishop to ordain alone, but they agreed that imposition of hands should be used.[5] As in the questions of election, the controversy arose from a difference of opinion as to whether the New Testament prescribed a definite pattern which could never be changed. In both cases the Puritans claimed that it did, but the bishops,

---

[1] Whitgift, *Works* I, pp. 339–425; see also Matthew Sutcliffe, *A Treatise of Ecclesiasticall Discipline* (1591), pp. 28–36.

[2] *Puritan Manifestoes*, p. 15; see also Udall, pp. 56ff.

[3] Whitgift, *Works* III, pp. 58–72; see also Sutcliffe, pp. 109–17.

[4] *Puritan Manifestoes*, p. 15; Udall, p. 47.

[5] Puritan proposals vary a little. Sometimes the imposition of hands is to be by both ministers and elders, sometimes by the ministers alone. In one case at least only one minister lays hands on the candidate, but this does not really conflict with the Puritan principle because he acts with the commission of the other ministers and elders and has no authority to ordain without this. See Udall, p. 41; *Puritan Manifestoes*, p. 97; *The Seconde Parte of a Register*, ed. Albert Peel (1915), I, pp. 165, 167, 307, and II, p. 218.

although willing to admit that the practices suggested by the Puritans were possible, refused to allow that the New Testament prescribed them as essential; the Church was free to order these matters as it saw fit, providing that it did nothing contrary to the word of God. Thus Whitgift did not attempt to argue that only bishops could ordain. Indeed he was ready to admit that "in the apostles' time there was divers manners of ordaining and electing ministers. For sometime one alone did choose and ordain, sometimes many, sometimes ministers only, and sometimes the people also." He was concerned only to defend the right of bishops to ordain without the assistance of others, and to insist that the New Testament did not require other ministers always to be involved in ordination. He attempted to justify this position by reference to 1 Tim. 5.22, "Lay thy hands rashly on none", and Titus 1.5, "that he should appoint ministers in every town". Cartwright maintained that these quotations did not prove anything. He was willing to admit that Timothy and Titus had the power of ordaining, but his claim was that they had not the power of ordaining alone, without the presbytery.[1] At the same time Whitgift insisted that episcopacy was "an institution apostolical and divine; and so always hath been held by a continued course of times from the Apostles to this very age of ours".[2] Others, such as James Pilkington, Bishop of Durham, were not prepared to make such high claims for it: "The privileges and superiorities, which bishops have above other ministers, are rather granted by man for maintaining better order and quietness in commonwealths, than commanded by God in his word."[3]

Whatever their views on the origin of episcopacy, however, hardly a single author can be found in the Elizabethan period who explicitly denied that priests could ordain. The Thirty-nine Articles, for example, do not assert the necessity of episcopal ordination. Article 36 states that the Ordinal contains all that is necessary for a valid ordination, and does not contain anything that is superstitious or ungodly, while Article 23 states that those are lawful ministers who are called and sent by men who have "publick authority" given to them to do this; it does not even say that prayer and the imposition of hands are necessary, and indeed Article 25 says that Orders, along with the other four "commonly called Sacraments", has not any visible sign or ceremony ordained of God. It would appear that this was yet another instance where it was

---

[1] Whitgift, *Works* I, pp. 425ff.
[2] John Strype, *The Life and Acts of John Whitgift* (1822) II, p. 170.
[3] *The Works of James Pilkington*, ed. James Scholefield (PS, 1842), p. 493.

thought that the Church was free to decide what method should be used. On the other hand, the care taken in the consecration of Matthew Parker as Archbishop of Canterbury at the beginning of Elizabeth's reign might seem to suggest that churchmen of the period did believe that only bishops could validly ordain, but it would appear from the documents connected with this ceremony that those involved were simply concerned to ensure that it was legal and canonical.[1] The cases of two men, Whittingham and Travers, are also sometimes cited as evidence that the Elizabethan bishops only accepted ordinations by bishops as valid, but in fact neither case supports this conclusion.

William Whittingham was Dean of Durham and the charge was brought against him that he was not properly ordained, but it would appear from Strype's account of the affair that it was not the validity of non-episcopal ordinations which was at question but whether there was sufficient evidence that Whittingham had been ordained at all. He claimed that he had been ordained while in exile at Geneva during Mary's reign according to the rite used there, and that this was suffic-ient to admit him to the ministry of the Church of England. The commissioners appointed to deal with the case objected to the first certificate that he produced because there was no indication where it had been made, there were no sworn witnesses, and because he claimed to have been ordained "by lot and election". In the second certificate he produced, the first two faults were corrected, and the third amended to "suffrages", but objections were again raised to the identity of the witnesses, and to the fact that "there were wanting *externae solennitates, authoritatem ordinantis*. Which, by Bucer's opinion, ought to be a bishop or superintendent. And the *formam ordinationis*, which chiefly consisteth in imposition of hands."[2] As Edwin Sandys, the Archbishop of York, pointed out, the validity of ordination at Geneva was not touched, "for he hath not received his ministry in that church, or by any authority or order from that church, so far as yet can appear".[3] Un-fortunately Whittingham died before the proceedings against him were concluded.

The case of Walter Travers was rather different. He had refused to be ordained in England and had received ordination in Antwerp. When he was nominated as Master of the Temple, Whitgift challenged his right to that position on the grounds that he was not rightly ordained.

---

[1] See below, pp. 75–6, for what actually happened at Parker's consecration.
[2] John Strype, *Annals of the Reformation* (1824) II, ii, pp. 170–2.
[3] Ibid. II, ii, p. 620.

However, it would appear that it was not the intrinsic power of presbyters to ordain which Whitgift was here denying, but their authority to ordain for the Church of England in this particular instance, for he drew a distinction between men such as Whittingham who "in time of persecution was ordained Minister by those who had authority in the Church persecuted", and men such as Travers who "in the time of peace, refusing to be made Minister at home, gaddeth into other countries to be ordained by such as had no authority: condemning thereby the kind of ordering Ministers at home".[1] Similarly, Edmund Grindal, who was Archbishop of Canterbury from 1575 to 1583, appears to have been willing to license a certain John Morrison to preach and to minister the sacraments, although he had received only Presbyterian ordination in Scotland. This suggests that Grindal regarded Scottish presbyters as having lawful authority to ordain.[2]

Thus, although the evidence is not conclusive, it would seem that the Elizabethan bishops did not argue that the New Testament demanded that only bishops should ordain, in the same way that the Puritans argued that it demanded that ordination must be by elders and ministers together, but they simply defended the position that ordination must be by men with lawful authority, and that in England this authority lay with the bishops alone. Nor is it until towards the end of this period that the belief emerges that grace is passed on from minister to minister in unbroken succession, although some earlier writers had maintained that the authority to ordain had been passed on in this way. Even William Fulke, a Puritan theologian, asserted that the office of a bishop had been passed on from the Apostles and that, had this chain been broken, the office would have ceased to exist. At the same time he denied that ordination was a sacrament or bestowed grace.[3] Another writer, John Bridges, defended the view that the Roman Church, in spite of its corruptions, still had valid ministers: "For if our brethren will make them but meere laye men, then are neither they nor wee any ministers at all, but mere laye men also. For who ordained us ministers but such ministers as were either their selves of their Ministrie; or at leaste were made ministers of those ministers?"[4] Thomas Bilson appears to have been the first to state that

---

[1] Strype, *Whitgift* III, pp. 182–6.
[2] John Strype, *The History of the Life and Acts of Edmund Grindal* (1821), p. 596.
[3] *Fulke's Answers to Stapleton, Martiall, and Sanders*, ed. Richard Gibbings (PS, 1848), p. 310; William Fulke, *Defence of the sincere and true translations of the Holy Scriptures into the English Tongue*, ed. C. H. Hartshorne (PS, 1843), pp. 468–9.
[4] John Bridges, *A Defence of the government established in the Church of England for Ecclesiastical matters* (1587), p. 1276.

the grace given in ordination was transmitted through the apostolic succession. He was also one of the few writers of the period to affirm that the power of ordaining belonged to bishops alone.[1]

It was over the question of the conferring of grace in ordination that another of the Puritans' objections to the Anglican Ordinal arose. They regarded the words "Receive the Holy Ghost" in the rite for the priesthood as ridiculous and blasphemous.[2] Whitgift maintained that it was no more ridiculous and blasphemous to use these words than it was to use the words which Christ used at the Last Supper:

> the bishop by speaking these words doth not take upon him to give the Holy Ghost, no more than he doth to remit sins, when he pronounceth the remission of sins; but by speaking these words of Christ, "Receive the Holy Ghost; whose sins soever ye remit, they are remitted, etc.", he doth shew the principal duty of a minister, and assureth him of the assistance of God's Holy Spirit, if he labour in the same accordingly.

Cartwright, however, argued that there was a difference between a pronouncement and a command:

> the minister doth not command that the bread be the body of Christ, but he saith that it is: neither doth he command that sins should be forgiven, but pronounceth in the behalf of God that they are forgiven. It is not unlawful also that he with the congregation should make a prayer for the assistance or increase of God his gifts upon him that is ordained, but to command that he should receive it is merely unlawful.

He went on to ask why, if they felt it necessary to use Christ's words, they did not also use his action and blow upon the candidates as he did. Whitgift answered him by saying that it was lawful for men to recite the words of Christ in the name of Christ. The bishop was not claiming to have authority to give the Holy Spirit himself, "but he speaketh them as the words of Christ used in the like action; who (as I said before) doth most certainly give his Holy Spirit to those whom he calleth to the ministry".[3] As Cartwright then pointed out to him, this was not really the point at issue; both agreed that God gave his gifts to those whom he called to the ministry, but the question was whether he gave them by the ceremony of the laying on of hands.[4]

---

[1] Thomas Bilson, *The Perpetual government of Christes Church* (1593), pp. 109, 316.
[2] *A full and plaine declaration of Ecclesiasticall Discipline owt off the word off God* (1574), pp. 68–9; *Puritan Manifestoes*, p. 34.
[3] Whitgift, *Works* I, pp. 489–90.
[4] Cartwright, *Second Replie*, pp. ccxciiff.

It might seem that Whitgift and Cartwright are in fundamental agreement, for Whitgift seems to be saying that the bishop is only quoting Scripture to assure the candidate that God will bestow the necessary gifts upon him. However, ten years later, he definitely went beyond this and said that something was given by the action of the bishop. When asked whether the use of these words meant that the bishop had authority to give the Holy Spirit, he replied that,

> the Bishop did not thereby take upon him to give the Holy Ghost, but only *instrumentaliter;* even as the Minister giveth baptism. ... The words are Christ's words, used in the admitting of the Apostles to the ministry. And therefore used by us in the like action, to signify that God by our ministry and imposition of hands, as by the instruments, doth give his Holy Spirit to all such as are rightfully called to the ministry.[1]

Thomas Cooper, who was Bishop of Lincoln from 1571 to 1584, also used the analogy of baptism to defend the use of these words. He pointed out that in both cases there was a distinction "betweene the inward operation of the Holy Ghost, and the outward action done by the Minister". The bishop did not

> blasphemously take upon himselfe to give the Holy Ghost, no more that the Minister doth take upon him to forgive sins, when he saith, Ego absolvo te etc. But he resteth upon the promise of Christ, who by ordinary meanes calleth Ministers to their functions in the Church and sealeth them with such spirituall graces of his Spirit as are convenient for the same. For as he giveth Pastors and Ministers, although they be outwardly called by men, so doth he give them the Spirit of his grace, though men outwardly lay on their hands, when the words be spoken.[2]

Richard Hooker also supported the use of these words on the ground that in ordination the same power was bestowed as Christ had bestowed on the Apostles, and therefore the same words could be used. He, however, interpreted "Holy Ghost" rather differently from the other two. They seem to have shared the Puritans' understanding of it as referring to the gift of certain personal qualities to the minister. Hooker, on the other hand, understood it to mean the gift of "such power as the Spirit of Christ hath endued his Church withal, such power as neither prince nor potentate, king nor Caesar on earth can give". This was "an holy and a ghostly authority, authority over the souls of men, authority

[1] Strype, *Whitgift* I, p. 258.
[2] Thomas Cooper, "Defence of the Ceremonies", in "The Seconde Parte of a Register", Dr Williams's Library, Morrice Mss. B.II, fols. 236–7.

a part whereof consisteth in power to remit and retain sins". He added
that the reason why they did not breathe on the candidates as Christ did
was so that "neither Spirit nor spiritual authority may be thought to
proceed from us, which are but delegates or assigns to give men
possession of his graces".[1]

Finally, the Puritans demanded that fasting should accompany all
ordinations, following New Testament practice;[2] that Roman priests
should not be treated as if they were ministers of the gospel;[3] and that
even the name "priest" should not be used, since it recalled either the
Old Testament priesthood, which had been abolished, or the "popish
priesthood of abomination", which was of Antichrist: "Suche oughte
not to have place amongste us, as the scriptures manifestly teache.
Besides that we never reade in the newe Testament, that this worde
priest as touching offyce, is used in the good parte."[4] Whitgift thought
that whether or not the name was used was an indifferent matter:
"priest" could signify a minister of the gospel just as much as a sacri-
ficer.[5] Hooker preferred the name "presbyter" because he had no wish
to offend those to whom the word "priest" was odious, but he also
thought that it really did not matter which word was used.[6]

The Puritans not only criticized the Ordinal but made positive efforts
to secure reforms. In 1581 they offered to the Queen a number of
articles requesting changes in matters connected with the ministry, and
asked that they might be enacted at the next Parliament. The Queen
submitted them to the bishops for their comments.[7] The articles
requested, among other things, that public notice of a candidate for
ordination be given to the congregation which was to have him and a
period of twenty days allowed for objections. The bishops replied that
"this is innecessarye and in vayne, unlesse he that is to be admitted had
bene dwellinge in that parishe before: which will happen verye
seldome". It would also waste time and give occasion for quarrelling.

---

[1] Richard Hooker, *Of the Laws of Ecclesiastical Polity* (1597) v, lxxvii, 5–8.
[2] *Puritan Manifestoes*, p. 97.
[3] Ibid., p. 9.
[4] Ibid., p. 25.
[5] *Works* III, p. 351.
[6] Hooker, v, lxxviii, 2–3.
[7] J. E. Neale, *Elizabeth I and her Parliaments 1559–1581* (1953), p. 400. Text of articles and
bishops' answers in Strype, *Whitgift* III, pp. 47ff, and also in his *Annals of the Reformation*
III, ii, pp. 302ff, but as another answer to the articles of 1584, see below, p. 49. This latter
version is reproduced by Edward Cardwell, *Documentary Annals of the Reformed Church of
England* (1839) I, pp. 417ff, who says that Strype must be wrong as they are obviously
not the same articles, and he suggests that they belong to a later date.

The Puritans also wanted to put an end to ordinations in private, and they asked that they should always be performed on a Sunday in the cathedral church of the diocese. The bishops agreed that it should be in public but were unwilling that it should be restricted to the cathedral. Finally, the Puritans asked that a bishop "shall not make any Minister, but suche as shall by the Deane and Chapiter, or the more part of them, or six learned preachers of the diocese then present be allowed for a man meete and sufficient, by subscription of their hands to some writinge, declaringe their assent in allowinge of him". The bishops, however, objected to this: "it will breed great trouble, and not worke that effect which is looked for, neyther can it in all places be performed".

A further attempt was made in 1584. A petition of sixteen articles was presented to the House of Lords by the Commons which tried to ensure that there should always be present at the ordination of priests a sufficient number of other priests to join with the bishop in laying their hands on the candidates, as was prescribed by the Ordinal. It asked that,

> no Bishoppe shall ordeyne any Ministre of the worde and sacraments, but with the assistance of six other Ministres, at the least; and thereto, suche only to bee chosen, as bee of good reporte for their lyfe, learned, continually resiant upon their benefices with cure; and which do give testimony of their care for the Churche of God, by their diligence in teaching and preaching in their charges. And that the sayd Ministres doo testifie their presence at the admission of such Ministres, by subscription of their handes to some act, importing the same. And furder, that this admission bee had and done publikely, and not in private house or chappell.

It also asked that notice be given to the parish and time allowed for inquiries to be made about the candidate and for objections to be lodged.[1]

Sandys replied to the petition in the name of the rest of the bishops and rejected both requests.[2] Strangely enough, Sandys had made a suggestion very similar to the first as early as 1562, but without success. His proposal went even further: no bishop should admit anyone to the ministry "without the consent of six learned ministers; who shall all lay their hands upon his head at his admission".[3] Whitgift made his own answers to the petition as well. He thought that the first request was neither necessary nor convenient. "It may tende to the nourishing of contention and schisme in the Churche: neither can it otherwise bee,

---

[1] Strype, *Whitgift* III, pp. 119–20.    [2] Ibid. I, pp. 350–1.
[3] Strype, *Annals of the Reformation* I, i, p. 506.

considering the wayward dispositions of many. It shall be therfore sufficient, that the Bishopp take unto him such as he thinketh to be meetest for the business, and which by law alreadie established are appointed for the same." He no doubt feared that to grant this request might be interpreted as an admission that the Church of England believed it necessary for a certain number of ministers to join in the ordination of a priest. As for their request for opportunity to object,

> it smelleth of popularitee, and of popular elections, long ago justly abrogated for the tumultuousnesse thereof; and indeed intolerable in a settled state, and where there is a Christian Magistrate. Neither could it work the effect which is pretended, the partie presented being altogether unknowen to them, and a meer stranger, as it must of necessity, for the most parte, come to passe. For how can the most parishes in the realme, take knoledge of the conversation of such, as have continually remayned in the Universitees, or in other places far from them?[1]

These reforms were modest, however, in comparison with the Bill which the Puritans presented to Parliament in the same year to replace the Prayer Book with a version of the service book which had been used by the exiles at Geneva.[2] It was, of course, defeated. There are a few differences between the ordination of ministers in this book and the original Genevan practice.[3] A period of at least twenty days is to be appointed instead of only eight for objections to be made to the candidates, and changes have been made in the ordination itself. The sermon begins the rite and it is to cover the duty of both the minister and the Church. Then the prayer of thanksgiving and petition for the candidate is made, instead of after the ordination, and the candidate is ordained by the imposition of hands of the "eldership", with these words being spoken by the minister who preached:

> According to this lawful calling, agreeable to the word of God, whereby thou art chosen Pastor in the name of God, stand thou charged with the pastoral charge of this people, over which the Holy Ghost hath made thee overseer, to govern this flock of God, which he hath purchased with his blood.

The second half of this charge is based on Acts 20.28. Like the Genevan service, the rite concludes with the singing of a psalm. The differences between the two are most probably to be accounted for by the influence

[1] Strype, *Whitgift* III, pp. 125-7.
[2] Horton Davies, *The Worship of the English Puritans* (1948), pp. 122ff.
[3] Text in *Fragmenta Liturgica*, ed. Peter Hall (1848), I, pp. 15-21.

THE PURITANS AND THE ORDINAL, 1550-1602

of the Anglican Ordinal upon the Puritans. This book also states that the election and ordination of doctors, elders, and deacons, is "as the Pastor's: the prayer, trial, and words of Ordination, respecting their special office". A revised version of this book was presented to Parliament in 1586, also with a Bill proposing that it should replace the Prayer Book, and when this again proved unsuccessful, the book was used by Puritans who fled into exile at Middleburgh.[1] A change is made in the method of selecting candidates for ordination in this edition. The congregation are now to select only one candidate, by fasting and prayer. He is then examined as before, except that he is also to preach to the congregation during the period of twenty days "that they may also discern of his fitness to communicate his gifts with them".

In a fourth edition of 1602 used at Middleburgh, full orders of service for the ordination of ministers, elders, and deacons are included, as well as the shorter instructions of the earlier editions.[2] As can be seen from Table 3 the ordination of ministers owes something to the rite drawn up by the reformer John a Lasco for the use of the exiled foreign congregations in London during the reign of Edward VI.[3] It is influenced directly by that rite and not by the version drawn up by John Knox in Scotland.[4] Unlike a Lasco's rite only one candidate is ordained at a time. It begins with an address describing the office and its duties, based in part on the description given by a Lasco at the election prior to the ordination. The examination is a shortened version of that in a Lasco's rite, but the blessing is drawn very closely from it:

God, our heavenly Father, who hath called you to this holy calling, illuminate you by his Spirit, strengthen you by his hand, and so direct you in your ministry, that you may walk in the same orderly, faithfully, and fruitfully, to the praise of his holy name, and the furthering and increasing of the kingdom of his Son Jesus Christ. Amen.

A marginal note states that the imposition of hands "is not used in the confirmation of those that have been ordained before, but only the giving of hands after the action". The admonition and prayer show

[1] Patrick Collinson, *The Elizabethan Puritan Movement* (1967), pp. 307-8. Text in *Reliquiae Liturgicae*, ed. Peter Hall (1847), I, pp. 71-5, 96-8.
[2] Text in *Reliquiae Liturgicae* I, pp. 75-96.
[3] John a Lasco, *Forma ac Ratio tota ecclesiastici ministerii, in peregrinorum, potissimum vero Germanorum, ecclesia: instituta Londini in Anglia per Edvardum Sextum* (n.p., n.d.), pp. 29-56.
[4] See below, pp. 55-6.

Table 3: The Influence of John a Lasco

| A Lasco's rite for ministers and superintendents | Puritan rite for ministers (1602) | Knox's rite for superintendents (1560) | Scottish Ordinal (1620), rite for ministers |
|---|---|---|---|
| (Description of office and duties) | Address describing office and duties | | Rubrics: Trial to be made of candidate and notice of ordination given to the parish |
| | | Sermon | SERMON |
| Question: Are candidates approved by the King? | | | PRESENTATION AND QUESTION AS TO SUITABILITY |
| | | Announcement: Candidate has been nominated and notice given to all concerned to attend | Question: Has trial been made and notice given to parish? |
| | | Objections asked three times | Reading of testimonial of trial and edict of notice |
| | | Consent of people asked | FINAL INQUIRY OF THE PEOPLE |
| | | | OATH OF SUPREMACY |
| | | | EXHORTATION TO CANDIDATE |
| Examination | Examination | Examination | |
| | | People asked if satisfied | EXAMINATION AND CONCLUDING PRAYER |

| | | | |
|---|---|---|---|
| Lord's Prayer | Lord's Prayer | Lord's Prayer | Lord's Prayer |
| Imposition of hands by ministers and elders accompanied by blessing | Imposition of hands by one or more ministers accompanied by blessing | Giving of right hand of fellowship by ministers and elders followed by blessing | IMPOSITION OF HANDS BY BISHOP AND MINISTERS accompanied by blessing |
| | | | DELIVERY OF BIBLE |
| | | (See above) | Giving of right hand of fellowship by bishop, ministers, and "Commissionars of the Church whereunto he is admitted" |
| Short admonition to people | Short admonition to candidate and people | | |
| Admonition to candidate | | Admonition to candidate | Admonition to candidate |
| | Prayer | | |
| | Lord's Prayer | | |
| A Psalm | | Psalm 23 | Psalm 23 |
| | | | FINAL COLLECT |
| Blessing | | | Grace |

little resemblance to a Lasco's. It is odd that the prayer should come at the end as in the original Genevan rite and not in the position in which it is found in both a Lasco's rite and the earlier Puritan rites. "The Manner of Ordaining Elders and Deacons" follows exactly the same pattern, except that there is no imposition of hands and the blessing reads: "The Almighty God and Father grant unto you all his grace, that in this your charge you may behave yourselves faithfully and fruitfully with comfort. Amen." There is no obvious resemblance to a Lasco who appointed separate services for elders and deacons on the same pattern as that for ministers, including an imposition of hands.

# 4. The Puritans and the Ordinal, 1603–1661

The situation in Scotland was different from that in England. There the Anglican Ordinal had never been introduced and the structure of ministry found in the continental reformed Churches had been adopted. The method of ordination was that prescribed in the Genevan service book, which had been brought back to Scotland by the Reformer John Knox in 1559 and which became the foundation of the Book of Common Order of the Church of Scotland.[1] In spite of efforts to prove the contrary, it seems assured that at first, as in Geneva, there was no imposition of hands in the ordination of ministers.[2] In addition to the normal offices of the reformed ministry, however, there was in Scotland the office of Superintendent, which appears to have been set up not as a type of permanent episcopacy but simply as a temporary expedient to organize the Presbyterian system, to take charge of vacant parishes, and to ordain suitable ministers for them. The superintendents had no power of ordination inherent in their office but simply acted under the commission of the General Assembly of the Church.[3] Knox drew up a rite for their "election", which could also be used for the ordination of other ministers besides superintendents, and this was first used in 1560.[4] In 1569 the General Assembly ordered it to be printed,[5] and it appeared in all subsequent editions of the Book of Common Order, although in 1570 the Assembly enacted that all ministers other than superintendents were to be ordained according to the original rite in the Book of Common Order.[6] As can be seen from Table 3, it was based upon the rite for ordaining ministers and superintendents drawn up by John a Lasco. It differed from that rite in that there was no

[1] See above, pp. 39–40, and *The Book of Common Order of the Church of Scotland*, ed. G. W. Sprott (1901), pp. 13–16.

[2] Duncan Shaw, "The Inauguration of Ministers in Scotland: 1560–1620", *Records of the Scottish Church History Society* XVI (1966), pp. 35–62.

[3] J. L. Ainslie, *The Doctrines of Ministerial Order in the Reformed Churches of the Sixteenth and Seventeenth Centuries* (1940), pp. 105–19.

[4] Text in *The Book of Common Order*, ed. Sprott, pp. 20–7.

[5] *Acts and Proceedings of the General Assemblies of the Kirk of Scotland from the year MDLX* (1839–45) I, p. 155.

[6] Ibid. I, p. 176.

imposition of hands and only one candidate was to be ordained at a time. The bidding was closely copied from a Lasco, the examination was an expanded version of his, and the prayer, blessing, and admonition showed much similarity, although they had all been extensively revised. An order for the admission of elders and deacons has also been preserved. This owes nothing to a Lasco's rites. After their election the candidates were to attend Church on a given Sunday and after the sermon their names were read aloud and they were admonished about the dignity of their vocation, their duty, and the duty of the people. Then a prayer was read, thanking God for the ministry and asking for the gift of the Holy Spirit. There followed the Lord's Prayer, the "Rehearsal of the belief", the singing of Psalm 103.19–22, the reading of a very brief exhortation to the candidates, and the service ended, rather strangely, with a short prayer for the King and the Regent.[1]

Gradually, however, the position changed. Firstly, the imposition of hands began to be adopted at the ordination of ministers. The Second Book of Discipline, which appeared shortly before 1580, stated that the ceremonies of ordination were fasting, prayer, and the imposition of hands by other ministers, elders, and doctors.[2] It did not immediately become the universal practice, however, and in 1597, under pressure from James VI, the General Assembly ordered "that there be ane uniformitie in the ordinatioun of the Ministrie throughout the haill countrey, impositioun of hands".[3] Yet even this did not secure complete uniformity. Secondly, episcopacy was introduced in 1610, again under pressure from the King. Three ministers were sent to England to be consecrated as bishops, and from this time onwards episcopal ordination became the rule in Scotland, although no attempt was made to reordain all those who had previously received ordination from ministers and superintendents only. At first no rites for the ordination of bishops and ministers were provided. In 1611 the King instructed "that no minister be admitted without an exact trial preceding, and imposition of hands used in their ordination by the bishop and two or three ministers whom he shall call to assist the action: and to the end an uniform order may be kept in the admission of ministers, that a form thereof may be imprinted and precisely followed of every bishop".[4] This was not immediately implemented and it is probable that the bishops simply adapted the method prescribed in the

[1] Text in *The Book of Common Order*, ed. Sprott, pp. 28–30.
[2] *Acts and Proceedings of the General Assemblies* II, p. 493.
[3] Ibid. III, p. 925.
[4] John Spottiswoode, *History of the Church of Scotland* (1851) III, p. 211.

Book of Common Order. In a list of "Articles required for the service of the Church of Scotland", drawn up in about 1615 by John Spottis-woode, one of the three bishops consecrated in 1610, it is noted that "Ane Ordour for electioun of Archbischops and Bischops, in times heirafter, must be establischit by law; and in the mean qhyl, if his Maiestie purpose the translatioun of any, by occasioun of this vacancie of St Androwis, the form usit in the translating of Bischops heir in England wold be kepit". The list also mentions the need for "Ane uniform Ordour for electing of Ministeris and their resavinge".[1]

It was not until 1620 that an Ordinal appeared.[2] It is particularly interesting as an example of a compromise between the Anglican Ordinal and the ordination practice of the reformed Churches. Had the climate of opinion been more congenial, such rites might well have been adopted in England as a concession to the demands of the Puri-tans, since they meet almost all their objections to the Anglican rites. The Ordinal contains only two rites—for bishops and ministers. The diaconate does not seem to have been abolished, but it apparently continued as before in Scotland and did not become the first step to the ministry of the Word. It begins with a new Preface, which says nothing about bishops, priests, and deacons having existed since the Apostles' times. Indeed the word "priest" does not occur anywhere in the Ordinal, but instead the office is called "the Spirituall office of a Pastor", or "the holy function of ministry". The Preface simply says that it has always been unlawful for a man to take upon himself the office of a pastor unless he was admitted by prayer and the imposition of hands, and therefore this order has been prescribed and shall be at all times observed by "these that have power to ordaine or consecrate", leaving it indeterminate whether these were bishops or ministers. Nor are there any instructions as to dress anywhere in the Ordinal.

As can be seen from Table 3, the "Forme and Maner of Ordaining Ministers" is mainly a compound of Knox's rite for superintendents and the Anglican rite for priests, those elements drawn from the latter being indicated in the Table by capital letters. As in Knox's rite only one candidate is ordained at a time. The parts drawn from the Anglican rite are copied almost exactly, except for the delivery of the Bible, which is accompanied by the words, "this is the Booke of Scripture,

[1] *Original Letters relating to the Ecclesiastical Affairs of Scotland, chiefly written by, or addressed to His Majesty King James the Sixth after his accession to the English Throne* (1851) II, p. 446.
[2] Text in *Scottish Liturgies of the Reign of James VI*, ed. G. W. Sprott (2nd edn, 1901), pp. 111–31.

which thou must studie continuallie, and mak the ground and reule of thy doctrine and living", and for the final collect, which is considerably modified and includes an element of thanksgiving for the calling of the candidate to the office. There are slight variations in the bidding from Knox's rite, but the prayer for the Holy Spirit follows his version very closely. Its central petition was:

> Looke upon us mercifullie, O Lord, thou that onlie art King, Teacher, and High Preist to thy owne flock, and send into this our brother, whome in thy name wee are now to admitte unto the ministrie of they Church, such a portion of thy Holy Spirite as thereby hee may rightlie devyde thy Worde, to the instruction of thy flock, and confutation of all pernicious errours, . . .

It then inserted the petition from the collect concluding the litany in the Anglican rite, omitted from this rite, before continuing with the text of Knox's prayer. In Knox's prayer the words, "are now to admitte unto the ministrie of they Church" had been "have charged with the chief care of Thy Church, within the bounds of . . .". The blessing also followed Knox very closely, but was prefaced by a statement of what was being given by the imposition of hands. It is to be noted that this is in the plural; the bishop speaks on behalf of all the ministers who share in the act of ordaining.

> In the name of God, and by the authoritie committed unto us by the Lord Jesus Christ, wee give unto thee power and authoritie to preach the Word of God, to minister his holie Sacraments, and exercise Discipline in such sort as is committed unto ministers by the order of our Church; and God, the Father of our Lord Jesus Christ, who hes called thee to the office of a watchman over His people, multiplie His graces with thee, illuminat thee with his Holie Spirit, comfort and strengthen thee in all vertue, governe and guide thy ministrie to the praise of His holie name, to the propagation of Christe's kingdome, to the comfort of his Church, and to the discharge of thy owne conscience in the day of the Lord Jesus, to whome, with the Father and the Holy Ghost, be all honour, praise, and glorie, now and ever. Amen.

The "forme and Maner of Consecrating an Archbishope or Bishope", perhaps rather surprisingly, owes almost nothing to Knox's rite. It retains the Communion service but omits the Epistle and Gospel, and also the litany and its concluding collect. It begins with rubrics directing that at least three bishops must consecrate a bishop, and four an archbishop, that there are to be public prayers first and then a sermon on the office and duty of a bishop, and after this objections to the candidate are to be asked three times, the last two features clearly the results of the influence of Knox's rite. The service proceeds as the Anglican rite as far as the hymn "Come Holy Ghost", with one alteration: the bidding which preceded the litany in the Anglican rite is transferred to a position after the hymn, so that it immediately precedes the prayer before the laying on of hands, the same position which the bidding occupies in the rite for ministers. It follows approximately the Anglican wording, with the additional ending, "and therefore wee will beseich you that are heer assembled, to assist us with your fervent devotione to Almightie God, saying:". The prayer that follows is a mixture of the Anglican one and the final collect from the Anglican rite, which is otherwise omitted from this service. The only other difference in the rite from the Anglican service is that in place of the imperative formula at the imposition of hands, there is:

> Wee, by the authoritie given us of God, and of his Sone the Lord Jesus Christ, give unto thee the power of Ordination, imposition of hands, and correction of maners, within the Dioceses whereunto thou art, or hereafter shall be called. And God Almightie bee with thee in all thy wayes, encresse his graces into thee, and guyde thy ministrie to the praise of his holie name, and the comfort of his Church. Amen.

This Ordinal is noteworthy not simply as a concession to Puritan requirements, but in some ways as an improvement on the original Anglican rites. The absence of the Communion service from the rite for ministers is to be regretted, but, on the other hand, the prayer before the imposition of hands in that rite, although it does not give thanks, as the Anglican one did, does pray for the Holy Spirit to be sent upon the candidate. The inclusion of a bidding before it also restores to the service a feature of the primitive rites, although the absence from both rites of provision for the prayer of the people, either in the litany and collect or in silence, is a loss. In the rite for the episcopate there are also improvements: the bidding is now more closely associated with the ordination prayer, and the prayer itself makes petition for the candidate at greater length. Finally, the formulas at the imposition of hands in both rites, although not naming the offices themselves, do make clear what powers are being conveyed, which the scriptural formulas of the Anglican rites fail to do very explicitly. In view of the limited knowledge of early ordination rites and practice at the time, these improvements must be attributed to good fortune.

Unfortunately, such a favourable view of the Ordinal was not shared by English Churchmen of the period. When it became known in England that it had no service for the diaconate and lacked the formula, "Receive the Holy Ghost", etc., in the rite for the priesthood, great concern was felt, as can be seen from a letter written by William Laud, the Archbishop of Canterbury, to James Wedderburn, Bishop of Dunblane, on 20 April 1636:

> Whereas you desire a copy of our Book of Ordination, I have here sent you one. And I have acquainted his Majesty with the two great reasons that you give, why the Book which you had in King James's time is short and insufficient. As, at first, that the Order of Deacons is made but as a lay office, at least, so that book may be understood. And secondly, that in the admission to priesthood, the very essential words of conferring order are left out. At which his Majesty was much troubled, as he had great cause, and concerning which he hath commanded me to write, that either you do admit of our book of Ordination, or else that you amend your own in these two gross oversights, or anything else, if in more it be to be corrected, and then see the Book reprinted. . . .[1]

Later in the same year Charles I sent instructions to the Scots for the revision of their Prayer Book, in which he specifically directed, "that in your Book of Orders, in giving Orders to Presbyters, you keep the words of the English Book without change; Receive the Holy Ghost, etc.".[2] A revised Ordinal appeared in 1636 and, although no copy of it is extant, it would appear from the exceptions made against it by the General Assembly of the Church of Scotland in 1638 that it was more or less identical with the English Ordinal.[3] It was, however, extremely short-lived. Within a year of its appearance, the Ordinal, the Prayer Book, and episcopacy were rejected by the Scots, and Presbyterianism was established.

Meanwhile, in England on the accession of James I in 1603 hopes had risen among Puritans that they might now be able to gain the concessions they had been denied under Elizabeth, and when at the beginning of 1604 the King called a conference at Hampton Court to discuss with them their objections to the Prayer Book and other grievances, they asked that bishops might always be assisted in the ordination of priests by "six grave preachers".[4] This met with some

---

[1] W. Prynne, *Hidden Workes of Darkness brought to publicke Life, or a necessary Introduction to the History of the Archbishop of Canterburies Traill* (1645), pp. 152–3.

[2] Ibid., p. 156.

[3] "Animadversiones upon the Bishopps Ther booke of Ordinatione of Presbyters and Deacons", in James Gordon, *History of Scots Affairs* (1841) II, pp. 92–3.

[4] Collinson, *The Elizabethan Puritan Movement*, p. 457.

success; in the Constitutions and Canons Ecclesiastical issued later in the year it was directed that the bishop should examine the candidates in the presence of members of his cathedral staff or other sufficient preachers of the diocese, at least three in number, who were also to assist in the imposition of hands. If he was prevented from examining the candidate himself, these ministers were to do it instead. The Canons also ordered that ordinations were to take place in the cathedral church in the time of divine service upon the Sundays immediately following the Ember Weeks, and they repeated other directions which had been made during the reign of Elizabeth or which were in the Ordinal itself: none was to be made deacon and priest on the same day, nor ordained without a Title; candidates for the diaconate were to be at least twenty-three years old and candidates for the priesthood twenty-four years old, and evidence of their learning and moral conduct was to be obtained.[1] This was by no means the end of Puritan objections to the Ordinal, as can be seen from the various petitions and pamphlets which appeared in the first part of the seventeenth century. All the old criticisms were repeated, and new ones added, such as the fact that priests were asked in their examination if they would exercise the discipline of Christ but were not allowed to do so in reality, nor were they even given authority to do so in their ordination.[2] No further concessions were obtained, however, and their criticisms were almost entirely ignored. The few who did enter into controversy with them did no more than restate the arguments used before in the reign of Elizabeth.[3]

The gulf between the Puritans and the rest of the Anglican Church was widening, largely owing to a change in attitude towards episcopacy among many Anglicans at this time. The Elizabethan churchmen on the whole had been content to regard episcopacy simply as one possible type of church government, but in the seventeenth century the

[1] Canons 31–35. Text in Edward Cardwell, *Synodalia* (1842) I, pp. 264–7. Although the Ordinal continued to state the minimum age for the diaconate as twenty-one, it had been raised to twenty-three by the Articles of 1575 (ibid. I, p. 133).

[2] *An abridgment of that booke which the Ministers of Lincoln Diocess delivered to his Majestie upon the first of December last* (1605), pp. 77ff; "A Petition of 22 London Ministers", in *A Survey Of the Booke of Common Prayer* (1606); Lewes Hewes, *Certaine grievances* (1641), p. 40.

[3] *The Second and Last Part of Reasons for Refusall of Subscription to the Booke of Common Prayer. . . . With an Answere to both at severall times returned them in publike conference, and in divers Sermons upon occasion preached in the Cathedrall Church of Exeter by Thomas Hutton* (1606), pp. 127ff; Thomas Sparke, *A Brotherly Perswasion to Unitie and Uniformitie in Iudgment and Practise touching the received and present Ecclesiastical government, and the authorised rites and ceremonies of the Church of England* (1607), pp. 75ff.

belief became widespread that episcopacy was of divine institution and therefore only bishops could validly ordain. Exceptions were possible when bishops could not be had, as in the foreign reformed Churches, and then priests might ordain. Such ordinations were not invalid, although they were less than perfect, as the episcopate was necessary only to the perfection, and not to the essence, of a Church.[1] This attitude can be seen in the case of the consecration of bishops for Scotland in 1610. Lancelot Andrewes, the Bishop of Ely, was unwilling to take part in the ceremony because he believed that they "must first be ordained presbyters, as having received no ordination from a bishop", but in the end he was persuaded to join in the consecration by Richard Bancroft, the Archbishop of Canterbury, on the grounds that in cases of necessity ordination by presbyters was valid.[2] Both John Cosin, who was Bishop of Durham, and Joseph Hall, Bishop of Exeter and later Bishop of Norwich, also affirmed that during the first half of the seventeenth century ministers ordained in foreign Churches were admitted to the ministry of the Church of England without reordination, but it is difficult to find much evidence for this.[3] An entirely different attitude, however, was taken towards those in England who refused ordination by bishops and were ordained by presbyteries or by congregations; no plea of necessity could be made in their case, and therefore all Puritan ordinations were regarded as invalid, and not simply as illegal, which had been the typical Elizabethan attitude. On the other hand, the Puritans too had changed their attitude towards episcopacy. Not all Puritans were originally convinced Presbyterians; some were Independents, but many would have been content with a more moderate episcopacy where the functions of the bishops were shared with the ministers, as they believed was the primitive practice. The uncompromising and hostile attitude of the English bishops towards them, however, made them determined to abolish episcopacy "root and branch", and establish the presbyterian system.

Much too late the episcopal party awoke to this threat and began

[1] Norman Sykes, *Old Priest and New Presbyter* (1956), pp. 58–84. For a fuller collection of the opinions of Anglican divines of this period see A. J. Mason, *The Church of England and Episcopacy* (1914), pp. 65–232.

[2] Spottiswoode, *History of the Church of Scotland* III, p. 209. A later version of the events states that Bancroft argued instead that consecrations could be performed *per saltum*. See Peter Heylyn, *Aerius Redivivus, or the History of the Presbyterians* (1670), p. 387. Since Spottiswoode was himself one of those consecrated, his evidence would seem the more reliable.

[3] Sykes, pp. 87–93.

to put forward various schemes to reduce episcopacy somewhat in the hope of reaching a compromise with the Puritans. In 1641 James Ussher, the Archbishop of Armagh, proposed a scheme for the government of the Church by the bishop together with his synod of clergy, which he believed was the practice of the early Church. The bishop would still remain the minister of ordination, but would act with the advice and consent of the other ministers.[1] Richard Baxter, the Puritan divine, later claimed that Ussher

> hath himself told me of his Judgment, that Bishops and Presbyters differ not as two Orders, but in Degree: and that *Ordinis est Ordinare*, so that he that hath the Order hath intrinsical power to Ordain; though he is regularly to do it under the Bishops oversight; And therefore it is not invalid and null, but only irregular or schismatical, when it is done disobediently against the Bishop (and so may be disabled *in foro exteriore*;)[2]

Baxter also said that Ussher had told him that he had argued this point to King Charles I and had shown him examples from the early Church of presbyters alone ordaining bishops.[3] Ussher's chaplain attributed similar views to him.[4] The theologian, Herbert Thorndike, writing at the same time as Ussher, also believed that in the ancient Church bishops had ordained with the advice and assistance of their presbyters and advocated the restoration of this practice.[5] A committee of the House of Lords was appointed on 1 March 1641, under the chairmanship of John Williams, the Bishop of Lincoln, to consider "all Innovations in the Church concerning Religion", and it was probably as a result of their deliberations that a Bill was introduced into the Lords in the July of that year which included in its proposals the provision that bishops should have twelve ministers in addition to the dean and chapter to assist them in conferring orders, and that no bishop should confer orders without the "presence and approbation" of four of them at least. It was read twice but went no further.[6]

[1] James Ussher, *Works*, ed. C. R. Elrington (Dublin 1864), XII, pp. 527–36.
[2] Richard Baxter, *A Treatise of Episcopacy* (1681), pt I, p. 69.
[3] *RB* II, 63.
[4] N. Bernard, *The Judgement of the Late Arch-Bishop of Armagh and Primate of Ireland of the Extent of Christs death, and satisfaction etc., Of the Sabbath, and observation of the Lords Day, Of the Ordination in other reformed Churches* (1657), pp. 125–6, and *Clavi Trabales* (1661), pp. 55–6. In this latter work Bernard also said that Ussher attached great importance to the inclusion of an imperative commission at the imposition of hands in ordination.
[5] Herbert Thorndike, *Theological Works* (LACT, 1844–56) I, i, pp. 75–7, 95–7.
[6] *Journal of the House of Lords* IV, p. 174; S. R. Gardiner, *The Constitutional Documents of the Puritan Revolution 1628–1660* (1889), pp. 97–8.

All this came much too late, however. The Puritans refused to compromise with the hated episcopate; the bishops were ejected from Parliament and imprisoned or forced to flee. Yet even then desperate attempts at compromise continued. The Oxford clergy suggested to Charles I in 1644 that he should concede that no bishop would ordain "without the counsell of the presbyters, that is the deane and chapter, and, if it bee thought fitt, any other grave ministers of the diocese"; ordination would always be in a solemn and public manner, and the bishop could grant the presbytery power to veto the ordination of any candidate, but not to compel him to ordain any candidate of whom he himself did not approve. These proposals were offered to the Puritans by the King's commissioners at Uxbridge, but the offer was refused,[1] and the King's final concessions went no further than this: in 1648 he proposed that after three years of presbyterian government, "the Power of Ordination shall not be exercised by Bishops, without the Counsel and Assistance of Presbyters".[2]

Thus episcopacy was abolished and the Westminster Assembly—a body of Puritan divines appointed by Parliament—was directed to frame an alternative system of church government and ordination. This caused considerable quarrelling and much debate between the Independents and Presbyterians in the Assembly.[3] The question was too urgent to wait for doctrinal agreement, however, as some machinery was needed to fill the vacancies left by the clergy of the episcopal party who had fled. The Presbyterians, therefore, being in the majority in the Assembly, forced through a "Directory for Ordination of Ministers" which followed the reformed model. This stated that it was expedient that no single congregation which could conveniently associate with others was to assume to itself the power of ordination, but that the examination and ordination properly belonged to the preaching presbyters. They were to ensure that a candidate was twenty-four years old and were to examine his learning, his calling, his life and conversation, and his ability in preaching. He was then to be sent to preach and converse with the people of the church where he was to serve so that they might judge his ability. After this the presbytery were to send to that congregation an announcement that on an appointed

---

[1] S. R. Gardiner, "A Scheme of Toleration propounded at Uxbridge in 1645", *English Historical Review* II (1887), pp. 340–2; John Rushworth, *Historical Collections* (1659–1701) III, ii, p. 873.

[2] *Journal of the House of Lords* X, p. 561.

[3] William A. Shaw, *A History of the English Church during the Civil Wars and under the Commonwealth 1640–1660* (1900) I, pp. 318–37.

day a competent number of its members were to appear before them to declare their consent or objections to his ordination. If they consented the ordination was to take place in their church and a solemn fast was to be kept by the congregation. Three or four presbyters were to attend and one of them was to preach a sermon on the duty of the minister and of the people. Then he was to examine the candidate on a specified number of points and ask the people about their willingness to receive, obey, and assist him. After this the presbyters were to lay their hands on him with a short prayer or blessing to this effect:

> Thankfully acknowledging the great mercy of God, in sending Jesus Christ for the Redemption of his People, and for his ascension to the right hand of the Father, and thence pouring out his Spirit, and giving gifts to Men, Apostles, Evangelists, Prophets, Pastors, and Teachers, for the gathering and building up of his Church, and for fitting and enclining this man to this great Work; To entreat him to fill him with his holy Spirit, to give him (whom in his Name we thus set apart to this holy Service) to fulfill the Work of his Ministry in all things, that he may both save himselfe and the People committed to his charge.

The service ended with an exhortation to the minister and the people, a prayer commending him and them to God, the singing of a psalm, and a blessing. The Directory also ordered that anyone already ordained by the rites of the Church of England was not to be reordained, as that ordination was valid, but was simply to be examined before being admitted to serve.[1]

Presbyterianism was hardly established, however, before the Independents gained the upper hand, and the ordination procedure was thrown into chaos; men were ordained either by presbyteries or by congregations, with imposition of hands or without, by the call of the Church or by their own sense of vocation. Eventually in 1660 Charles II was restored to the throne, and the bishops and clergy in exile returned to England. Even prior to this some had advocated the adoption of one of the schemes for a reduced episcopacy to secure agreement with the Puritans: Thorndike repeated in 1659 what he had said in 1641; John Gauden, who was later to become Bishop of Worcester, supported Ussher's scheme; and Edward Stillingfleet, who was also destined for that bishopric at a later date, did the same, asserting that no particular structure of government was prescribed for

---

[1] *Propositions Concerning Church-government and ordination of ministers* (1647), pp. 24–9.

the Church.[1] There was, however, not only a question of the modification of future practice but also the problem of those who had been ordained during the intervening period. This was recognized by George Morley, later Bishop of Winchester, who was sent to England in 1660 to negotiate with the Puritans prior to the return of Charles II. He wrote to Lord Clarendon:

> I forsee the main difficulty will be touching their ordination by presbyters without bishops, which we cannot acknowledge to be lawful, nor will they, I am afraid, be brought to acknowledge to be unlawful, and much less to be mere nullities. In this case I have thought of two expedients; the one that no notice be taken whether there have been any such ordinations or no; the other, that there may be an hypothetical reordination, by bishops, of such as were so ordained, which reordination, as it will be a provision against the nullity of such ordinations, so it will not conclude them to be nullities, but only irregular and uncertain. And this is much the better salvo of the two, if they can be brought to it.[2]

Thorndike proposed another way of overcoming this problem. While claiming that ordinations by presbyters against the authority of their bishops were null, he thought that it was not necessary that those so ordained should be reordained; their ordinations could be made valid by the consent of the Church, although he left it to his superiors to determine "the form and solemnity, in which the consent of the Church to their ordinations shall be celebrated".[3] There was, as might be expected, no suggestion that the ordinations of Independents should be recognized in any way.

The majority of the bishops, however, were in no mood to make concessions to the Puritans. Their exile on the continent might have made them feel more charitable towards the reformed Churches there, but it had the reverse effect on their feelings towards those who had driven them out of England. They ignored these suggestions and immediately embarked upon a policy of reordaining those who had not received episcopal ordination, sometimes going so far as to demand a full renunciation of their former orders from them. This gave rise to serious problems of conscience for those who believed that their first ordination was valid and had been vindicated by the grace they had

---

[1] Thorndike, *Theological Works* IV, i, pp. 363ff; *A Collection of the State Papers of John Thurloe*, ed. Thomas Birch (1742) V, pp. 598–601; Edward Stillingfleet, *Irenicum. A Weaponsalve for the Churches Wounds* (1661).

[2] *State Papers collected by Edward, Earl of Clarendon* (1767–86) III, p. 738.

[3] Thorndike, *Theological Works* V, pp. 42–3. He later changed his opinion and demanded their reordination (ibid. V, pp. 203, 420–6).

received in their ministry.[1] Nevertheless, many Puritans, encouraged by the King's attitude towards them on his return, were still hopeful that a compromise might be reached and were now ready to accept Ussher's scheme for a modified episcopacy. They offered this to the King, and at the same time they asked that, until a settlement should be reached, no "Renunciation of their Ordination by meer Presbyters, or confessing it to be sinful, be imposed on, or required of any, as necessary to their Ordination, Institution, Induction or Confirmation by the Seales". Now it was the turn of the bishops to reject Ussher's scheme, as the Puritans had done almost twenty years earlier. In their reply they stated that "the Bishops of this Realm have constantly (for ought we know, or have heard to the contrary) Ordained with the Assistance of Presbyters, and the Imposition of their Hands, together with the Bishops", and they refused to go into the question of whether the episcopate was a distinct order or had the power of sole ordination.[2]

Hopes of a compromise rose again among the Puritans with the King's Declaration concerning Ecclesiastical Affairs on 25 October 1660. The first draft of this had been shown on 4 September to three leading Puritan divines, Richard Baxter, Edmund Calamy, and Edward Reynolds, and in it the King had said that no bishop would ordain without the advice of the presbyters, and that,

> As the Dean and Chapters are the most proper Council And Assistants of the Bishop both in Ordination, and for the other Offices mentioned before; so we shall take care that those Preferments be given to the most Learned and Pious Presbyters of the Diocess, that thereby they may be always at hand and ready to advise and assist the Bishop; And moreover, That some other of the most Learned, Pious, and Discreet Presbyters of the same Diocess (as namely the Rural Deans, or others, or so many of either as shall be thought fit, and are nearest) be called by the Bishop to be present and assistant together with those of the Chapter, at all Ordinations, and at all other Solemn and Important Actions in the Exercise of Ecclesiastical Jurisdiction, especially wherein any of the Ministers are concerned. And our will is, that the great work of Ordination be constantly and solemnly performed by the Bishop in the Presence, and with the Advice and Assistance of his aforesaid Presbytery at the four set Times and Seasons appointed by the Church for that purpose.[3]

[1] See G(iles) F(irmin), *Presbyterial Ordination Vindicated in a Brief and Sober Discourse concerning Episcopacy* (1660); Zachary Crofton, *A Serious Review of Presbyters Reordination by Bishops* (1661); John Humfrey, *The Question of Reordination, whether, and how, a Minister Ordained by the Presbytery, may take Ordination also by the Bishop?* (1661), and *A second discourse about reordination* (1662).

[2] *RB* II, 91–101.    [3] Ibid. II, 105.

These provisions did not satisfy the Puritans, however, and they commissioned Baxter to draw up a petition to the King expressing their criticisms. In this Baxter said that,

> the Bishop which your Majesty declareth for, is not *Episcopus Praeses*, but *Episcopus Princeps*; indued with *sole* Power both of *Ordination* and *Jurisdiction*. For though it be said, That (the Bishop shall do nothing without the Advice of the Presbyters) yet their *Consent* is not made necessary, but he might go *contrary* to the Counsel of them all. And this *Advice* is not to be given by the *Diocesan Synod*, or any *chosen Representatives* of the *Clergy*, but by the *Dean and Chapter*, and so many and such others as *he* please to call.

He therefore asked that the bishop should not ordain without the consent of the majority of the diocesan synod, and he added the request that "none be urged to be reordained, or denied Institution for want of Ordination by Prelates, that was ordained by Presbyters".[1]

When this petition was delivered to Clarendon, the Lord Chancellor, he refused to present it to the King, but instead he instructed the Puritans to draw up a list of specific alterations which they wanted to be made in the Declaration. This they then did. They proposed that the section relating to ordination should read that ordinations were to be performed by the advice and consent of the presbyters, and in place of the paragraph on the assistance of the chapter and others chosen by the bishop, they wished to insert:

> To the end that the Deans and Chapters may be the better fitted to afford Counsel and Assistance to the Bishops; both in Ordination, and in the other Ordinances mentioned before, we will take care that those Preferments be given to the most learned and pious Presbyters of the Diocess. And moreover, that at least an equal Number of the most learned, pious, and discreet Presbyters of the same Diocess, (annually chosen by the major Vote of all the Presbyters of that Diocess) shall be assistant and consenting together with those of the Chapter at all Ordinations, and all other Acts of spiritual Jurisdiction. Nor shall any Suffragan Bishop ordain, or exercise any act of spiritual Jurisdiction, but with the Consent and Assistance of a sufficient Number of the most Judicious and pious Presbyters, annually chosen by the major Vote of all the Presbyters in his Precincts: And our will is, that the great Work of Ordination be constantly and solemnly performed at the four set times and Seasons appointed by the Church for that purpose.

They also wanted to add to the Declaration the condition that "such as have been ordained by Presbyters, be not required to renounce their

[1] *RB* II, 106 (italics in original).

Ordination, or to be reordained, or denied Institution and Induction for want of Ordination by Bishops".[1]

When the Puritans met the King and some of the bishops to discuss their proposals, however, they found that the King was adamant in refusing to accept the necessity of the consent of presbyters in ordination, "because it gave the Ministers a negative Voice". There was also considerable debate over the validity of ordinations performed by presbyters. The final revision was then left to two bishops and two Puritan divines, and in the published Declaration there was no mention of the consent, but only of the advice and assistance, of presbyters in ordination. The revised paragraph proposed by the Puritans was accepted with a number of modifications; all reference to consent was omitted, and the provision was included that "the number of the ministers so elected, and those present of the chapter shall be equal, and not exceed one the other, and that to make the numbers equal, the juniors of the exceeding number be withdrawn, that the most ancient may take place". The proposed clause dispensing with reordination was not accepted, but in its place was inserted the provision,

> "that none be judged to forfeit his presentation or benefice, or be deprived of it, upon the statute of the thirteenth of queen Elizabeth, chapter the twelfth, so he read and declare his assent to all the articles of religion, which only concern the confession of the true Christian faith, and the doctrine of the sacraments comprised in the Book of Articles in the said statute mentioned".[2]

The implications of this are not entirely clear. The statute referred to allowed priests who had not been ordained according to the Ordinal to receive livings without reordination on subscription to the Articles of Religion, and had originally been framed to cover the case of Roman priests, although some believed that it would also cover those ordained in the reformed Churches. It was possibly proposed by the bishops because of its ambiguous nature, as it did not commit them explicitly to accept ordination by presbyters as valid, while at the same time it might still seem to hold out hopes of this to the Puritans. Yet the latter clearly did not regard it as the equivalent of their own proposal, for in a "humble and grateful Acknowledgement of many Ministers of the Gospel in and about the City of London, to his Royal Majesty for his

---

[1] Ibid. II, 107.
[2] Ibid. II, 108–11. Text in Edward Cardwell, *A History of Conferences and other proceedings connected with the revision of the Book of Common Prayer* (3rd edn, 1849), pp. 292–93, 297.

gracious Concessions in his Majesty's late Declaration concerning Ecclesiastical Affairs", they added the further request that there might be no reordinations.[1]

Unfortunately, a Bill to make the King's Declaration effectual was rejected by Parliament, and Puritan hopes were dashed. The Ordinal was not even discussed at the Savoy Conference in 1661, which restricted itself to the Prayer Book, although Baxter did again plead

> that it be not imputed to them as their unpardonable Crime, that they were born in an Age and Country which required Ordination by Parochial Pastors, without Diocesans: and that Reordination (whether absolute or hypothetical) be not made necessary to the future exercise of their Ministry. But that an Universal Confirmation may be granted of those ordained as aforesaid, they being still responsible for any personal insufficiency or crime.[2]

The plea fell on deaf ears. The bishops were determined to pursue their policy of reordaining all who had not received episcopal ordination, and would not be swayed by anyone. This policy was maintained when episcopacy was restored to Scotland in 1661. Two of the four candidates for the episcopate had not previously received episcopal ordination as priests and deacons. They were therefore first ordained to these orders privately before all four candidates were publicly consecrated as bishops in Westminster Abbey. Apparently the English bishops justified this difference from the procedure adopted in 1610 on the grounds that then the Scots were in a defective state through necessity, whereas in 1661 they had been in schism and revolted from their bishops.[3] The bishops had made episcopal ordination necessary de facto; it only remained for them to revise the Ordinal and make it necessary de iure, and victory over the Puritans would be complete.

---

[1] RB II, 129.

[2] Richard Baxter, A Petition for Peace with the Reformation of the Liturgy. As it was presented to the Right Reverend Bishops by the Divines appointed by his Majesties Commission to treat with them about the Alteration of it (1661), p. 2.

[3] G. Burnet, History of his Own Time (1724, 1734) I, pp. 139–40. Burnet also says that the reason for the change of procedure was partly the new Act of Uniformity which made episcopal ordination a necessity, but this can hardly be true as the Act did not come into force until the following year. The rite used at the ordinations and consecrations would have been the Edwardine Ordinal as the work of revising it had not been completed at this time. For ordination procedure in Scotland after this date see Gordon Donaldson, "Scottish Ordinations in the Restoration Period", Scottish Historical Review XXXIII (1954), pp. 169–75; W. R. Foster, Bishop and Presbytery. The Church of Scotland 1661–1688 (CHS, 1958), pp. 38–42, 97–100.

## 5. *Roman Catholics and the Ordinal, 1553–1662*

Throughout the whole of the Anglican Orders controversy the question of the policy adopted during the reign of Queen Mary towards those ordained by the Anglican Ordinal has been a major issue because it has been felt by Roman Catholics that the attitude of the Roman authorities so close in time to the Ordinal's composition would be decisive in the question of its validity. Almost every single author has included a lengthy section on this subject, Anglicans maintaining that no distinction was drawn between such men and those ordained by the Pontificals,[1] Roman Catholics insisting that from the first Anglican Orders were condemned as invalid.[2] The fact is that the information is so limited and the available documents so ambiguous that it is quite impossible to make a clear decision whether or not the Anglican Ordinal was regarded as a valid rite, still less to determine on what grounds, if any, it was rejected.

If the evidence of a contemporary Roman Catholic apologist, Nicholas Sanders, can be trusted, it would appear that at least at the beginning of Mary's reign there was no settled policy with regard to Anglican Orders. He records that at first priests were allowed to minister without any examination being made as to who ordained them, how they were ordained, or whether they were limited by censures or irregularities.[3] On the other hand, it is clear from the episcopal registers of the period that some of those ordained by the Anglican Ordinal were reordained during Mary's reign.[4] Since, however, the registers do not give any reasons for the reordinations, it is by no means certain that they were performed because the Anglican rite was regarded as invalid; the ordinands themselves could have asked to be reordained, claiming that their own defect of intention, or that of the ordaining bishop, had invalidated their former orders.

---

[1] See, for example, Frere, *Marian Reaction*, pp. 147–62.
[2] See, for example, Messenger, *The Reformation, the Mass and the Priesthood* II, pp. 3–167.
[3] Nicholas Sanders, *De origine ac progressu schismatis Anglicani* (Ingolstadt 1586), p. 248.
[4] Frere, *Marian Reaction*, pp. 88–121.

On 4 March 1554 the Queen issued a number of injunctions to her bishops, the fifteenth of which read:

> Item, Touching such persons as were heretofore promoted to any orders after the new sort and fashion of orders, considering they were not ordered in very deed, the bishop of the diocese finding otherwise sufficiency, and ability in those men, may supply that thing, which wanted in them before; and then according to his discretion admit them to minister.[1]

What was meant by this is disputed. Roman Catholics have argued that it implies that Anglican Orders were invalid and that reordination was intended, but the language more naturally suggests that only some supplementary ceremony was necessary, although which particular ceremony is not specified. It may have been the absence of minor orders which was thought of as a defect, or the change in the *porrectio instrumentorum*, or the omission of unction of the candidates. Alternatively, no specific defect may have been intended and it was to be left to each bishop to determine what supplementary ceremonies were required. James Pilkington seems to suggest that the ceremony in question was unction, but it may be that he is not speaking only of a supplementary ceremony but referring contemptuously to a complete reordination:

> They would make men believe that the oil hath such holiness in it, that whosoever wanteth it is no priest nor minister. Therefore in the late days of popery our holy bishops called before them all such as were made ministers without such greasing, and blessed them with the pope's blessing, anointed them, and then all was perfect; they might sacrifice for quick and dead.[2]

Similarly, one of the visitation articles of Edmund Bonner, Bishop of London, issued later in 1554, does not clearly state whether Anglican Orders are invalid or not:

> Item, Whether any such as were ordered schismatically, and contrary to the old order and custom of the catholic church, or being unlawfully and schismatically married after the late innovation and manner, being not yet reconciled nor admitted by the ordinary, have celebrated or said either mass or divine service within any cure or place of this city or diocese?[3]

This seems to make no distinction between those with Anglican Orders and those ordained according to the Pontificals but after the

[1] Cardwell, *Documentary Annals* I, p. 114.
[2] Pilkington, *Works*, p. 163.
[3] Cardwell, *Documentary Annals* I, pp. 132–3.

breach with Rome, and to imply that all that was necessary was "reconciliation" and not reordination. It is known, however, that Bonner did regard Anglican Orders as invalid, for in a book written by him in 1555 he stated that those ordained by the Anglican Ordinal had "no authority at all given to them to offer in the Mass the Body and Blood of our Saviour Christ".[1] This suggests that he rejected the Ordinal because it did not contain the words which had accompanied the *porrectio instrumentorum* in the medieval rites for the priesthood, *Accipe potestatem offerendi sacrificium in ecclesia pro vivis et mortuis.* According to Ridley, it was widely held by Roman Catholics at the time that these words constituted the essential form of the rite for the priesthood.[2]

The instructions given by Pope Julius III to Cardinal Pole, who was sent to carry out the reconciliation of England to the Holy See, do not contain a clear condemnation of Anglican Orders as invalid. They speak of two classes of clerics, those who before their lapse into heresy had been "rite et legitimite promoti vel ordinati", who may be allowed to exercise their orders, and those who were "non promoti", who could be ordained.[3] Who were the latter? Roman Catholics have claimed they were men with Anglican Orders, Anglicans have argued that they were men who had received no ordination of any sort. The evidence does not permit a decision. A later Brief issued to Pole by the Pope extended his faculties to cover bishops consecrated by heretical or schismatical bishops, "aut alias minus rite et non servata forma ecclesiae consueta",[4] but it does not say what was to be done with them. Were they to be ordained again or simply allowed to exercise their orders?

On 20 June 1555, the new Pope, Paul IV, issued a Bull, *Praeclara carissimi*, in which he confirmed all that Pole had done. In this was inserted the statement that anyone ordained by a bishop who was not "rite et recto ordinato" was to be ordained again.[5] This apparently caused some confusion in England as to who these bishops were, and on 30 October 1555 a Brief, *Regimini universalis*, was issued by the Pope to make it clear. It declared that "eos tantum episcopos et archiepiscopos qui non in forma ecclesiae ordinati et consecrati fuerint, rite et recte ordinatos dici non posse", and that all bishops who had been consecrated "in forma ecclesiae", in spite of the fact that it was in

---

[1] Edmund Bonner, *A Profitable and necessarye doctryne* (1555), no pagination.
[2] *The Works of Nicholas Ridley*, ed. Henry Christmas (PS, 1841), p. 19.
[3] Cardwell, *Documentary Annals* I, pp. 118–19.
[4] Messenger, *The Reformation, the Mass and the Priesthood* II, p. 85.
[5] Ibid. II, p. 141.

schism, were validly consecrated.[1] It apparently was left to the bishops in England to decide whether the Anglican Ordinal lacked the essential form. Pole simply passed on to them instructions similar to those which he himself had received; they were to accept as valid orders received "etiam ab haereticis et schismaticis episcopis, etiam minus rite, dummodo in eorum collatione ecclesiae forma et intentio sit servata", and the "non promoti" were to be ordained.[2] There is no indication as to what Pole thought would constitute a valid intention, but one of the decrees promulgated by him at the Synod of Lambeth in 1555 upheld the doctrine of the sacraments put forward by Eugenius IV, which included the statement that the essential matter and form of ordination were the *porrectio instrumentorum* and the accompanying formula.[3] If, therefore, Pole thought that the Anglican Ordinal was invalid, which is not certain, it was on the grounds that Bonner also had rejected it, that it did not have as its form the formula which had accompanied the *porrectio instrumentorum* in the medieval rites, or a suitable equivalent. It is strange, however, that his instructions make no mention of the possibility of a defect of matter; he may have regarded the *porrectio instrumentorum* of the 1550 rite for the priesthood as the equivalent of the ceremony of the Pontificals, but it seems unlikely that he would have so regarded the ceremony in the 1552 Ordinal.

Thus the evidence for the Roman Catholic attitude towards the Anglican Ordinal during Mary's reign is extremely limited. The same is true for the reign of Elizabeth. There is no shortage of polemical writings by Roman Catholics which deny that Anglicans had valid orders, but not one of them mentions the insufficiency of the rites themselves as a reason for this. Some claimed that the absence of the minor orders made them mere laymen,[4] others that the absence of papal confirmation of the episcopal appointments had caused a break in the succession of bishops.[5] Some criticized the Anglicans for changing the rites without the authority of the pope, but did not say that the rites themselves were invalid.[6] One Roman Catholic, Thomas Heskyns, did say that those ordained by the Anglican Ordinal lacked the lawful authority to consecrate the body and blood of Christ, but it would appear that he did not mean that the Anglican form for the

---

[1] Ibid. II, pp. 147-8.    [2] Ibid. II, pp. 122-3.
[3] Cardwell, *Documentary Annals* I, p. 146. See above, p. 7.
[4] *A Brief Discours contayning certayne Reasons why Catholiques refuse to goe to Church* (Douai 1580), fol. 41. The author was Robert Parsons, a Jesuit.
[5] *The Works of John Jewel*, ed. John Ayre (PS, 1845-50), III, pp. 320-35.
[6] Pilkington, *Works*, pp. 578ff.

priesthood was defective, but that those ordained by it were outside the Catholic succession.[1] The main reason, however, given by all writers for denying the validity of Anglican Orders was that there had been a break in the episcopal succession because the Anglicans had been unable to find enough bishops to consecrate their new bishops at the beginning of the reign.[2] This was, of course, hotly denied by the Anglicans.[3] Some Roman Catholics even claimed that the Anglican bishops had received no consecration at all but had obtained all their authority from Parliament, and they were dubbed "Parliamentary bishops".[4]

These allegations seem to have arisen because of the circumstances surrounding the consecration of Matthew Parker as Archbishop of Canterbury in 1559. The Queen was unable to find four diocesan bishops who were prepared to consecrate him, so she issued the letters patent for the consecration to other bishops. This did not affect the sacramental validity but was thought to be contrary to the law enacted by Henry VIII. Furthermore, there were doubts whether the use of the Ordinal was legal. The Act of Uniformity which had authorized the Prayer Book in 1559 had not explicitly mentioned the Ordinal. For these reasons the Queen inserted in the letters patent a clause in which she claimed to supply by her royal authority anything lacking in the bishops or in what was required by law. Probably because there were still doubts whether this action was legal, the consecration took place before 6 a.m. on Sunday, 17 December 1559, and apparently no attempts were made to publicize the facts.[5] This secrecy almost certainly was

---

[1] Thomas Heskyns, *The Parliament of Chryste* (Antwerp 1566), fols. cccxx, cccxxvii.
[2] Thomas Stapleton, *A Fortresse of the Faith first planted amonge us englishmen, and continued hitherto in the universall Church of Christ* (Antwerp 1565), fol. 141, and his *A Counterblast to M. Hornes vayne blaste against M. Fakenham* (Louvain 1567), fols. 7–8 301, 458.
[3] *Fulke's Answers to Stapleton, Martiall, and Sanders*, p. 118.
[4] Sanders, p. 298.
[5] V. J. K. Brook, *A Life of Archbishop Parker* (1962), pp. 81–6. In spite of the attempt by J. C. Whitebrook, *The Consecration of Matthew Parker* (1945), to prove that the consecration took place on a different date, by different consecrators and with the Pontifical rite, the true facts of Parker's consecration now seem assured. See the reply to this by F. J. Shirley, *Elizabeth's First Archbishop* (1948). The only variation from the Anglican rite, according to Parker's register, was that all four bishops, and not just the chief consecrator, recited the formula, "Take the Holy Ghost", etc. Why this change was made, and why it was thought worthy of recording in the register, is a mystery. Was it because this was thought to be the essential form and the validity of the consecration would be the more assured if all said it? Was it because there was no archbishop among the consecrators and so they were uncertain who should say it? Or, perhaps less likely, was it a result of the

the cause of the rise of the stories that sufficient consecrators could not be found. The legality of the use of the Ordinal was later challenged by Bonner, now deprived of his bishopric and imprisoned. This so embarrassed the government that a special Act of Parliament was passed in 1566, declaring all consecrations since Elizabeth's accession to be good and perfect and the use of the Ordinal to be legal.[1] This was undoubtedly the cause of the claims that the Anglican bishops derived their authority from Parliament, although the law was clearly intended to rectify only a legal, and not a sacramental, deficiency.

Allegations against the valid succession of Anglican bishops continued to be made in the seventeenth century, and fuel was added to the fire by the invention of the famous "Nag's Head Fable", first published by an Irish Jesuit, Christopher Holywood, in 1604.[2] This legend asserted that Parker had been consecrated in the Nag's Head Tavern, Cheapside, by the imposition of a Bible on his head accompanied by the words, "Take thou authority to preach the word of God sincerely", or some such formula. It was immediately taken up and elaborated, and from then onwards it found a regular place in the polemic against Anglican Orders for almost three centuries. By this time the use of the Roman Pontifical, instead of the local medieval variations, had become universal in the Roman Catholic Church, and this led to a number of erroneous views about ordination. It became widely believed that the formula, *Accipe Spiritum Sanctum*, at the imposition of hands in the rite for the episcopate was the form, and that the matter and form for the priesthood were in two parts, the *porrectio instrumentorum* and its formula, and the final imposition of hands and its formula, *Accipe Spiritum Sanctum, quorum peccata*, etc., since it was not known that these had not been features of all earlier rites. It was in 1608 that the first explicit condemnation of the Anglican Ordinal as defective in matter and form appeared. It was made by a certain Matthew Kellison, but he offered no reasons in support of his judgement.[3]

In 1613 the Archdeacon of Norfolk, Francis Mason, made an attempt to produce a comprehensive answer to the Roman objections to the

---

influence of the Exeter Pontifical which directed that all consecrators should recite, *Accipe Spiritum Sanctum* (see above, p. 4)?

[1] Procter and Frere, p. 115.

[2] Christopher Holywood, *De Investiganda vera ac visibili Christi ecclesia* (Antwerp 1604), p. 17.

[3] Matthew Kellison, *A Reply to Sotcliffe's Answer to the Survey of the new Religion* Rheims 1608), fol. 31b.

validity of Anglican Orders. Among other things he tried to refute the Nag's Head Fable by quoting from Parker's register to show that Parker had been consecrated by four bishops, all of whom were themselves validly consecrated. He dealt with Kellison's claim that the Ordinal was defective in matter and form by pointing out that there were a number of views in the Roman Church as to what constituted the essential matter, and the noted Roman theologian, Robert Bellarmine, maintained that it was the imposition of hands, which was certainly the only matter found in the Bible. A variety of forms were possible: the Eastern Church conferred orders by prayer, the Roman Church by an imperative formula. The Church of England had retained the Roman form for the episcopate, *Accipe Spiritum Sanctum*, had rejected the first part of the form for the priesthood, *Accipe potestatem*, etc., since the Christian priesthood was not a sacrificing priesthood, and had retained the other part, "Receive the Holy Ghost, whose sins", etc.[1]

Mason's book met with strong criticism from Roman Catholics. They did not regard Parker's register as conclusive evidence of the fact of his consecration, but claimed that it was a forgery. In 1616 further doubts were thrown on the validity of Parker's consecration by a Roman priest, Anthony Champney, who pointed out that there was no record of the consecration of William Barlow, Parker's chief consecrator. If he had not been consecrated, he argued, then Parker's consecration was invalid.[2] Along with the Nag's Head Fable, this became a favourite weapon against the validity of Anglican Orders and it has been brought forward even in the present century, in spite of the fact that the evidence in favour of Barlow's consecration far outweighs any doubts raised by the absence of any record of the ceremony.[3] Champney also took up Mason's liturgical arguments. He agreed that there were a number of different views as to what constituted the essential matter and form for the episcopate, but he claimed that for this reason it was impossible to be sure that the imposition of hands and the words, "Take the Holy Ghost", were all

---

[1] Francis Mason, *Of the Consecration of the Bishops in the Church of England* (1613), pp. 95–6, 121–32, 207ff, 244ff, 261.

[2] Anthony Champney, *A Treatise of the vocation of bishops and other ecclesiasticall ministers* (Douai 1616), pp. 191ff.

[3] See A. S. Barnes, *Bishop Barlow and Anglican Orders, a study of the original documents* (1922), and the refutation by Claude Jenkins, *Bishop Barlow's Consecration and Archbishop Parker's Register, with some new documents* (1935), reprinted from the *Journal of Theological Studies* (October 1922).

that were necessary. The Anglican bishops could at the most be no more than probable bishops since some of the traditional ceremonies of ordination, which might be part of the essential matter and form, had been omitted in their consecration. At the same time he firmly denied that they were in any case true priests because he believed that the matter and form for the priesthood were not in doubt; they were the *porrectio instrumentorum* and the words which accompanied this, which were omitted from the Anglican Ordinal.[1]

Other Roman Catholics added further reasons for rejecting the validity of Anglican Orders. At least two authors, Henry Fitzsimon and Sylvester Norris, both Jesuits, claimed that there were defects not only in matter and form but also in intention; neither those who ordained nor those who received ordination believed in a sacrificial priesthood and the judicial power to remit sins.[2] Kellison repeated his claim that the Ordinal was defective in matter and form, this time giving his reasons. He agreed that the matter of episcopal ordination was the imposition of hands by three bishops and the form was *Accipe Spiritum Sanctum*. Although these words did not by themselves denote that the episcopate was being conferred, yet they were sufficient for the purpose, since the fact that they were said while the three bishops laid on their hands made it clear which order was being conferred, and he cited the Spanish theologian, Gabriel Vazquez, in support of this view. Nevertheless, although the Anglicans had retained the matter and form, their orders were still invalid because those who laid on their hands were not validly ordained bishops through a break in the succession, and because they did not have the full matter and form of the priesthood, having omitted the *porrectio instrumentorum* and its formula.[3]

Mason prepared a second enlarged edition of his work, in Latin, in order to answer the criticisms made by his opponents, and this was published posthumously in 1625. In it he reaffirmed that the matter for all orders was the imposition of hands; this was not only the sole ceremony mentioned in the Bible but also in the consecration of bishops was the only one which was performed by all three bishops. On the

[1] Champney, pp. 158–65, 242.

[2] Henry Fitzsimon, *Britannomachia Ministrorum in plerisque fidei fundamentis et articulis dissidentium* (Douai 1614), pp. 306, 319; Sylvester Norris, *The Guide of Faith, Or, A Third Part of the Antidote against the Pestiferous writings of all English Sectaries* (n.p. 1621), pp. 180–5.

[3] Matthew Kellison, *Examen reformationis novae praesertim Calvinianae in quo synagoga et doctrina Calvini, sicut et reliquorum huius temporis novatorum, tota fere ex suis principiis refutatur* (Douai 1616), pp. 171–7.

other hand, he believed that the form was not prescribed in Scripture, nor was there any example of the words that the Apostles used. This did not mean that any words at all could be used, but providing that they expressed the power of the order being conferred, a variety of different expressions was possible. As to the change in intention, he agreed that they did not intend to confer the popish priesthood, but they still intended to do what the true Church did, which Bellarmine had said was sufficient.[1]

At about the same time there was a similar debate on the Ordinal between a certain James Wadesworth, a convert from Anglicanism to the Roman Church, and William Bedell, an Anglican priest. Wadesworth stated that Anglican Orders were invalid because the minor orders were lacking and the matter, form, and intention were defective; the *porrectio instrumentorum* and the accompanying words were omitted, and neither those who ordained nor those who were ordained believed in a sacrificial priesthood. Bedell in reply pointed out that the primitive Church did not have the minor orders, nor could the delivery of the book of Gospels possibly be the matter in the ordination of deacons, since the Gospels were not written when the first deacons were ordained. The *porrectio instrumentorum* in the ordination of priests was not mentioned in Scripture nor in the ancient authors, and hence it was a later ceremony and not the essential matter. As for the intention of sacrificing, if "sacrifice" was understood as "a memorie and representation of the true Sacrifice and holy immolation made on the Altar of the Crosse", then the Anglicans did not lack intention, for "we do offer sacrifice for the quick and dead, remembring, representing and mystically offering that sole sacrifice for the quicke and dead, by the which all their sins are meritoriously expiated, and desiring that by the same, wee and all the Church may obtaine remission of sinnes, and all other benefits of Christs passion".[2] On the other hand, one Roman Catholic author used the fact that deacons existed before the Gospels were written as an argument *against* the validity of Anglican Orders! The chief office of a deacon could not be to read the Gospel, since deacons existed before the Gospels were written, but was to assist in sacrifice, and because Anglican deacons received

---

[1] Francis Mason, *Vindiciae Ecclesiae Anglicanae* (1625), pp. 216–40.
[2] *The Copies of certaine letters which have passed betweene Spaine and England in matter of Religion, Concerning the generall Motives to the Romane obedience. Betweene Master James Wadesworth, a late Pensioner of the Holy Inquisition in Sivill, and W. Bedell a Minister of the Gospell of Jesus Christ in Suffolke* (1624), pp. 12–13, 139–57.

only the power to read the Gospel, they were not true deacons. Their priests were not true priests because there was no intention of conferring on them power to sacrifice, nor did their form express the giving of this power, and their bishops were not true bishops because they were not true priests and because in the formula at the imposition of hands no grace was given to them.[1]

During the reign of Charles I hopes of a possible reunion with Rome grew, but the question of Anglican Orders remained one of the major obstacles. To further the cause of reunion a Franciscan, Christopher Davenport, published a book which attempted to interpret the Thirty-nine Articles in a Catholic sense. Under Article 36 he discussed the validity of the Ordinal and, although he believed that the Anglicans had erred in changing the prescribed rites, he thought that their forms might be sufficient to confer valid orders. Vazquez and others thought that imposition of hands and the words, *Accipe Spiritum Sanctum*, were sufficient for episcopal ordination. Innocent IV had said that the Apostolic Church used only the imposition of hands and prayer in the ordination of priests and that the Church had subsequently produced the forms now used; therefore a variety of forms was possible and the Anglican one, because it included the power of sacrificing and absolving, would seem to be sufficient. As for the Anglican rite for the diaconate, it seemed to many that nothing essential was omitted.[2] He later changed his views and in a subsequent book he argued that Anglican Orders were invalid through a defect of intention; they had changed the rites to declare that they did not do what the Church intended, and they had denied the power of sacrificing.[3] Dom. Leander of St Martin, one of the papal agents sent to England in 1634 in the hope of securing reunion, thought that Anglican Orders were either invalid or dubious, and that, if the Anglicans were reunited with the Roman Church, this problem might be solved by conditional reordination, or by the Anglican clergy continuing to hold their benefices and other positions *in commendam*, without exercising their ministries.[4] Another papal envoy, Gregorio Panzani, very wisely

---

[1] Richard Broughton, *The Iudgement of the Apostles, and of those of the first age, in all points of doctrine questioned betweene the Catholikes and Protestants of England as they are set downe in the 39 Articles of their Religion* (Douai 1632), pp. 353–75.

[2] Christopher Davenport, *Deus, Natura, Gratia* (Lyon 1634), pp. 322–7.

[3] Christopher Davenport, *An Enchiridion of Faith* (2nd edn, Douai 1655), pp. 86–94.

[4] *State Papers collected by Edward, Earl of Clarendon* I, p. 208. Leander gave his opinion on what was necessary for a valid consecration of a bishop in a letter to Francis Windebank, the Secretary of State, in April 1635: the consecrator must be a true bishop and

refused to commit himself to any statement on the validity of Anglican Orders.[1]

As a consequence of the controversy with Roman Catholics over the sufficiency of their forms, there developed among Anglicans a belief that the imperative formula, "Receive the Holy Ghost, whose sins", etc., was absolutely essential to the validity of the rite for the priesthood. The importance attached to this formula as "the very essential words of conferring order" in relation to the revision of the Scottish Ordinal has already been noted.[2] This idea appears to have been advanced first of all by Lancelot Andrewes. Earlier Anglicans had said that these words were most suitable for this purpose, because they had been used by Christ himself, and probably also by the Apostolic Church, but none of them had suggested that they were absolutely necessary. Andrewes, however, in a sermon preached on 19 May 1616 said that by these words were Holy Orders given to the Apostles, "and are to us, even to this day, by these and by no other words; which words had not the Church of Rome retained in their ordinations, it might well have been doubted, for all their *Accipe potestatem sacrificandi pro vivis et mortuis*, whether they had any Priests at all, or no. But as God would, they retained them, and so saved themselves. For these are the very operative words for the conferring this power, for the performing this act."[3]

John Cosin also appears to have shared the view that this formula was essential. In a letter written about 1650, which describes a conference he had in the year 1645 with a certain Father Robinson, Prior of the English Benedictines in France, he said that, when asked what he regarded as the matter and form for the priesthood, he replied that,

we held nothing necessary either to the matter and form of it, but prayers and imposition of hands, together with the words that our Saviour said to His disciples, when He made them the dispensers of holy things, and ministers of His Church, in the xxth chap. of S. John, "Receive the Holy Ghost: whose sins ye do remit, they are remitted," etc.: —by virtue of which words and

---

intend to perform what Holy Church intends, to confer the power and office of a bishop, using the matter and form received in the Church, imposition of hands by one or more bishops (one would do in case of necessity) and words expressing that episcopal power was being conferred, accompanied "for more expression" by other signs, *traditio baculi pastoralis*, *mitrae*, etc. Both the consecrator and he who was consecrated must also have received the power of priesthood, i.e., of sacrificing and absolving (ibid. I, pp. 253–4).

[1] Joseph Berington, *The Memoirs of Gregorio Panzani* (1793), pp. 243, 247.
[2] See above, p. 60.
[3] Lancelot Andrewes, *Works* (LACT, 1841–54) III, p. 263.

benediction our holy orders are given us;—and that not only the ancient fathers, but even their own best authors among the Roman Catholics themselves, were of the same mind.

Father Robinson maintained that the matter and form were the *porrectio instrumentorum* and the accompanying words.[1] Cosin also prepared a paper for the conference in which he set out his arguments for his view, and in this he actually quoted the passage from Andrewes' sermon, and supported it with references to patristic authors; he believed that St Hilary, St Jerome, St Augustine, St Cyprian, and others taught that these words conferred the power of order, and many other scholars claimed that the matter was imposition of hands and not the *porrectio instrumentorum*.[2] In a second paper prepared for this conference he went further into the question, maintaining that there was no example, command, or custom in Scripture to support the *porrectio instrumentorum*, nor was there any trace of it in the ancient Pontificals.[3] Nevertheless, in spite of his use of the quotation from Andrewes, it would not seem that Cosin really meant that no ordination was valid without the formula, "Receive the Holy Ghost", etc. For in this second paper he admitted that he was aware that the Eastern Church used different rites of ordination. Indeed, that was one of his arguments why the *porrectio instrumentorum* could not be the essential matter, since it was not observed in the Eastern Church, which both Anglicans and Roman Catholics believed to have valid orders. Therefore he could hardly believe that "Receive the Holy Ghost" was absolutely essential, when he knew that it too was not used in the Eastern Church. It would seem more likely that he meant that the form must in some way express the bestowal of the Holy Spirit, and that the traditional form in the West had been the words which Christ used.

A similar position appears to have been adopted by John Bramhall, who was later Archbishop of Armagh. He did not say that this formula was the absolutely essential form for the priesthood, but he did believe that it was the form used by Christ and by the primitive Church, whereas the *porrectio instrumentorum* was "an upstart custom or innovation, confirmed but the other day by the decree of Eugenius the Fourth". He was aware that the Eastern Church used a different form which was also valid, but he believed that the scriptural form was superior to this.[4] He also dealt with the allegation of a defect of

---

[1] John Cosin, *Works* (LACT, 1843–55) IV, pp. 245–6.
[2] Ibid. IV, pp. 254–8.     [3] Ibid. IV, pp. 266–76.
[4] John Bramhall, *Works* (LACT, 1842–45) I, pp. 271–2, and V, pp. 214–19.

intention which had been made by Sylvester Norris. He asserted that the interior intention of those who ordained was not necessary. All that was required was that they should have the implicit intention "to do what the Catholic Church doth, and to do whatsoever Christ instituted; though they are far from believing, that the Roman Church is the Catholic Church: and this is sufficient, our adversaries being judges, to the validity of holy Orders".[1] Here he was simply repeating what the Roman theologian, Bellarmine, had said.

On the other hand, it must not be thought that all Anglicans of this period thought that their imperative formula was the only form for the priesthood which had been used and could be used in the Western Church. Henry Fern, who was later Bishop of Chester, wrote:

> We grant, there is a certain Ceremony to be used (according to the constant practice of the Apostles), Imposition of hands, and that a certain Form is to be used; not certain for Words and Syllables (it being not necessary to have it, in all places and all times, so certainly the same) but for substance and meaning; that, in the conferring of Orders, such Words be used as do aptly express the Institution, purpose and intention of the Office, and the designation of the person to it, and such prayers withall, as do expressly concern that sacred action, in the imploring of help and grace. And thus we maintain our Forms of Ordination to be conformable to Scripture, and the Antient Church. . . .[2]

It is to be noted, however, that even he shared the view held by other Anglicans that some formula was necessary in addition to prayer and did not think of prayer as constituting the essential form itself.

After 1655 it became very difficult for Roman Catholics to use the absence of the *porrectio instrumentorum* and its formula as the ground for declaring the Anglican Ordinal invalid. For in that year Jean Morin, a French Roman Catholic theologian, published a work in which he set out a large collection of ordination rites of both the Eastern and Western Church and examined various questions connected with them, one of which was the controverted subject of the matter and form of ordination. Following the principle that the matter and form must be something which was common to all rites, he conducted a comparison of them and he concluded that the matter for the episcopate could not be the imposition of the book of Gospels, the form

[1] Ibid. v, pp. 210–14.

[2] Henry Fern, *Certain Considerations of present Concernment touching this reformed Church of England with a particular Examination of Anthony Champny (Doctor of Sorbon) his exceptions against the Lawful Calling and Ordination of the Protestant Bishops and Pastors of this Church* (1653), pp. 213–14.

could not be *Accipe Spiritum Sanctum*, the matter and form for the priesthood could not be the *porrectio instrumentorum* and its formula nor the imposition of hands accompanied by the words, *Accipe Spiritum Sanctum, quorum peccata*, etc., at the end of the Roman rite, and the matter for the diaconate could not be the delivery of the book of Gospels nor its form, *Accipe Spiritum Sanctum*, since none of these was ancient or universally observed, but the matter and form for all three orders must be the one thing which was common to all rites, the imposition of hands and prayer for the Holy Spirit.[1]

Subsequent attacks on the Ordinal, therefore, concentrated on the claim that it was invalid because there was no mention in the forms for the priesthood and episcopate of the particular office being bestowed:

> It is a knowne principle common to both Protestants, and Catholicks, that in the forme of Ordination there must be some word expressing the authority, and power given to the person ordained; the intention of the Ordainer expressed by generall words, indifferent, and applicable to all, or divers degrees of holy Orders, is not sufficient to make one a Priest, or a Bishop. As for example, *Receive the Holy Ghost*, these words being indifferent to Priesthood, and Episcopacy, and used in both Ordinations, are not sufficiently expressive of either in particular; unlesse Protestants will now at length professe themselves Presbyterians, making no distinction betweene Priests, and Bishops; but they are as farre from that, as we Catholicks. In the words, or forme whereby Protestants ordaine Bishops, there is not one word expressing Episcopall power, and authority. . . . Let Protestants search all Catholick Rituals not onely of the West, but of the East; they will not finde any one forme of consecrating Bishops, that hath not the word *Bishop* in it, or some others expressing the particular authority, and power of a Bishop, distinct from all other degrees of holy Orders.

The writer then referred his readers to Morin's book as proof of this thesis. He also made the same charge against the form for the priesthood:

> The forme, or words whereby men are made Priests, must expresse authority, and power *to consecrate*, or make present *Christs* Body and Bloud . . . words giving power to remit sinnes, doth not include power to consecrate all Sacraments ordained for remission of sinnes, as some Protestants endeavour to make the ignorant believe. In all formes of ordaining Priests that ever were used in the Easterne, or Westerne Church, is expressly set downe the word

[1] Jean Morin, *Commentarius de Sacris Ordinibus* (Paris 1655), pt. III, pp. 3–31, 123–57, 168–75.

Priest, or some other words expressing the particular, and proper function, and authority of Priesthood.[1]

John Bramhall, evidently unaware of Morin's research, replied to these charges by claiming that the Anglican and Roman forms for the episcopate were identical—the words, *Accipe Spiritum Sanctum*. It was true that, if these words were considered on their own, there was nothing which distinctly expressed the episcopal power and authority, yet, if they were taken in the context of the rest of the rite, there could be no doubt what it was intended to confer. He also denied that all forms for the priesthood contained the word priest: "It is set down expressly in the Eastern Church, it is not set down expressly in the Western Church. Both the Eastern and Western forms are lawful, but the Western cometh nearer to the institution of Christ." In any case, the word priest did appear if the rite was taken as a whole. Moreover, if general words were sufficient in baptism, without the minister expressing in the form the effect of baptism, why were general words not sufficient in ordination? Finally, he maintained that by the words, "Receive the Holy Ghost", etc., was meant, "receive grace to exercise the office of a priest".[2]

These arguments, however, did not satisfy the Roman Catholics. The author of *A Treatise of the Nature of Catholick Faith and Heresie* replied that, although Vazquez and others had believed that the words, *Accipe Spiritum Sanctum*, were sufficient to confer the episcopal order, it was no more than a probability and ought not to be relied upon. He then reaffirmed that only the Anglican forms did not express the office being conferred, referring Bramhall to Morin's book again.[3] Another anonymous writer treated Bramhall's claims at greater length, also referring to Morin's book in support of his statements. He argued that the fact that the rite as a whole expressed the particular order was irrelevant; the rest of the rite was not part of the essential form. Roman Catholics did not have the same form for the episcopate as the Anglicans, as Bramhall claimed, since their form was not "Receive the Holy Ghost", but prayer. It was not true that the word priest was not set

---

[1] *A Treatise of the Nature of Catholick Faith and Heresie*, by N.N. (Rouen 1657), pp. 22–4. It is usually attributed to Peter Talbot, the titular Archbishop of Dublin.

[2] Bramhall, *Works* III, pp. 162–8.

[3] *The Nullity of the Prelatique Clergy, and Church of England Further discovered in answer to the plaine prevarication, or vaine presumption of D. John Bramhall in his Booke, intituled The Consecration and Succession of Protestant Bishops justified*, etc., by N.N. (Antwerp 1659), pp. 39–40.

down "expressly" in the Western Church; it was set down "equivalently" in the words, *Accipe Potestatem*, etc., and it was set down "expressly" in the prayer. The general words of baptism were sufficient because they had been instituted by Christ, whereas the general words of the Anglican form had not been instituted by Christ for bestowing the priesthood. Nor was it any good Bramhall saying what it was intended to express by those words, when the form itself did not signify it.[1]

Thus, the grounds of the Roman objections to the Anglican forms had shifted. The alleged defect of intention, however, remained constant, although it is interesting to note that many who criticized the lack of belief in a sacrificial priesthood in the ordainers and the ordained argued that it was necessary "to intend what the Church intends" whereas the Council of Trent had said that it was only necessary to "intend what the Church does",[2] which was very different. It is also to be noted that those who alleged that the episcopate was invalid because those consecrated were not validly ordained priests clearly did not consider the possibility of consecrations *per saltum*. The Anglican defence of their orders in this first period of the controversy was on the whole disappointing. They accepted the Roman theories of form without question, although on the subject of intention their awareness of Bellarmine's claim that it was only necessary to intend what the true Church did gave them a strong line of argument.

---

[1] *Erastus Senior, Scholastically Demonstrating this Conclusion, that (admitting their Lambeth Records for true) those called Bishops here in England are no Bishops, either in Order, or Jurisdiction, or so much as Legal* (n.p. 1662), pp. 1-12, 21-30. This is sometimes attributed to Peter Talbot, but its author was more probably another controversialist, John Lewgar.

[2] Denzinger, no. 1611.

# 6. Revision in 1662
## and Subsequent Attempts at Comprehension

The work of revising the Prayer Book and Ordinal had already been undertaken by Matthew Wren, Bishop of Ely, during his imprisonment in the Tower of London from 1641 to 1660. The manuscript containing his proposals has unfortunately been damaged by fire, and of the Ordinal only the first few pages remain.[1] Thus it is not possible to ascertain what changes he would have made, or the full extent to which he influenced the later work of revision. However, as his suggestions for revising the rest of the Prayer Book are mainly concerned with minor alterations and the removal of archaisms, it is unlikely that he suggested any drastic changes. From the portion of the manuscript which remains, it would appear that he proposed only two significant alterations in the Ordinal. One was that the title should be amended from "The Forme and Manner of Making and Consecrating Bishops, Priestes and Deacons", to "The Manner of Ordering, Making, and Consecrating Bishops, Preists, and Deacons", and he also wanted to insert the words "Ordering or" before the word "Consecrating" in the title of the rite for the episcopate. He gave as his reasons for this:

1. Bycause (Form, & Manner) in effect are both ye same.

2. Bycause ye words (Ordering & Ordination) in an Act that is confined to Persons, are much more proper, then is the word (Consecrating,) which may be applyed unto Dead or Inaminate things, To Bread, & Wine, to Places, & Times.

3. Bycause the Church from the beginning hath used it, by ye word of (Holy Orders) onely to signify these Spirituall Functions.

4. Bycause, when we have used the word (Ordring) for Preists, & Deacons, then to use the word (Consecration) alone for Bishops, As it is suspected, to relish a little too much of the Pomp of ye Church of Rome, So hath it bin abused in way of argument, by 2 contrary Factions; Both by ye Canonists, thereby to draw Episcopacy to a dependency wholy on the Pleasure, and Power of ye Papacy, as but his Commissioners; and also by ye Aërian

[1] Text in *The Durham Book*, ed. G. J. Cuming (1961), pp. 265–89.

Faction, from thence to pretend, that Episcopacy is not a distinct Order in ye Church of Christ, but onely a Degree, in nature no otherwise above Presbytery, then as Archiepiscopacy is above Episcopacy. By ye very same Paralogism also, this Faction hath made their Deaconry to be in itself nothing else but a Laicall Faculty, that thereby they may give a little more colour to their Lay Presbytery.[1]

The other alteration was the reversal of the order of the three services, putting the rite for the episcopate first. His reasons were:

1. Bycause this is consonant both to ye Title of the former Book, & also to ye words of ye Preface, where it is twise so put.

2. Bycause the Institution of Christ himself was so: For in ye beginning He gave unto His Apostles, *Matth. 28.* all plenary Power over His Church, by them to be derived to their Successors & Substitutes unto ye worlds end, & this was Episcopacy, being *Specialis Potestas, ad omnes Actus Sacros*; Afterward, the Apostles (by ye guidance of the Holy Spirit) found cause by way of Distribution to Ordayn Partiary Powers also, & so by them were introduced the Orders of Preisthood, & of Deaconry.

3. Bycause the doing of this will conduce to some prevention of error in those, who being little able to judg, and reading first, (as the book of Ordination now hath it) what is sayd in ye Ordring of Preists, are easily mistaken, when in that which followes for ye Ordring of Bishops they find so little difference (to their apprehensions) & thereby run into a surmise, That there is little or no need of ye latter of these, or (at the best) that by ye Institution of both they are but One Order, & in some small Degree onely differing.

4. Bycause this order accords with the example of our Liturgy, which hath set ye Communion Service before that of Baptismes & Confirmation.

Other proposals were chiefly minor alterations in wording, such as the substitution of "Church" for "Congregation", "who" for "which" when referring to persons, and "are" for "be" when the mood was indicative. He also wanted a "more elegant" translation of "Come

[1] The "Aërian Faction" were the Puritans who claimed that the Ordinal had not intended the episcopate to be a separate order because, "when it speaks of the making of Bishops, it calls that a Consecration, and not an Ordination; as it doth, when it speaks of making Deacons, and Presbyters, which it calleth Priests: calling one, The form and manner of Ordering Deacons; the other, the form of Ordering Priests. For, even in that very Preface, it speaks of Consecrating, not of Ordaining a Bishop, as the Book all along doth of Ordering, that is, Ordaining of Deacons and Priests: but never of other then of Consecrating of Archbishops and Bishops, that is, of setting them over the rest in degree, to be the mouth and hand of the rest, in executing what by the rest is agreed upon" (*Reasons shewing the Necessity of Reformation of the Public Doctrine, Worship, Rites and Ceremonies, Church Government and Discipline, by Divers Ministers of sundry Counties* (2nd edn, 1660), pp. 42–3); see also W. K. Firminger, *The Alterations in the Ordinal of 1662: Why were they made?*, CHS XXXI (1898), pp. 26–42.

Holy Ghost", but he did not know one, except that "I heare, that at ye King's Coronation, there was another".

Apart from Wren's proposals, however, little preparatory work was done on the Ordinal prior to its revision by Convocation in 1661, as Cosin's interest in revising the Prayer Book does not appear to have extended to the Ordinal. He apparently began to make some changes in the Ordinal in the "Fair Copy" of his "Durham Book" drawn up by William Sancroft, his chaplain, but went no further than the end of the rite for the diaconate, probably through shortage of time. There are twenty entries in his hand, about half of which are corrections already suggested by Wren, although, because the portion of Wren's manuscript covering the rite for the diaconate is missing, it is possible that almost all were originally proposed by him. Only one is certainly an original suggestion by Cosin, and that is the tentative proposal in the Preface that the minimum age for the diaconate should be amended from twenty-one to twenty-three years of age to bring it into line with the requirements of the Canons.[1]

Sancroft continued the work of revising the Ordinal in the "Fair Copy".[2] He incorporated more of Wren's suggestions and made other minor changes in wording and rubrics, many of which may well have been drawn from the now missing part of Wren's manuscript. His alteration of the title to "The Forme and Manner of Making, Ordeyning, and Consecrating of Bishops, Priestes and Deacons" was obviously influenced by Wren, as was his inclusion of "ordeyning, &" before the word "Consecrating" in the title of the rite for the episcopate. He added the words, " & hath bin confirmed" to the age requirements in the Preface; this had not been suggested by Wren. He restored the special suffrage in the litany in the rites for the diaconate and priesthood, omitted since 1559, and amended it slightly so that it mentioned the particular order being conferred. He rearranged the rite for the priesthood, transferring the presentation and litany to the very beginning, as they were in the rite for the diaconate, almost certainly in order to make it easier for the two orders to be conferred on the same occasion, as F. E. Brightman has suggested,[3] since he also amplified the rubric at the end of the rite for the priesthood so as to describe in detail how this was to be done. Previously the rubric had simply directed that the litany need be said only once. Sancroft now added the instruction that the candidates for the diaconate and the priesthood were to be pres-

[1] Cuming, *The Durham Book*, pp. 264–70 and Appendix D, p. 297.
[2] Ibid., pp. 264–84.    [2] Brightman, *The English Rite* I, p. ccxxiii.

ented in succession and the litany said once. The Communion service was then to be begun and the deacons were to take the Oath of Supremacy and to be examined and ordained after the Epistle, and the priests after the Gospel. Brightman has also suggested that Sancroft transferred the hymn, "Come Holy Ghost", in the rite for the priesthood from its place immediately after the Gospel to a place immediately before the prayer preceding the imposition of hands for exactly the same reason, to make it easier to combine the services for the diaconate and priesthood, but this is hardly a satisfactory explanation; it could have been left in its old position and the two rites combined without any difficulty. Possibly it was simply done so that it would be in the same position as it already was in the rite for the episcopate, or possibly there was a more serious theological reason. Cosin, in describing the doctrine and discipline of the Church of England to foreign Christians in a Latin treatise written about 1652, said that,

> Presbyteri . . . ab uno Episcopo per invocationem Spiritus Sancti, impositionem manuum, sacri Codicis traditionem, et verborum Christi, 'Accipe Spiritum Sanctum: quorum peccata', etc., prolationem, solenni more ordinantur.[1]

It would seem likely that by "invocationem Spiritus Sancti" he meant the hymn, "Come Holy Ghost", particularly as he used the same phrase to describe the consecration of bishops, where the hymn also occurred, whereas he said that deacons were ordained "Nominis Divini invocationem". If this was so, then he, and perhaps Sancroft too, may have regarded this hymn as an important, if not essential, element in the rite and wanted it to be more closely associated with the imposition of hands. Another change made by Sancroft in the rite for the priesthood was the addition of a fourth alternative Gospel, Luke 12.35–48. He also apparently followed Wren's suggestion and included a different translation of "Come Holy Ghost", but on a separate paper which cannot now be found. It was probably the version by Cosin, which had been sung at the coronation of Charles I,[2] and which was included in the 1661 revision of the Ordinal, although it may have been only the amended version of the earlier translation which also appears in that final revision, as Sancroft describes it as "corrected". Finally, he proposed that in the imperative formula at the imposition of hands in

---

[1] Cosin, Works IV, p. 352.
[2] Ibid. II, p. 175; The Manner of the Coronation of King Charles the First of England, ed. Charles Wordsworth, HBS II (1892), p. 57.

the rite for the episcopate, after the words "Holy Ghost", there should be inserted the phrase, "by whom the Office, & Authority of a Bishop is now committed unto thee", but he suggested no change in the similar formula in the rite for the priesthood.

The major work of revision, therefore, was left to Convocation itself. Unfortunately, almost nothing is known of their deliberations except the results, in the shape of the Book annexed to the Act of Uniformity in 1662.[1] Almost all the proposals in the "Fair Copy" were accepted, and a large number of additional changes were made. Only two of Sancroft's major proposals were not included, the phrase in the Preface requiring confirmation as a condition for ordination and the additional Gospel from St Luke in the rite for the priesthood. Most of the significant changes made by Convocation were designed to exclude a Puritan interpretation of the Ordinal and to make episcopal ordination a *sine qua non* for admission to the ministry of the Church of England. The Preface was reworded to demand episcopal ordination as essential. A new Epistle, Eph. 4.7–13, describing the varying gifts of grace for the ministry, was appointed for the rite for the priesthood in place of the two alternatives previously provided, since the Puritans had argued that the reading at this service of 1 Tim. 3, which described the qualities required in a bishop, showed that bishops and priests were regarded as belonging to the same order, and Ussher had appealed to the one from Acts to show that the church at Ephesus was ruled by many elders in common and that the Church of England intended her priests to do the same under the presidency of a bishop. This latter Epistle was transferred to the rite for the episcopate, as were two of the three alternative Gospels from this service, that from Matt. 28, which described Jesus commissioning his Apostles to baptize all nations, and that from John 20, which described the commission to the Apostles to forgive sins, presumably to indicate that bishops and not priests were the successors of the Apostles. Another Gospel, Matt. 9.36–8, was added to the rite for the priesthood. Cosin had proposed in his "Durham Book" that the suffrage in the litany in the Prayer Book, "that it may please thee to illuminate all Bishops, Pastours, and Ministers", etc., be changed to "Bishops, Priests, and Ministers", because he believed that in the ancient Church only bishops and not priests were termed pastors.[2] Convocation now altered this to "Bishops, Priests, and Deacons", and made this change in the litany in the Ordinal too, which Cosin had,

[1] Text in Brightman, *The English Rite* II, pp. 928–1017.
[2] Cuming, *The Durham Book*, pp. 88–9.

presumably inadvertently, failed to do. The word "Pastors" was also removed from the exhortation to the candidates in the rite for the priesthood, so that the Puritans could no longer argue that the Church of England taught that priests as well as bishops were to rule their flocks. An additional question was included in the examination of candidates for the episcopate: "Will you be faithful in ordaining, sending, or laying hands upon others?" The reason for this may have been the fact that towards the end of the Commonwealth the number of bishops had sunk dangerously low, and Lord Clarendon had been unable to persuade the remaining bishops of the urgency of filling their places.[1] On the other hand, it may have been included to stress that ordination was the function of the bishop and not of the presbytery. Finally, and perhaps most important of all, changes were made in the formulas at the imposition of hands in the rites for the priesthood and episcopate. The former was expanded to include the phrase, "for the Office and Work of a Priest in the Church of God, now committed unto thee by the Imposition of our hands", after the words, "Receive the Holy Ghost". In the formula for the episcopate Sancroft's proposal underwent further changes in order to make it quite clear that grace was being bestowed by that imposition of hands:

> Receive the Holy Ghost, *for the Office and Work of a Bishop in the Church of God, now committed unto thee by the Imposition of our hands; In the Name of the Father, and of the Son, and of the Holy Ghost, Amen.* And remember that thou stir up the grace of God which is *given* thee by *this* Imposition of *our* hands: for God hath not given us the spirit of fear, but of power, and love, and soberness.[2]

These alterations in the formulas were made to counter the claims of the Puritans who, according to Humphrey Prideaux, later Dean of Norwich, had argued that the old Ordinal recognized "no difference between a Bishop and a Priest because their offices were not at all distinguished in the words whereby they were conferred on them when ordained or any new Power given a Bishop which he had not afore as a Priest".[3] Roman Catholics, however, immediately made the claim that these changes had been made as a result of their criticisms of the

---

[1] Cuming, *A History of Anglican Liturgy*, p. 164.

[2] Words here italicized are those which differ from the earlier Ordinal; cf. above, p. 25, n. 2.

[3] Humphrey Prideaux, *The Validity of the Orders of the Church of England* (1688), p. 9. Prideaux also says that Peter Gunning and John Pearson in the Lower House of Convocation were the "prime advisers" of the changes (p. 43).

Anglican forms in the hope of making the ordinations valid, and this
became a feature of the polemic for many years.[1] Gilbert Burnet, later
Bishop of Salisbury, made the reply that the alterations were not an
admission of any previous defects, since it was obviously too late to try
to remedy any alleged deficiency if the succession had already died out,
but they were only meant as explanations of the meaning of the
formulas,[2] and this line of argument was adopted by all subsequent
Anglican replies to Roman Catholic attacks. Yet, it is not unlikely that
Roman Catholic objections as well as the Puritan interpretation suggested the idea of expanding these formulas, not to remedy their alleged
invalidity, but to improve and clarify them. It might seem surprising
that these formulas were retained at all when Morin had shown that
they were not ancient,[3] and when they had attracted so much criticism.
However, there is no evidence that Morin's work was known to
Anglicans at this time and there is evidence to show that the scriptural
formula, "Receive the Holy Ghost, whose sins", etc., was still regarded
as "the authoritative and commissionating words of Ministeriall
Ordination".[4]

A number of other minor alterations were made by Convocation.
"Making" was substituted for "Ordering" in the title of the rite for the
diaconate, although not in the head-lines of the pages, to correspond
with the new title of the Ordinal proposed by Sancroft; previously
"Making" in the title had referred to the ordaining of both deacons and
priests, but now it was to refer only to the former, "Ordering" was to
refer to the latter, and "Consecrating" to the ordaining of bishops. A
special Gospel was appointed for the rite for the diaconate instead of
that for the day—Luke 12.35-8, the first part of the Gospel originally
suggested by Sancroft as another alternative for the rite for the priesthood. The original version of "Come Holy Ghost" was slightly modified and Cosin's version was included as an alternative. The rubrics
were amplified in places and directions concerning vesture were
restored, although they merely said that candidates for the diaconate
and priesthood were to be "decently habited", and a candidate for the
episcopate was to be "vested in his Rochet" and was to put on "the
rest of the Episcopal habit" after the examination. The concluding

---

[1] This charge was first made on an extra leaf pasted inside the cover of *Erastus Senior,*
which appeared in 1662.
[2] Gilbert Burnet, *A Vindication of the Ordinations of the Church of England* (1677), pp. 71-4.
[3] See above, pp. 83-4.
[4] John Gauden, *Considerations touching the Liturgy of the Church of England* (1661), p. 20.

collect of the litany in the rites for the diaconate and priesthood became the collect of the Communion service, which was a pity since it impoverished the prayer of the people in the rites. In the rite for the episcopate it remained as before, except that it now included a reference to the bishop's "well-governing" of the Church, and a new collect was added to the Communion service based on the collect of St Peter's Day in the Prayer Book. The Presentation in the rite for the episcopate was now to come after the Creed and Sermon, instead of simply after the former, and all three rites had the collect, "Prevent us, O Lord", from the Communion service inserted before the final blessing. The instruction was added to the Preface that the diaconate and priesthood were to be conferred "at the times appointed in the Canon," and only "on urgent occasion" on another Sunday or Holy-day, and the explicit direction was added to the title of the rite for the episcopate, "which is always to be performed upon some Sunday or Holy-day". The final rubric in the rite for the priesthood, relating to the conferring of the diaconate and priesthood on the same occasion, was further amplified from the version in the "Fair Copy"; it now directed that both collects were to be used, that the Epistle was to be Eph. 4.7–13 and not the whole of 1 Tim. 3 as was previously ordered, and the Gospel was to be either Matt. 9.36–8, from the rite for the priesthood, or Luke 12.35–8, from the rite for the diaconate. Only one change was made which might be thought of as a concession to Puritan criticism; in the question in the examination of deacons dealing with their duties, the words "to baptize" were amended to "in the absence of the Priest to baptize infants", thus conceding that this was not a part of their normal duties but something which they could only do in case of emergency; presumably it was not imagined that adult baptism might need to be administered when a priest could not be obtained.

At this revision an alteration relating to ordination was also made in the Prayer Book itself. The Scottish Prayer Book of 1637 had included a version of the concluding collect of the litany in the rite for the priesthood which was to be said during the Ember Weeks for those who were then to be admitted into Holy Orders. Cosin, no doubt influenced by this, inserted in his "Durham Book" a similar prayer composed by himself, Sancroft added the one from the Scottish Prayer Book as an alternative, and both were included in the 1661 revision of the Prayer Book.[1] There seems to be no precedent for this provision.

[1] Cuming, *The Durham Book*, pp. 94–7.

It will be clear that the most notable feature of this revision of the Ordinal is the requirement of episcopal ordination as an absolute necessity for admission to the ministry of the Church of England. Previously the Preface had required that anyone who was not already a bishop, priest, or deacon should be ordained by the rites of the Ordinal, but it had left it indeterminate as to what constituted a true bishop, priest, or deacon. It is sometimes argued that the change in 1661 merely made explicit what had always been the intention of the Preface. Yet this does not really seem to be the case. As the question of non-episcopally ordained men had not really arisen when the Ordinal was drawn up, it can hardly be maintained that it was intended to exclude them. It may be true that many had understood the Ordinal in this sense, but, as has already been said, there were cases in which some were prepared to accept as valid ministers men who had not received episcopal ordination, and there were undoubtedly many men ministering in the Church of England who interpreted it differently and believed that it did not deny the validity of other ministers and rites of ordination. On the other hand, the alteration now made in the Preface definitely asserted that all non-episcopal ordinations were invalid. When this was suggested at the time, according to Lord Clarendon, "it was answered, that the church of England judged none but her own children, nor did determine that other protestant churches were without ordination. It is a thing without her cognisance."[1] Nevertheless, although the intention may not have been to pass judgement on them, it did indeed do just that. The Preface required episcopal ordination for all, both those in England who had refused to be ordained by bishops and those from foreign reformed Churches, and thus, although perhaps unintentionally, it declared that non-episcopal ordination was invalid in the opinion of the Anglican Church. For compelling a man to submit to a second ordination could only mean that the sufficiency of his first ordination was being denied. The argument, often used since, that he was only submitting to the legal requirements of the Act of Uniformity, which cast no doubts on his former ordination, does not avoid the issue. Why was the law made, if the sufficiency of non-episcopal ordinations was not being questioned? Nor is it true that all that was being implied was that there was some uncertainty as to the sufficiency of the former ordination; its validity was being explicitly denied. If the Anglican divines had wished to leave

---

[1] *The Life of Edward, Earl of Clarendon written by himself* (1857) I, p. 555.

the validity of non-episcopal ordination simply as an open issue, they could have done this by proposing that candidates who had been so ordained should receive only a conditional ordination.

In 1662, therefore, a large number of ministers who were unable in conscience to accept that their non-episcopal ordination was invalid were compelled to leave the ministry of the Church of England. Among these and among Anglicans too, however, there were many who did not regard this schism as a final break and who entertained high hopes that a compromise might be reached which would secure the comprehension of the Dissenters within the Church of England. Thus throughout the rest of the seventeenth century various schemes were proposed for uniting the presbyterian and episcopal ministries.

John Bramhall, although finding it necessary to ordain again men in presbyterian orders because of the law, was prepared to insert into their Letters of Orders a clause to show that he did not deny the validity of their former ordinations,[1] in the hope of making it easier for them to conform. Such an expedient, however, would never have been acceptable to the majority of Dissenting ministers who were not prepared to tolerate anything which might suggest that their former ordination had in any way been imperfect. On the other hand, many Anglicans would never have allowed the proposal made in a Bill of Comprehension drawn up in 1667 that those with Presbyterian ordination should be accepted into the ministry of the Church of England without any further ordination.[2] It was never presented to Parliament, but it would undoubtedly have been rejected by those who could not believe in the validity of non-episcopal ordinations. Clearly, therefore, some other way would have to be found.

A scheme for comprehension which tried to do just this was drawn up in a series of conferences between two Anglicans, John Wilkins, later to be Bishop of Chester, and Hezekiah Burton, and three leading Presbyterians, Richard Baxter, William Bates, and Thomas Manton. Wilkins proposed that:

> such persons, as in the late times of disorder have been ordained by Presbyters, shall be admitted to the Exercise of the Ministerial function by the Imposition

---

[1] "Non annihilantes priores ordines (si quos habuit) nec invaliditatem eorum determinantes, multo minus omnes ordines sacros ecclesiarum forinsecarum condemnantes, quos proprio Judici relinquimus, sed solummodo supplentes quicquid prius defuit per canones ecclesiae Anglicanae requisitum, et providentes paci ecclesiae, ut schismatis tollatur occasio, et conscientiis fidelium satisfiat, nec ulli dubitent de eius ordinatione, aut actus suos presbyteriales tanquam invalidos aversentur" (Bramhall, *Works* I, p. xxxvii).

[2] Thorndike, *Theological Works* v, p. 302.

of Hands of the Bishop, with this, or the like form of words: Take thou
Authority to Preach the Word of God and to Minister the Sacraments in any
Congregation of the Church of England where thou shalt lawfully be
appointed thereunto.[1]

Baxter, however, was far from satisfied with this and wanted to
amend the proposal so as to read:

> those who have been ordained only by meer Presbyters, or the Presidents of
> their Synods shall be instituted, and authorized to exercise their Ministry (and
> admitted to Benefices) therein in such manner and by such persons as by his
> Majesty shall be thereto appointed, by this form and words alone (Take etc.)
> provided that those who desire it, have leave to give in their professions that
> they renounce not their Ordination, nor take it for a nullity, and that they
> take this as the Magistrates License and Confirmation, and that they be not
> constrained to use any words themselves which are not consistent with this
> profession.[2]

Baxter put forward these amendments because he suspected that the
original proposal had been intended as a reordination, and he wished
any possible ambiguity to be removed. The circumlocution "such
persons as by his Majesty shall be thereto appointed" in place of the
word "bishops" was to remove any suggestion that those who admitted them did so by any intrinsic power which they possessed.
Similarly, he did not want an imposition of hands to be considered an
essential part of this ceremony, and the inclusion of the phrase "or the
Presidents of their Synods" was intended "to avoid Dispute, whether
such were meer Presbyters, or (as some think) Bishops". "Times of
disorder" was omitted because that restriction would have excluded
all who had received Presbyterian ordination after 1660, which Baxter
did not want to do.[3]

These amendments were not satisfactory to Wilkins, who insisted
that "those Consciences must be accommodated who took them for no
Ministers who were ordained without Bishops". Nor was he willing to
restore the Ordinal as it had been before 1662, which Baxter also
requested.[4] Eventually a compromise was reached. The Dissenters
would not be allowed to make an explicit declaration of their understanding of the ceremony, but the word "legal" would be inserted
before the word "authority" in the formula at the imposition of
hands.[5]

---

[1] RB III, 66. Wilkins also proposed that the ordination services be shortened by the
omission of the hymn "Come Holy Ghost".
[2] Ibid. III, 68.    [3] Ibid. III, 70.    [4] Ibid. III, 71–2.
[5] Ibid. III, 75–6.

It is extremely unlikely, even if the whole scheme had not been rejected by Parliament, that this compromise would have been acceptable to many Anglicans, as the amended formula seems to make it very difficult for them to have understood the ceremony as an ordination. Other unsuccessful schemes for comprehension in which Baxter was involved suggested methods which it is even less possible to regard as in any sense ordinations. The first, in 1673, proposed that those who were ordained by presbyters should simply "upon proof of their fitness for the Ministry, receive by word, or in a written Instrument, a Legal Authority to exercise their Ministry in any Congregation in his Majesty's Dominions, where they shall be lawfully called".[1] Again in 1675 he helped to draw up a proposed Act for comprehension with a similar clause. Those ordained by presbyters,

and are qualified for that Office as the Law requireth, shall receive power to exercise it from a Bishop by a written Instrument (which every Bishop in his Diocess is hereby impowered and required to Grant) in these words and no other (To A. B. of C. in the Country of D. Take thou Authority to exercise the Office of a Presbyter, in any place and Congregation in the King's Dominions whereto thou shalt be lawfully called.) And this practice sufficing for present Concord, no one shall be put to declare his Judgment, whether This, or That which he before received, shall be taken for his Ordination, nor shall be urged to speak any words of such signification; but each party shall be left to Judge as they see cause.[2]

Later schemes offered no new methods but merely reiterated earlier proposals; a Comprehension Bill of 1680 proposed that those ordained by presbyters between 1644 and 1660 should be accepted without reordination,[3] and another Bill, of 1689, contained a clause, struck out in Committee in the Lords, which proposed that they should be admitted by the imposition of hands by a bishop with the formula, "Take thou authority to Preach the word of God and administer the Sacraments and to performe All other Ministerial Offices in the Church of England."[4] Yet another Bill, introduced into the Commons at the same time, proposed that anyone ordained "according to the course used in any Reformed Churches" should be capable of being a minister in the Church of England, and this was not only to apply to the past.[5]

[1] RB III, 256.   [2] Ibid. III, 288.
[3] Roger Thomas, "Comprehension and Indulgence", in From Uniformity to Unity 1662–1962, ed. Geoffrey F. Nuttall and Owen Chadwick (1962), pp. 225–7.
[4] Text in Appendix T of the Report of the Clerical Subscription Commission (1865).
[5] Thomas, p. 249.

Needless to say, none of these was successful. It is interesting to note that all of these schemes which involved any sort of ceremony proposed the use of an imperative formula as the necessary form; nobody seems to have suggested the use of a prayer. This is further evidence that the researches of Morin had not penetrated into Anglican theology. Yet the use of an ambiguous imperative formula was clearly not proving an acceptable way of uniting the ministries, and some other method needed to be sought. When, therefore, later in 1689 a commission was appointed to revise the Prayer Book to facilitate comprehension, John Tillotson, then Dean of Canterbury and a member of the commission, prepared a list of concessions which might be made and among them he suggested that all future ordinations should be episcopal but that those who had been ordained in reformed Churches abroad should be accepted into the ministry of the Church of England without re-ordination, and that those who had received only presbyterian orders in England should undergo a conditional ordination.[1]

When the commission met, however, this question was the subject of considerable debate.[2] Those seeking admission to the ministry of the Church of England and claiming a previous ordination were divided into three categories—those from the Church of Rome, those from foreign reformed Churches, and English Dissenters. Objections were raised against admitting Roman Catholics without further ordination because, it was claimed, the matter, form, and intention of their former ordination were in doubt: hands were not laid upon them and the words, "Receive the Holy Ghost, whosoever sins", etc., said until after their ordination, and the correct intention could never be proved. Others urged caution in condemning Roman Orders because they had always been regarded as valid by the Church of England in the past and because Anglican Orders were ultimately derived from them. Henry Compton, the Bishop of London, then said that it was not the validity of their orders that was being questioned, but the sufficiency of the evidence; imposters had often presented themselves for admission to the ministry of the Church of England, claiming Roman Orders, and the Church of Rome was not willing to confirm the doubtful cases. It was therefore proposed that such men should receive conditional ordination. In the discussion over those ordained in foreign Churches,

---

[1] Cardwell, *History of Conferences*, pp. 413–14.
[2] An account of the deliberations of the commission is given in a diary written by one of its members, John Williams, later Bishop of Chichester. Text in *Parliamentary Paper* 283 (1854), pp. 94–108.

various examples were brought forward to justify their admission without reordination, including that of the Scottish bishops in 1610 who were not ordained priests before being consecrated. Eventually it was proposed to draw up a rubric "to signify that it was sufficient tho' imperfect Ordination; and that they shou'd be received by imposition of the hands of the Bp only to Officiate in the Church of England". Over the question of admitting English Dissenters, Gilbert Burnet brought forward the case of the Donatists to justify accepting them; notwithstanding the Canons of the Church against admitting two bishops to one altar, the Donatists had been received into the same city and it had been agreed that the one who survived the longer should be the bishop, in spite of the fact that the Donatists had been very troublesome to the Church. The objection was raised that this was no precedent, since the Donatists had been episcopally ordained.

> But it was answer'd, that there could be no more two Bps than a Presbyter be Ordained without a Bishop, and if necessity of affairs was a Reason for the One, it was a Reason for the other; and that the Stopping of the prt Schism made it a necessity. It was then queried how it should be done; and it was agreed that it shou'd be only for this turn, those that were in Orders, but not to proceed further.[1]

When the commission next met, a draft rubric was read which proposed that Dissenters should be admitted with a conditional ordination. This gave rise to some discussion. William Beveridge, later Bishop of St Asaph, felt that it "lookt like Equivocation on the part of the Ordainer and Ordained: Of the Ordainer, because it is likely he believ'd him not ordained before; of the Ordained, because he questioned not his former Ordination". Burnet replied that there was no reason for this because a declaration that each should reserve his opinion was annexed to the rubric. Bramhall's treatment of those with presbyterian ordination was also mentioned in the discussion, and the distinction between imperfect and invalid ordinations was again brought up; it was suggested that the Dissenters' ordinations could not be regarded as invalid, because that would render all actions done by them null and void, which they would never allow, but they could be called imperfect, and then they could be treated in the same way as ordinations in the foreign Churches. Tillotson maintained, however, that the principle must be preserved that episcopal ordination was necessary where it could be had. It was then proposed that it be thought

---

[1] Parliamentary Paper 283, pp. 102–3.

of, not as a reordination, but as supplying what they lacked, as in
Queen Mary's time the Roman Catholics had supplied what they
thought lacking in Anglican ordinations. "To this it was reply'd that
then the question only was as to the matter of fact (as in Baptism)
allowing their right, if prov'd; but here it was matter of right. After
this it was proposed and carryed (Dr Bev. & Scot dissenting) to be
hypothetically expressed, and after examination of the Phrase it was
also agreed, that the like Phrase should be inserted at the Archdeacons
Presentation in Ordination."[1]

Another subject which gave rise to considerable debate in the
revision of the Ordinal by this commission was the formula, "Receive
the Holy Ghost", etc., in the rite for the priesthood. Some wished to
retain it as they thought it was fitting, although they admitted that
when it was used by Christ it was used in a different sense; yet, they
insisted, the ordinary was conveyed with the extraordinary. They
interpreted it to mean no more than, "Receive ye Commission to
preach the Word and Administer the Sacraments, in the due Use of
which the Holy Ghost is conveyed". Others thought that it was the
essential form, and Mason and Bramhall were cited in support of this
view. Burnet, however, who was probably the only member of the
commission to be aware of the discoveries of Morin, said that this did
not appear to be so. If it had been the essential form, then there would
have been no ordinations when it had not been used, and Morin had
shown that it had not been used for the first thirteen hundred years of
the Church's history, nor was it used in any Church other than the
Anglican one at the present day; In the Church of Rome the form was
the prayer, *Exaudi nos*, etc.; so Mason and Bramhall had been
mistaken. Tillotson then produced a quotation from St Augustine
(*De Trinitate*, l.15, c. 27) which said Christ was God because he gave
the Holy Ghost and the Church only prayed for it, and William Lloyd,
the Bishop of St Asaph, pointed out that the Apostles prayed that the
Holy Ghost might be conferred by the imposition of their hands,
quoting Acts 8.15–17. It was then suggested that an alteration in the
form might be imprudent, but it was replied that some alterations had
been made in 1661 and the Church of Rome had made many changes
in its forms.[2]

This is all that is known of the deliberations of the commission
about the Ordinal, and for the rest the only evidence is the interleaved

[1] Ibid., pp. 103–4.     [2] Ibid., pp. 104–6.

copy of the Prayer Book containing their suggestions and amendments.[1] On an interleaf after the Preface to the Ordinal are added two new rubrics, the first apparently intended as a concession to those Dissenters who felt that the examination of the candidates and the provisions for objections to them were inadequate, and the second referring to the attitude to be taken to converts from Rome, which had been discussed by the commission:

> The Persons who desire to be ordained shall send their Testimonials to the Bishop from the place of their present residence at least a month before; and come themselves to be examined at least a week before. After the receipt of the Testimonials, the Bishop shall give order that public notice be given of their desiring Holy Orders in the Church, Chapel, or College where they reside, the Lord's-day before the Ordination.

> Whereas we have often been imposed upon by men pretending to Orders in the Church of Rome, it is therefore humbly proposed whether, since we can have no certainty concerning the instruments of Orders which they show, they may be admitted to serve as Deacons or Presbyters of this Church without being ordained according to the following Offices.

Immediately after these rubrics comes the statement, "the commissioners proceeded no further for want of time; the Convocation being met". Nevertheless, the book contains other alterations and amendments after this point, most of which follow suggestions made in the discussions of the commission. It may be supposed, therefore, that these were inserted after the discussions but never finally approved by the whole commission. A number of notes are added on the interleaves opposite the rite for the priesthood, but with no indication where it was proposed to insert them into the text. They refer to the attitude to be taken towards those ordained abroad and the Presbyterians in England. The former were to be received into the ministry of the Church of England by the imposition of the bishop's hands "in these or such like words: Take thou authority to preach the Word of God, and to minister the Holy Sacraments in this Church, as thou shalt be lawfully appointed thereunto".[2] English Presbyterians were to be admitted by a conditional ordination into the Church of England,

> By Which as she retains her opinion and practice, which make a Bishop necessary to the giving of Orders when he can be had; so she does likewise leave all such persons as have been ordained by Presbyters only the freedom

---

[1] Text: Parliamentary Paper 283, pp. 84–8.
[2] A query is marked against the word "as", and "where" is suggested as an alternative.

of their own thoughts concerning their former Ordinations. It being withal
expressly provided that this shall never be a precedent for the time to come,
and that it shall only be granted to such as have been ordained before
the —— day of ——.[1]

The Letters of Orders in such cases were to adopt the wording used
by Bramhall, as had been suggested in the discussions of the commission. Also in the rite for the priesthood, against the imperative
formula at the imposition of hands, is written the quotation from St
Augustine mentioned in the discussion about this and on the interleaf
is added a prayer intended as a possible replacement for the formula:

> Pour down, O Father of Lights, the Holy Ghost on this thy servant, for the
> office and work of a Priest in the Church of God, now committed unto him
> by the imposition of our hands, that whose sins he does forgive, they may be
> forgiven, and whose sins he doth retain, they may be retained, and that he
> may be a faithful dispenser of God's holy word and sacraments, to the edifica-
> tion of his Church, and the glory of his holy name, Through Jesus Christ, etc.

The invocation of the Trinity thus displaced was to be prefixed to the
words at the delivery of the Bible. No change was suggested for the
formula in the rite for the episcopate, probably through shortage of
time. Other changes made in this proposed revision were the alteration
of the word "Priests" to "Presbyters (commonly called Priests)" in the
title of the Ordinal, and the addition of the expression, "i.e. Presbyters", to the title of the rite for the priesthood. New hymns were to be
composed in place of "Come Holy Ghost" and a number of other very
small changes were also proposed.

Nothing came of this scheme, however, and, although attempts at
comprehension continued to be made, there do not seem to have been
any more serious attempts in this century to find ways of reuniting the
ministries or of revising the Ordinal to make it acceptable to both
parties, except for what appears to be another proposed Bill for Comprehension found among the Burnet papers in the Bodleian Library,
Oxford. This has a clause which enacts,

> that no minister ordained only by presbyters since the year of our Lord 1660,
> shall be admitted to any benefice or promotion unless he receive a second
> imposition of hands from some bishop, to recommend him to the grace
> of God for the work or exercise of his office, in the place or charge unto
> which he is called; and the bishop shall frame his words and testimonial

---

[1] The condition was to be added to the presentation and the final inquiry of the people,
as well as to the imperative formula itself.

accordingly, to the mutual satisfaction of himself and the ordained, till a form be by a convocation and a law established.[1]

From the rest of the Bill it would seem that this was a later proposal than that made in 1689, but nothing more appears to be known of it.

[1] Cardwell, *History of Conferences*, p. 458.

# 7. *Attempts at Revision, 1700–1900*

The failure of the movement towards the Comprehension of Dissenters in 1689 and the growth of the idea of Toleration considerably weakened the desire to find ways of reuniting episcopal and non-episcopal ministries. Compromise gave way to controversy. Among Anglicans in the early years of the eighteenth century can be seen a growing belief in the idea of the Apostolic Succession and a consequent total rejection of the validity of non-episcopal ministries.[1] From now onwards the need to make the Ordinal acceptable to Dissenters ceases to be a driving force in attempts at its revision.

Criticism of the Ordinal can be traced throughout the eighteenth century, almost all of it centring round the formula, "Receive the Holy Ghost", etc. Both Thomas Comber, Dean of Durham, and Gilbert Burnet, writing at the very end of the previous century, mention the objections which had been raised by the Puritans to this formula as though the controversy was still alive, and they defend its use.[2] William Nicholls, the author of a commentary on the Prayer Book in the first half of the eighteenth century, did the same,[3] and one revised Prayer Book, published in 1753, although containing no Ordinal, remarked about it in its preface: "I believe it is not so concise and correct, as to want no Emendation. I forbear entering into Particulars; only must observe, that instead of saying 'Receive thou the Holy Ghost'; it would be better to change it into a Wish or Prayer;

---

[1] J. Wickham Legg, *English Church Life from the Restoration to the Tractarian Movement* (1914), pp. 382–90. For the controversy between Anglicans and Dissenters over ordination see James Owen, *A Plea for Scripture Ordination* (1694), *Tutamen Evangelicum* (1697), and *The Validity of the Dissenting Ministry* (1716); E. Wells, *The invalidity of Presbyterian Ordination* (1707); John Thomas, *An Answer to James Owen's arguments for Ordination by Presbyters without Bishops* (1711); James Peirce, *Presbyterian Ordination prov'd regular* (1716), and *A Defence of the Dissenting Ministry and Presbyterian Ordination* (1717); J. Jackman, *Success no Rule* (1718), and *Presbyterian Ordination presumptuous* (1719).

[2] Thomas Comber, *A discourse upon the Form and Manner of Making, Ordaining and Consecrating Bishops, Priests and Deacons According to the Order of the Church of England* (1699), pp. 262–3; Gilbert Burnet, *An Exposition of the Thirty-Nine Articles of the Church of England* (1699), p. 378.

[3] William Nicholls, *A Supplement to the Commentary on the Book of Common Prayer* (1711).

or else leave it entirely out."[1] The formula also came under criticism from those who denied the orthodox teaching on the Trinity. Dr Samuel Clarke, who had strong Unitarian leanings, produced a revised Prayer Book which altered all references to the Trinity to conform to his beliefs. In the Ordinal, in addition to striking out all the trinitarian conclusions to prayers, substituting the Grace for the Blessing, and amending references to the Trinity in the litany, Clarke turned the formulas at the imposition of hands in the rites for the priesthood and the episcopate into prayers:

> Grant, O Lord, that this person may receive the Holy Ghost for the Office and Work of a Priest in the Church of God, now committed unto him by the imposition of our hands: That, under the Direction of the Spirit of Truth and Holiness, whose soever sins he forgives, may be forgiven; and whose soever sins he retains, may be retained: And that he may be a faithful Dispenser of the Word of God, and of His Holy Sacraments, in the Church where he shall be appointed to minister. Amen.

> Grant, O Lord, that This thy Servant may receive the Holy Ghost, for the Office and Work of a Bishop in the Church of God, now committed unto him, by the imposition of our hands: And that he may continually remember to stir up thy Gifts which are in him, to Thy Glory and to the good Government of Thy Church, and the Salvation of the Souls of men. Amen.

He also omitted the hymn, "Come Holy Ghost", from the rite for the priesthood, substituting a psalm for it, and both the hymn and the Creed from the rite for the episcopate, substituting a psalm for the latter, and made a small change in the bidding to prayer in the rite for the episcopate: "fall to Prayer" became "offer up our Prayers".[2] Another anti-trinitarian writer later in the century, stating his objections to the Thirty-nine Articles, objected to Article 36 because it approved of a formula in the ordination of priests which gave an "extraordinary power, not warranted by Scripture". He also objected to the two versions of the hymn because they were directed to the Holy Ghost as eternal God, which he believed was superstitious as there was no direct invocation of the Holy Spirit in the New Testament. One of the versions also had "the gross Athanasian doctrine of three co-equal Persons and one God".[3]

[1] *A New Form of Common-Prayer, with the Offices thereto belonging, to which are prefixed Reasons for the Proposed Alterations, by a Clergyman of the Church of England* (1753), p. 30.
[2] A copy of the Book of Common Prayer with Ms. alterations by Samuel Clarke in the British Museum.
[3] *Queries Recommended to the Consideration of the Public with regard to the Thirty-Nine Articles* (1772), pp. 37–8.

Apart from these criticisms, however, little was done to revise the Ordinal and only two other revised Ordinals appeared in England during the eighteenth century, and they were not motivated primarily by a dislike of the imperative formulas but were composed for rather different reasons. One was drawn up by a nonjuring bishop, Thomas Deacon. The Nonjurors were a group of bishops and priests who considered that they were still bound to their Oath of Allegiance to James II, even after his deposition, and were therefore unable to take the Oath to William and Mary. They were ejected from their benefices and forced to continue to minister in schism. They apparently followed the Anglican Ordinal in their ordinations, but no doubt if the schism had lasted longer, attempts would have been made to revise this. Deacon's attempt is the only one known, and it is most unlikely that this was ever used, except for the ordination to the diaconate of a certain Thomas Podmore on 11 December 1748, of which there is an official record.[1] This Ordinal is basically an amalgamation of the Anglican rites with those of the fourth-century *Apostolic Constitutions*, the earliest ordination rites then known.[2] The rites appear in it in the reverse order from the Anglican, the service for bishops coming first, as in the *Apostolic Constitutions*. There is also a rite for deaconesses, which was probably included only because it existed in the *Apostolic Constitutions* and not because Deacon had any intention of reviving the order. The Anglican Preface to the Ordinal is omitted.

Each of the four rites begins with lengthy rubrics composed by Deacon himself. The candidates for each order are to be elected, in the case of the episcopate by the clergy and faithful of the diocese with the approval of the majority of the bishops of the province, two of whom are to examine him, together with the metropolitan or senior bishop, and present him at his consecration; in the case of the priesthood the election is by the clergy with the agreement of the faithful of the parish concerned, and the candidate is examined by two priests, who present him at the ordination, and by the bishop; in the case of deacons and deaconesses, the election is by the faithful of the parish, the candidate is examined by two deacons and the bishop and, after the

---

[1] Henry Broxap, *A Biography of Thomas Deacon* (1911), p. 157. This is the only existing record of Deacon's episcopal acts.

[2] Text in Hall, *Fragmenta Liturgica* VI, pp. 254–300. Deacon's text of the *Apostolic Constitutions* is almost certainly based on the translation made by William Whiston in *Primitive Christianity Reviv'd* (1711–12), vol. II, as there are close similarities between the two, although at times Deacon appears to correct Whiston's translation from the Greek text which Whiston also prints.

bishop has consulted with his college of presbyters and given his approval, is presented by the same two deacons. Other rubrics direct that notice of the ordination is to be given and that between then and the ordination itself, except in the case of deaconesses, a prayer is to be said on Wednesdays and Fridays, the prayer being an adaptation of the first Ember Collect from the Book of Common Prayer, mentioning the particular order to be conferred. Candidates for the episcopate are to be at least forty years of age "unless upon a particular occasion", for the priesthood thirty, deacons twenty-five, and deaconesses forty. In the case of a consecration to the episcopate, the majority of the bishops of the province must either be present or have sent their consent in writing, "nor shall there be any Consecration unless three Bishops be present, except in the case of persecution, or some such other very necessary occasion", and the metropolitan or senior bishop present is always to be the consecrator. All four rites presuppose only one candidate at a time.

All the elements from the Anglican rites are included, except for the alternative Epistles and Gospels, the Oath of Supremacy, the litany, the hymn, "Come Holy Ghost", and the formulas at the imposition of hands, and there are a number of minor variations in other elements. The giving of the Bible and of the New Testament is also omitted from the rites for the priesthood and diaconate respectively, and the space for silent prayer is omitted from the rite for the priesthood. In some cases elements from one Anglican rite are also included in other rites in this version. Thus the rite for the episcopate has at the beginning a sermon on the duty of a bishop, the necessity of the order, and the esteem in which he should be held, following the practice of the Anglican rite for the diaconate. The same rite also adopts a question as to the candidate's suitability, based on that in the Anglican rite for the diaconate, and the rites for the episcopate and priesthood both include questions on the duties of the office similar to that in the rite for the diaconate and adopt similar wording in the question on belief in the Scriptures to that in the question put to deacons. The examination in the rite for deacons and deaconesses is prefaced with a short address similar to that in the rite for the episcopate, and concludes with the prayer which ends the examination in the rite for the priesthood. The rite for deaconesses is based very closely on that for deacons, except that no sermon is to be preached, the phrase in the collect referring to Stephen is replaced by the words, "And didst admit thy servant Phoebe and others into the order of Deaconesses", the Epistle is to be Rom.

16.1–2, and the Gospel is to be Luke 2.36–8. Following the structure of the rite for the episcopate, the ordination now comes after the Creed in all the other rites, except for the presentation which remains in its old position.

From the *Apostolic Constitutions* have been drawn the ordination prayers in each rite, said at the imposition of hands in place of the Anglican formulas; that in the rite for the episcopate is an abbreviated version of the original, and it is accompanied by two deacons holding the book of Gospels open over the candidate's head, as the *Apostolic Constitutions* prescribe. The Anglican prayers before the imposition of hands in the rites for the episcopate and priesthood now become mere preliminaries; they are recited facing the altar and in the rite for the episcopate the candidate does not put on the "episcopal habit" until after it. In all the rites the ordination prayer is preceded by a signing of the candidate with the sign of the cross and a proclamation, during which the imposition of hands begins. In the rite for the episcopate it reads:

> With the suffrage and consent of the Bishops of the Province of N. and of the Clergy and people of the Diocese of N. the Divine grace, which always healeth what is infirm, and supplieth what is wanting, promoteth the Reverend Priest N. to be Bishop of the Church and See of N. Let us pray for him, that the grace of the most Holy Spirit may descend upon him.
>
> *Answ.* Lord have mercy: We beseech thee to hear us, good Lord.

The same formula, with suitable alterations, was used in the other rites. This practice was not drawn from the *Apostolic Constitutions* but was based upon the later usage of the Eastern Church. In each rite the ordination prayer from the *Apostolic Constitutions* was followed immediately by the special final collect for that rite from the Anglican Ordinal, except for the rite for the episcopate which had the giving of the Bible and of the pastoral staff, as in the 1550 Anglican Ordinal, intervening between the two. The collect in the rite for the episcopate omitted the petition, "and so endue him with thy Holy Spirit", presumably because it was thought that the Spirit had already been received, and the collect in the rites for deacons and deaconesses omitted the clause relating to advancement to higher office, probably because in the case of deacons this had already been said in the preceding prayer and in the case of deaconesses it was not applicable. In the rite for the episcopate there then follow directions drawn from the *Apostolic Constitutions*; the candidate receives the kiss of peace from the other bishops, is enthroned, pronounces a benediction, preaches, and continues the celebration of the Eucharist. The only difference from the *Apostolic Constitutions* is that the benediction prescribed is not the Grace but the Blessing from the Anglican Ordinal, with the addition of the response, "And with thy spirit", which also appeared in the *Apostolic Constitutions*. Deacon also introduced similar ceremonies into the other rites. A priest received the kiss of peace from the bishop and other priests and was put into his stall; the bishop then pronounced the blessing, the newly ordained priest preached, and the bishop celebrated the Eucharist; candidates for the diaconate received the kiss of peace from their fellow-deacons or deaconesses, and the bishop pronounced the blessing and celebrated the Eucharist.

Certain other changes were also made in the rite for the episcopate. The question as to the candidate's suitability was followed by an appeal for the consent of the clergy and people, derived from the *Apostolic Constitutions*, and occupying the place taken by the final inquiry of the people in the other rites. In the place of the litany in this rite, Deacon introduced a bidding and response, drawing the wording mainly from the special suffrage of the Anglican litany but adapting it to the pattern of a supplication in the Eastern type of litany, and following it with the concluding collect of the Anglican litany. Thus there are in effect two biddings in this rite, the original bidding from the Anglican rite followed immediately by this. Finally, instead of the Oath of Canonical Obedience there is a question in the examination asking if the candidate will pay canonical obedience to the metropolitan. This is omitted at the consecration of an archbishop and in its place is provided a question stating the duties of a metropolitan and asking if the candidate will perform them faithfully and diligently.

This Ordinal was a genuine, if somewhat uncritical, attempt to draw up rites of ordination which would correspond more closely with those of the primitive Church. The main criticism which can be levelled against it is that it was too elaborate; the retention of almost all of the existing Anglican Ordinal together with the introduction of material from the *Apostolic Constitutions* and elsewhere resulted in something nearer to the complexity of the medieval rites than the simplicity of the primitive Church. Its main gain was the restoration of a prayer at the imposition of hands, its main loss was the absence of any provision for the prayer of the people, apart from the brief response to the bidding in the rite for the episcopate. It is perhaps worth noting, in view of the current discussion on the use of the term "presbyter", that Deacon freely interchanges it with the word "priest" in his rites.

The other attempt to revise the Ordinal in the eighteenth century was by John Wesley in 1784. Influenced mainly by two books, Stillingfleet's *Irenicum* and Peter King's *An Enquiry into the Constitution, Discipline, Unity and Worship of the Primitive Church*, which had appeared in 1691, Wesley came to believe that bishops and priests differed only in degree and not in order. He therefore thought that as an Anglican priest he had the right to ordain in cases of necessity, and when the English bishops would do nothing about providing a bishop for America, he ordained a "superintendent" and "elders" to serve in America, and later other "elders" for Scotland, and eventually for England, adapting the Anglican Ordinal for this purpose.[1] The Preface was entirely omitted, and "superintendent" substituted for "bishop" and "elder" for "priest" throughout. All oaths and directions about vestments were also omitted, and in the litany the expression "Bishops, Priests and Deacons", was amended to "Ministers of thy gospel". In the rites for deacons and elders an elder presented the candidates to the superintendent, the question as to their suitability was omitted, and in the rite for the diaconate the reading of the candidates' names replaced it. Also in the rite for the diaconate the alternative Epistle from Acts 6 was omitted, and a rubric directing that there should be a space for silent prayer was added after the examination, identical with the one in the Anglican rite for the priesthood. The Bible was given to the candidates, instead of the New Testament, with the words, "Take thou authority to read the holy Scriptures in the church of God, and to preach the same", and the rubric at the end of the service requiring a year in the diaconate was omitted, as Wesley sometimes ordained a man as an elder on the following day. In the service for elders the alternative Gospel from Matt. 9 and the earlier version of "Come Holy Ghost" were omitted, as was the phrase, "whose sins thou dost forgive, they are forgiven; and whose sins thou dost retain, they are retained", from the formula at the imposition of hands. The expression, "Receive the Holy Ghost", was, however, retained, so apparently Wesley did not share the objections which had been made to this. In the "Form of Ordaining a Superintendent", all mention of "consecrating" was omitted, the phrase in the collect, "Bishops, the Pastors of thy Church", was altered to "all the Ministers and Pastors

[1] A. B. Lawson, *John Wesley and the Christian Ministry* (1963), esp. pp. 130ff. Text in Appendix 2, pp. 182–98.

of thy Church", and the Epistle from 1 Tim. 3 and the Gospel from John 20 were omitted.

Revisions of the Ordinal in other parts of the world can be dealt with briefly. The Episcopal Church of Scotland used the English Ordinal at this time, but in America a revised version appeared in 1792. The main change was the provision of another formula as an alternative to "Receive the Holy Ghost", etc. in the rite for the priest-hood as a consequence of the objections which had been raised:

> Take thou Authority to execute the Office of a Priest in the Church of God, now committed to thee by the Imposition of our hands. And be thou a faithful Dispenser of the Word of God, and of his holy Sacraments; In the name of the Father, and of the Son, and of the Holy Ghost. Amen.

There were also a number of other small changes. In the question in the examination of priests concerning the Scriptures the word "suffic-iently" was omitted, and in the bidding to prayer in the rite for the episcopate the phrase, "offer up our Prayers to Almighty God", was substituted for "fall to prayer", and the example of the Apostles at the ordination of Matthias for that of the disciples at Antioch at the sending forth of Paul and Barnabas, it no doubt being realized that the latter was not a good precedent for an ordination to the episcopate as a separate order. The other changes were such as were made necessary by the pastoral situation in America. There being no archdeacons, a priest presented the candidates for the priesthood and diaconate; as there was no archbishop, a "Promise of Conformity to the Doctrine, Discipline and Worship of the Protestant Episcopal Church" was substituted for the oath of obedience to the archbishop in the rite for the episcopate; and the Oath of Supremacy was omitted from all the rites.[1]

In the nineteenth century objections to the Ordinal, as to the rest of the Prayer Book, grew considerably, mainly in reaction to the Oxford Movement. Yet even prior to the publication of *Tracts for the Times* there was agitation for revision of the Ordinal. The main target for attack was again the imperative formulas in the rites for the priest-hood and episcopate, which presented serious problems of conscience for some who thought it presumptuous for men to pretend to have power to confer the Holy Spirit, and could not see how the use of these words could be defended. One such troubled churchman, Charles Nourse Wodehouse, drew up a petition to the House of Lords in 1824

---

[1] Text in William McGarvey, *Liturgiae Americanae* (Philadelphia 1895), pp. 420–40.

in which he listed the several parts of the Book of Common Prayer which he could not conscientiously affirm to be sanctioned by Scripture, among them these formulas, but did not specify what he wanted to put in their place.[1] When, in 1840, he supported a similar petition to his own presented to the House of Lords by Richard Whately, the Archbishop of Dublin, he seemed to favour the substitution of a prayer.[2] Another writer, W. W. Hull, pressed for the adoption of the American formula for the priesthood as an alternative. He was also troubled by the terms in which ordinands were required to express their belief in Scripture, and wanted the word "sufficiently" omitted from the question concerning Scripture in the rite for the priesthood, as in the American Ordinal, and the question put to deacons made identical to this question. Finally, he wanted the question concerning obedience to superiors in the examination in the rites for the diaconate and priesthood to be amended to indicate that it was "limited to things lawful and expedient", and the Preface altered so as not to appear to preclude the ordination of those who were not learned in Latin.[3] Pressure for revision also continued to come from those who held unorthodox views about the Trinity. Richard Littlehales, who rejected the doctrine of the eternal generation and procession of the Son and of the Holy Spirit, wanted the hymn, "Come Holy Ghost", omitted from the rites for the priesthood and episcopate and proposed to substitute for it a prayer for the Holy Spirit. He also suggested a number of small alterations in the examination of deacons.[4]

After the publication of *Tracts for the Times*, however, objections to the imperative formulas rose greatly. For in the very first tract John Henry Newman had quoted the formula in the rite for the priesthood and said,

> Thus we have confessed before God our belief, that through the Bishop who ordained us, we received the Holy Ghost, the power to bind and loose and administer the Sacraments, and to preach. Now how is he able to give these great gifts? Whence is his right? Are these words idle, which would be

---

[1] C. N. Wodehouse, *A Petition to the House of Lords for Ecclesiastical Improvements, with Explanations* (1832), pp. 10, 35-42.

[2] J. Hull and W. W. Hull, *Observations on a Petition for the Revision of the Liturgy* (1840), p. 46.

[3] W. W. Hull, *An Inquiry concerning the Means and Expedience of proposing and Making any changes in the Canons, Articles, or Liturgy, or in any of the Laws affecting the Interests of the Church of England* (1828), pp. 186-7.

[4] Richard Littlehales, *A Review of the Liturgy and Articles of the Church of England* (1813), pp. 19-20.

taking God's name in vain, or do they express merely a wish, which surely is very far below their meaning, or do they not rather indicate that the speaker is conveying a gift? Surely they can mean nothing short of this. But whence, I ask, his right to do so? Has he any right, except as having received the power from those who consecrated him to be a Bishop? He could not give what he had never received. It is plain then that he but transmits; and that the Christian Ministry is a succession. And if we trace back the power of ordination from hand to hand, of course we shall come to the Apostles at last. We know we do, as a plain historical fact: and therefore all we, who have been ordained Clergy, in the very form of our ordination acknowledged the doctrine of the Apostolical Succession. . . . I do not see how any one can escape from this plain view of the subject, except, as I have already hinted, by declaring that the words do not mean all that they say. But only reflect what a most unseemly time for random words is that, in which Ministers are set apart for their office.[1]

This formula, therefore, came to be used by the Tractarians and the later Ritualists as their warrant for the doctrine of apostolic succession and for the practice of private confession. As Edward Pusey remarked, "So long as those words of Our Lord, 'Whose sins thou dost forgive, they are forgiven', are repeated to us when we are ordained, so long will there be confession in the Church of England."[2] Many who did not share the Tractarian views interpreted the formula rather differently: "receive" was to be understood as meaning "mayest thou receive", and "Holy Ghost" merely meant "ministerial authority", while the commission to forgive sins was intended to be exercised only in declaring the Absolution at Morning and Evening Prayer.[3] A few, however, were unable to accept this interpretation and found it difficult to see how the words could mean anything other than Newman had said they meant, although they could not believe those doctrines to be true.[4] Others, while adopting a different interpretation of the formula from the Tractarians, realized that the words did give grounds for their beliefs. Both these groups, therefore, began vehement agitation for revision. The Ordinal as it stood seemed to vindicate Tractarian ideas; therefore the Ordinal must be changed. Hence there was a continuous flow of publications throughout the rest of the

[1] *Tracts for the Times*, No. 1 (9 September 1833), p. 3.
[2] In a letter to *The Times*, 29 November 1866.
[3] C. Green, *A Letter to C. N. Wodehouse* (1843), pp. 24–6; J. R. Pretyman, *Thoughts on the Revision of the Prayer-Book, and of the Terms of Clerical Conformity* (1855), p. 16.
[4] "Miles Coverdale", *The Exeter Diocesan Synod Reviewed* (1851), p. 17; see also John C. Fisher, *Liturgical Purity our Rightful Inheritance* (1857), pp. 38ff.

century, almost entirely from extreme Evangelicals, pressing for alterations to the imperative formulas, especially that in the rite for the priesthood.

A wide range of suggestions was made as to what should replace them, almost all being alternative formulas rather than prayers, indicating that the results of the research by Morin and others into primitive ordination rites were not widely known or appreciated. Indeed, at least one author suggested that an imperative formula was more suitable than a prayer.[1] Some suggested a formula which was a mixture between an imperative commission and a benediction:

> Receive the office of a Presbyter in the Church of God, now committed unto thee by the imposition of our hands. May the Holy Ghost be given to thee for the fulfilment of the same.

The same formula, with "Bishop" substituted for "Presbyter", was to be used in the rite for the episcopate.[2] Others suggested straightforward alternative imperative commissions. Richard Bingham, who produced not only revised formulas but a complete revised Ordinal, suggested:

> Take thou authority to hold the Office and execute the Work of a Presbyter in the Church of God now committed unto thee by imposition of our hands; and be thou a faithful dispenser of the Word of God and of his holy Sacraments, in the Name of the Father, and of the Son, and of the Holy Spirit, Amen.

> Take thou authority to hold the Office and execute the Work of a Bishop in the Church of God, now committed unto thee by imposition of our hands; In the name of the Father, and of the Son, and of the Holy Spirit. Amen. And remember that thou stir up the grace of God which is given thee, as signified by the imposition of our hands. For God hath not given us the spirit of fear, but of power, and of love, and of a sound mind.

The other main changes he proposed in the Ordinal were the substitution of "presbyter" for "priest" throughout, the omission of the litany from all three rites, and the inclusion of a sermon at the beginning of the rite for the episcopate. The Preface was to be lengthened to explain how Christ instituted a fourfold ministry, of which apostles and prophets had disappeared, evangelists remained as the modern missionaries and itinerant preachers, and the pastors and teachers existed under the names of bishops, priests, and deacons. A rubric was to be

[1] Philip Gell, *The difficulties of an Honest and Conscientious Use of the Book of Common Prayer considered as a loud and reasonable call for the only remedy*, Revision (1860), p. 16.
[2] George G. Lawrence, *A Few Thoughts on the Revision of the Liturgy* ( 1859), pp. 15-16.

included to the effect that, if there was doubt whether someone had been "legally ordained before, in some other Church", the bishop could administer a conditional ordination.[1]

One author who did suggest a prayer instead of a formula was Christopher Benson, Master of the Temple. He believed that the original saying in John 20.22–3 had intended to confer power on the Apostles alone and not on their successors, and that the Church of England had adopted it not in this original sense but as a prayer for the Holy Spirit and a commission to pronounce the Absolution in the Prayer Book. If, however, this was not thought sufficient to justify retaining it, he proposed that something similar to the ordination prayer of the Greek Church could be substituted:

> O God, great in power, unsearchable in wisdom, and wonderful in thy counsels towards the sons of men; O Lord, who hast been pleased to grant unto this thy servant the order of a Presbyter, replenish him with the gifts of thy Holy Spirit; that he may be worthy to stand before thy holy altar unblameably, to preach the gospel of thy kingdom, to minister the word of thy truth, to present unto thee spiritual gifts and sacrifices, and to renew thy people by the laver of regeneration; that at the second coming of the great God and our Saviour Jesus Christ, thine only begotten Son, he may receive the reward of the faithful servant of the Lord's house, through the multitude of thy goodness.[2]

C. H. Davis, who wrote prolifically on the subject of the revision of the Ordinal, sometimes under the pseudonym "Philecclesia", proposed a number of different alternative formulas in his various works, and made many other suggestions for alterations in the Ordinal. Some of these were the changes which had already been made in America, but others were his own suggestions. They included the substitution of "presbyter" for "priest" throughout, of "ordain" for "order", and of "a presbyter appointed" for "Archdeacon". The word "infants" was to be omitted from the statement about baptizing in the question put to deacons about their duties, because in Acts 8 there was evidence of the deacon Philip baptizing adults. The collects in the rites for the priesthood and episcopate were to begin "by thy Divine

---

[1] Richard Bingham, *Liturgiae Recusae Exemplar, The Prayer Book as it might be* (1863), pp. 184–201.

[2] Christopher Benson, *Discourse upon the Powers of the Clergy, Prayers for the Dead, and the Lord's Supper, preached at the Temple Church* (1841), pp. 43–56. He quoted the ordination prayer from John Glen King, *The Rites and Ceremonies of the Greek Church in Russia* (1772), p. 287.

Providence", instead of "by thy Holy Spirit", to bring them into line with the collect in the rite for the diaconate. The first question put to deacons would be more appropriate for priests. Deacons ought to receive authority to read not only "the Gospel", but "the Word of God", since they promised to read in Church the Scriptures of the Old and New Testament in their examination. The word "ordained" should be removed from the rite for bishops, and the word "lawful" substituted for the word "episcopal" before "ordination" in the Preface, to restore the situation as it had been before 1662. The rubric referring to deacons and priests being ordained at the same time might be transposed to the end of the Preface. The bidding to prayer in the rite for the episcopate was to include the example of the ordination of Matthias as well as the sending of Paul and Barnabas, and not instead of it as in the American Ordinal.[1]

In 1859 an "Association for Promoting a Revision of the Book of Common Prayer", later called "the Prayer-Book Revision Society", was formed under the leadership of Lord Ebury and other prominent Evangelicals which included among its aims a revision of the imperative formulas at the imposition of hands in the rites for the ordination of priests and bishops. It had on its Council most of the authors quoted above, but contrary to their own proposals it suggested prayer should be substituted and not alternative formulas, although it did not suggest a particular form of prayer. In spite of the efforts of this Society and of individuals, however, the movement to revise the Ordinal was unsuccessful.[2] It attracted the support of only a minority, almost entirely Evangelicals. The majority of Anglicans were indifferent, and the Anglo-Catholic element were obviously opposed to any change which would weaken their position.

The situation in Ireland was slightly different. Here there was the same pressure for reform of the Ordinal and the prime motive was again the exclusion of Anglo-Catholic doctrines, but because of the strongly evangelical character of the Irish Church, the movement made more progress. A "Liturgical Amendment Society" suggested a large

[1] C. H. Davis, *Moderate Revision of the Prayer-Book, on the orthodox principles of its preface, advocated and illustrated in a Conciliatory Spirit, to promote the union of sound Protestant–Catholic Churchmen holding no extreme opinions* (1853), pp. 66–70; *Liturgical Revision illustrated and Vindicated on Orthodox Principles* (1859), pp. 22, 29; and *Hints and Suggestions on a Revision of the Liturgy by Philecclesia* (n.d.), p. 18.

[2] The only change made during this century was not of any liturgical or doctrinal importance. By the Clergy Subscription Act of 1865 the Oath of Supremacy was removed from the services and taken beforehand.

number of minor changes as well as the adoption in the rite for the priesthood of the prayer at the imposition of hands proposed in 1689, with the omission of the clause referring to the remission and retention of sins, and the inclusion of a similar prayer in the rite for the episcopate:

> Pour down, O Father of Lights, the Holy Ghost on this thy servant, for the office and work of a bishop in the United Church of England and Ireland, now committed unto him by the imposition of our hands, and grant him thy grace faithfully to fulfil the same to the edification of the Church of God, and the glory of thy holy name, through Jesus Christ our Lord, to whom, with thee, O Father, and the Holy Ghost be all honour and glory, world without end.[1]

When, however, a committee was appointed to find ways of "checking the spread of novel doctrines and practices opposed to the principles of our Reformed Church", known as "Master Brooke's committee" from the name of its chairman, it reported to the General Synod in 1871 that, because the formula for the priesthood had led to grave error in some and was not ancient, the Church of Ireland would be justified in changing it to

> Almighty God, our Heavenly Father, grant unto thee the gift of the Holy Ghost for the Office and Work of a Priest in the Church of God, now committed unto thee by the Imposition of our hands. And be thou a faithful dispenser of the Word of God, and of His holy Sacraments: In the Name of the Father, and of the Son, and of the Holy Ghost. Amen.

It also proposed that the Gospel John 20.19–23 should be included in the rite for the priesthood, but suggested no change in the rite for the episcopate. Some members of the committee dissented from these proposals.[2] When a committee was appointed by the General Synod to revise the Prayer Book and Ordinal, it adopted the first of these proposals, against considerable opposition, but the second was not mentioned. The prayer was proposed in the committee by Master Brooke and seconded by Charles Parsons Reichel, who had submitted to the committee a paper strongly arguing that the imperative formula had been retained in 1550 through the ignorance of the compilers of the Ordinal that this was not the essential form.[3] When this paper was

---

[1] *Amendments in the Book of Common Prayer prepared by the Committee of the Liturgical Amendment Society (Ireland)* (1861), pp. 19–21. For the 1689 proposal, see above, p. 103.

[2] *Church of Ireland, Report of Master Brooke's Committee for the General Synod, 1871* (Dublin 1871), pp. 32–44.

[3] Charles Parsons Reichel, *Shall we alter the Ordinal? A Paper originally submitted to the Revision Committee of the Church of Ireland* (Dublin 1872).

published, it provoked the reply from Richard Travers Smith which observed the similarity between the Anglican Ordinal and Bucer's rite,[1] and which argued that the Ordinal was a true product of the Reformation, that the imperative formula had not been retained through ignorance, and that there were good reasons for its continued retention. It was also proposed in the committee that the imperative formula should be kept as an alternative, but without success, and an attempt was made to substitute another prayer for the one proposed:

> The Lord Jesus Christ, who, after his resurrection and before he ascended into heaven, did charge his Disciples, saying,—"All power is given unto me in heaven and earth; go ye therefore and make disciples of all nations, baptizing them in the name of the Father and of the Son and of the Holy Ghost; teaching them to observe all things whatsoever I have commanded you; and, lo, I am with you alway even unto the end of the world": and who, in the same days, after he had breathed upon them, did say unto them, "Receive ye the Holy Ghost; whose soever sins ye remit, they are remitted unto them and whose soever sins ye retain, they are retained": who also, after his Ascension, did, on the day of Pentecost, send down from heaven upon them great and mighty gifts of the Holy Ghost: Give thee the Holy Ghost for the office and work of a Priest in the Church of God now committed unto thee by the imposition of our hands, and make thee a faithful Dispenser of the Word of God and of his Holy Sacraments. Amen.

A rubric was to be added which stated that after the first candidate it would suffice to say, "The Lord Jesus Christ give thee the Holy Ghost", etc. This attempt was rejected, as was an attempt by Master Brooke and Reichel to secure a similar change in the formula for the episcopate as they had proposed for the priesthood. Reichel also tried unsuccessfully to have the formula at the giving of the New Testament in the rite for the diaconate altered to:

> Receive this Book of the Gospel; read and study it, and impart it to others; and see that thou follow its holy teachings in thy life and conversation.[2]

When the proposals were put to the General Synod in 1873, however, the change in the formula for the priesthood was rejected, partly because of legal doubts whether those so ordained could be accepted as priests in England, and only a few insignificant changes were approved. Nevertheless, in the revised Prayer Book of the Church of Ireland,

[1] See above, p. 20.
[2] *General Synod of the Church of Ireland, Revision Committee, Report of Progress* (Dublin 1872), pp. 89, 105–10, 174–8.

published in 1878, it was thought advisable to insert a paragraph concerning the Ordinal in the Preface to the book:

No change has been made in the formula of Ordination of Priests, though desired by some; for, upon a full review of our Formularies, we deem it plain and here declare that, save in the matter of Ecclesiastical censures, no power or authority is by them ascribed to the Church or to any of its Ministers, in respect of forgiveness of sins after Baptism, other than that of declaring and pronouncing, on God's part, remission of sins to all that are truly penitent, to the quieting of their conscience, and the removal of all doubt and scruple; nor is it anywhere in our Formularies taught, or implied, that confession to and absolution by a Priest are any conditions of God's pardon; but, on the contrary, it is fully taught that all Christians who sincerely repent, and unfeignedly believe the Gospel, may draw nigh, as worthy communicants, to the Lord's Table without any such confession or absolution; which comfortable doctrine of God's free forgiveness of sins is also more largely set forth in the Homily of Repentance and in that of the Salvation of Mankind.

The Irish proposal for the rite for the priesthood was, however, included in a Bill drawn up in 1880 by the Prayer-Book Revision Society in England and presented to Parliament by Lord Ebury, although without success. The Bill also proposed to replace the formula in the rite for the episcopate with a similar composition.[1]

Before leaving this period, mention must be made of the use made of the Anglican Ordinal by the Wesleyan Methodists. They adopted the imposition of hands at the ordination of ministers in England in 1836 and began to use a rite which included parts of the Anglican rites for the priesthood and episcopate, there being no superintendents in England. The service was conducted by the President of the Conference and began with the singing of a hymn, extemporary prayer, the reading of the names of the candidates, and the reading of a number of prescribed passages of Scripture. The President then read the Exhortation to the candidates and conducted the examination as in the Anglican rite for the priesthood, apart from a few small changes in the latter; the first question was replaced by the first question from the rite for the diaconate and there were two additional questions which concerned the candidates' belief in the doctrine contained in Wesley's Sermons and Notes on the New Testament, and their willingness to

---

[1] *Auricular Confession and Priestly Absolution, Lord Ebury's Prayer-Book Amendment Bill, with letters containing reasons and authorities in support of it* (1880), p. 4.

enforce the discipline of the Conference. After the examination came the bidding to prayer from the rite for the episcopate, followed by the rubric directing a space for silent prayer from the rite for priests. "Come Holy Ghost" was omitted and instead there was the collect from the beginning of the rite for priests, with slight emendations; the phrase, "who by thy Holy Spirit hast appointed divers Orders of Ministers in the Church", was omitted and the office was described as "the office and work of Ministers and Pastors in thy Church". There followed the long prayer from the rite for priests and then the equivalent prayer from the rite for bishops, omitting the section, "who of thine infinite . . . perfect his Church". The imposition of hands was performed by the President and other ministers present with the words:

> Mayest thou receive the Holy Ghost for the office and work of a Christian Minister and Pastor, now committed unto thee by the imposition of our hands. And be thou a faithful dispenser of the Word of God, and of his holy Sacraments; In the Name of the Father, and of the Son and of the Holy Ghost. Amen.

This was followed by the giving of the Bible with both the words used at this ceremony in the rite for priests and the words used at the same ceremony in the rite for bishops, with minor alterations. The service concluded with the final collect from the rite for bishops and a rubric directing that the Lord's Supper should follow.[1] Later in the century this rite was very slightly altered; "Come Holy Ghost" was restored before the collect, and a hymn was included immediately before the imposition of hands. The final rubric also directed that a Charge should be delivered to the candidates by the Ex-President after the Lord's Supper.[2]

It can be seen, therefore, that liturgical factors played virtually no part in the movement to revise the Ordinal in the nineteenth century; the main aim was not to restore the primitive structure of the rites, of which the majority of reformers appear to have been ignorant, but to exclude Anglo-Catholic doctrines and practice from any foundation in the official formularies of the Church of England. Only a few were motivated by a desire for the comprehension of Dissenters. None of the

---

[1] *Order of Administration of the Lord's Supper and Baptism: the forms of Solemnization of Matrimony, and of the Burial of the Dead; together with the Ordination Service: As used by the Wesleyan Methodists* (1848), pp. 93ff.
[2] *The Book of Public Prayers and Services for the use of the people called Methodists* (1883), pp. 269–79.

proposals was really any improvement on the imperative formulas already present. With the exception of Christopher Benson's suggestion, none of them was a true ordination prayer but was simply a benediction or alternative imperative formula. It is therefore perhaps fortunate that the movement was not successful.

# 8. Roman Catholics and the Ordinal, 1662–1896

Attacks on Anglican Orders by Roman Catholics after 1662 followed the same lines as before. The "Nag's Head Fable" and the absence of any record of Barlow's consecration continued to be the main features of the polemic, and the documents from the reign of Queen Mary were cited as evidence that from the first the Roman Church had condemned Anglican Orders. Other reasons for doubting their validity, such as the heretical views of many of the Reformers and the supposed laxity of some Anglicans in the administration of baptism, were also added to the controversy in the course of time. With regard to the Ordinal itself, the attack continued to be centred round the rites for the episcopate and priesthood in the Ordinals of 1550 and 1552; the rite for the diaconate was almost completely ignored, and, although the 1662 revision was cited as evidence that Anglicans had come to realize that their earlier forms were invalid, very few claimed that it was deficient.[1] Unless otherwise stated, therefore, all criticisms and defences described in these next two chapters are of the Ordinal prior to 1662.

Various answers were given by Anglicans to the charge that their forms for the priesthood and episcopate were invalid. Gilbert Burnet believed that it was within the power of the Church to determine and alter the forms, and he cited Pope Innocent IV in support of this. Morin was alone in his opinion that the form for the priesthood in the Roman Pontifical was prayer and the majority thought that it was *Accipe Spiritum Sanctum, quorum peccata*, etc. Although this was only a recent addition to the ordination rites, the Church of England had retained it because it was used by Christ himself, and, "though we do not annul Orders given by any other Form, yet we have all reason to conclude that used by our Saviour to be not only sufficient, but absolutely the best and fittest". The objections that it did not expressly mention the order being conferred or the power to consecrate the

---

[1] See, for example, Thomas Ward, *The Controversy of Ordination truly stated; As far as it concerns the Church of England by Law Established* (1719), pp. 1–14; *An Epistle Apologetical of S. C. To a Person of Honour Touching his Vindication of Dr Stillingfleet* (1674), pp. 92–5. The author was Hugh Paulin de Cressy, an ex-Anglican who had become a Roman Catholic.

Eucharist had no force; the form used by Christ himself must be sufficient, and Morin had shown that neither the ancient Western rites, nor any of the Eastern rites explicitly mentioned the power to consecrate the Eucharist, which in any case was always implicitly included in the conferring of the priesthood. Moreover, the rite as a whole showed clearly which order was meant. The Roman form for the episcopate consisted only of the words, *Accipe Spiritum Sanctum*, and Vazquez had argued that this was sufficient because, although these words did not express the episcopal power, the other circumstances which accompanied them did.[1] Similar arguments were advanced by others.[2] One author, Luke Milbourne, claimed that the Anglican forms were as good as the Eastern forms, which also did not specify the order at the imposition of hands, and that they were an improvement on the Roman rite for the priesthood, where the imposition of hands was in silence and so had no words to determine the order being conferred.[3]

Others took a rather different line and did not accept that the imperative formulas were the essential form. Humphrey Prideaux argued that the formulas did express clearly enough which order was being conferred, but that this did not matter, as they were not essential elements in ordination but only recent additions, as Morin had shown. He believed that nothing was absolutely essential to ordination, but that the Church had followed the Apostolic practice of conferring orders by prayer and the imposition of hands and in the Anglican rites the prayers were the collects.[4] Thomas Brett, the eminent Nonjuror, regarded the essentials of ordination as the imposition of hands by a bishop with a prayer denoting that the bishop was appointing the candidate to a particular office. The prayers in the Anglican rites were the collects. They declared which office was being conferred, and the rest of the rites, including the formulas, also made it sufficiently clear.[5]

---

[1] Burnet, *Vindication of the Ordinations of the Church of England*, pp. 20–42, 62–6.

[2] *A Defence of the Ordinations and Ministry of the Church of England* (1688), pp. 12–19; A. T. Browne, *Concio ad clerum Habita coram Academia Cantabrigiensi Junii 11° Anno 1687. Pro Gradu Baccalaur. in S. Theologia. Ubi Vindicatur Vera et Valida Cleri Anglicani, Ineunte Reformatione, Ordinatio* (1688), pp. 14–24.

[3] Luke Milbourne, *A Legacy to the Church of England, Vindicating her Orders from the Objections of Papists and Dissenters, Fully explaining the Nature of Schism, and cautioning the Laity against the Delusion of Imposters* (1722) I, pp. 314–25.

[4] Prideaux, *Validity of the Orders of the Church of England*, pp. 10, 25–6, 46–52, 68–9.

[5] Thomas Brett, *The Divine Right of Episcopacy, and the Necessity of an Episcopal Commission for Preaching God's Word, and for the valid Ministration of the Christian Sacraments, Proved from the Scriptures, and the Doctrine and Practice of the Primitive Church* (1718), pp. 155–61.

A similar position was adopted by another Nonjuror, Daniel Williams.[1] Some Roman Catholics, however, were prepared to see the Ordinal in a more favourable light. In the negotiations which were carried on between William Wake, the Archbishop of Canterbury, and Dr Louis Dupin, a French Roman Catholic theologian, early in the eighteenth century in the hope of securing a union between the Anglican and Gallican Churches, Dupin was willing to regard Anglican Orders as valid,[2] and in 1723 a detailed defence of the Ordinal and of the English episcopal succession was published by another French theologian, Pierre Francois Le Courayer, who had also been in correspondence with Wake. Citing Morin and others as authorities he claimed that it was the invocation of the Holy Spirit upon the candidates rather than the reciting of any particular prayer which constituted the essential form of ordination, and he contended that the Anglican rites had retained this both in the invocation of the Holy Spirit in the collect[3] and in the formula at the imposition of hands, which he thought could be regarded as an invocation even though it was in the imperative mood. Although these formulas did not explicitly mention the order being conferred, they were sufficiently determined by the preceding prayers, to which they were morally joined as part of the essential forms. The heretical views of the Reformers on the subject of Order were not sufficient to render invalid the rites which they drew up, because firstly not all had heretical views and the error of some could not be imputed to all, and secondly the validity of a rite did not depend upon the views of those who devised it; providing that it retained the essential matter and form, it was sufficient to confer valid orders. He also argued that the omission of any explicit mention of the bestowing of the power to offer sacrifice did not render invalid the rite for the priest-hood, since it was also absent from the ancient rites. Anglicans believed in the Eucharistic Sacrifice in the same sense in which the patristic authors had, and they received the power to offer sacrifice in the general commission given to them to administer the sacraments and perform all the functions of the priesthood.[4]

Le Courayer's work met with strong criticism from other Roman

---

[1] Daniel Williams, *The Succession of Protestant Bishops Asserted; or, the Regularity of the Ordinations of the Church of England Justify'd* (1721), pp. 8–19.

[2] Norman Sykes, *William Wake, Archbishop of Canterbury, 1657–1737* (1957) I, pp. 308–9.

[3] Strictly speaking the collects do not invoke the Holy Spirit; they simply refer to him.

[4] P. F. Le Courayer, *Dissertation sur la Validité des Ordinations des Anglois, et sur la succession des Évêques de l'Église Anglicane* (Brussels 1723) I, pp. 103–140, 179–201, and II, pp. 32–46.

Catholics. Michel Le Quien, a French Dominican, published a reply in which he argued that the primary function of the ministry was to offer the sacrifice instituted by Christ, and to abolish the sacrifice was to abolish the priesthood. The essential form of ordination was a prayer recited at the imposition of hands which must express both the particular order being bestowed and the principal function of the ministry, to offer sacrifice. The Anglicans, having rejected the sacrifice of the Mass, had no intention of continuing the sacrificial ministry of the Catholic Church and so they had removed from their Ordinal all references to the sacrificial functions, thus demonstrating that they lacked the intention of doing what the Church did in ordaining. Their forms were inadequate because the words pronounced at the imposition of hands did not express the order being bestowed, and the preceding collects could not be part of the forms since the form had to accompany the matter. Yet, even if these collects were the forms, they were not adequate as they did not express the principal function of the ministry, the offering of sacrifice, which all the ancient rites did.[1] Another critic, Jean Hardouin, a French Jesuit, also alleged that there was a defect of intention; the Anglican rejection of the Eucharistic Sacrifice and the changes made in the rites of ordination showed that they did not intend to ordain men to the Catholic priesthood. Moreover, he refused to accept Morin's claim, adopted by Le Courayer, that the matter and form of ordination were the imposition of hands and prayer; the consensus of opinion in the Church still thought otherwise; and he even included a lengthy appendix in which he criticized Le Quien for accepting in principle Morin's views.[2] Similar criticisms of Le Courayer's thesis were also voiced by John Constable, an English Jesuit writing under the pseudonym of "Clerophilus Alethes".[3]

The claim that Anglicans did not believe in the Eucharistic Sacrifice and therefore lacked an adequate intention in ordaining appears to have been regarded by Le Courayer as a real weakness in his argument; for he repeatedly pressed Archbishop Wake for more evidence with which to refute the charge, but Wake was not very helpful, evidently regarding this allegation as not very important.[4] In 1726 Le Courayer published a defence of his work against the criticisms which had been

[1] Michel Le Quien, Nullité des Ordinations Anglicanes (Paris 1725) II, pp. 1–156.
[2] Jean Hardouin, La Dissertation du P. Le Courayer, Sur La Succession des évêques Anglois, et sur la validité de leurs ordinations, réfutée (Paris 1725), vol. II.
[3] "Clerophilus Alethes", Remarks upon F. Le Courayer's Book in Defence of the English Ordinations (n.p., n.d.), pp. 248–86.
[4] Sykes, William Wake I, pp. 352–4.

made. He claimed that the forms need only express the principal effect of the sacrament in general terms, no explicit mention of sacrifice being necessary, and he quoted several ancient rites in support of this. Nor was it essential that the form should be pronounced at the imposition of hands; it was only necessary that the two should constitute one moral action. The changes made by the Anglicans in the rites of ordination did not constitute a defect of intention; it was not essential that they should have right beliefs on priesthood and sacrifice, but only that they should still intend to ordain bishops and priests, which they did. Thus, although he devoted considerable space to proving that the Anglicans did believe in the Eucharistic Sacrifice, he claimed that this did not affect the validity of their orders. Finally, the fact that a variety of views was still current about what were the essential matter and form of Order did not invalidate the Ordinal; only prayer and the imposition of hands had been universally practised and so only these could be essential.[1] Both Hardouin and Le Quien wrote further replies to this, and Le Courayer in turn composed yet another answer to these, but none of them made any new points and merely reiterated what they had already written.[2]

So the controversy continued. Periodic attacks by Roman Catholics appeared, alleging defects of matter, form, and intention in the Anglican Ordinal, but few specified the precise nature of these or gave the subject any detailed treatment. On the whole, Anglicans exhibited little interest in the question, and of the few replies which appeared hardly any went beyond the vague assertion that the only essentials of ordination were prayer and the imposition of hands, which the Ordinal contained. None of them faced up to the important questions raised by earlier controversialists: What was the specific content of the form of ordination? What in the Anglican Ordinal corresponded to this? Did form and matter have to be simultaneous or could they be separated? What constituted a valid intention, and whose intention was required? It was not until late in the nineteenth century that there was a revival of interest in the subject among Anglicans. This was brought about mainly by the growth of the Anglo-Catholic movement, the adherents of which attached great importance to their

---

[1] Le Courayer, *Défense de la Dissertation sur la validité des Ordinations des Anglois* (Brussels 1726) II, i, pp. 1–307.

[2] Hardouin, *La défense des Ordinations Anglicanes réfutée* (2 vols., Paris 1727); Le Quien, *La Nullité des Ordinations Anglicanes demontrée de nouveau contre la Défense du R. P. Courayer* (Paris 1730); Le Courayer, *Supplément aux deux Ouvrages fait pour la Défense de la validité des ordinations Anglicanes* (Amsterdam 1732).

claim to possess the same priesthood as the Roman Church, and it led to an intensifying of attacks on Anglican Orders by Roman Catholics who vehemently denied that Anglicans were true priests in the same sense in which they were. On the whole, Anglicans came off worse in the debate because the majority failed to grasp the precise points of the Roman arguments. For example, Frederick George Lee, the Vicar of All Saints, Lambeth, and a leading Anglo-Catholic, simply claimed that the Anglican Ordinal was in substantial harmony with all the ancient rites and failed to state what specific part of the rites was the essential form. In various parts of his book he seemed to incline to different opinions on this, and he may even have regarded the whole rite, rather than a particular part, as the form. On the subject of intention he said that, since the unworthiness of the minister did not hinder the sacrament, erroneous opinions held by any bishop could not invalidate the orders he conferred; by participating in an ordination he signified his intention to do what Christ enjoined, and that was sufficient.[1]

Lee's vagueness with regard to the form was criticized by Wilfrid Raynal, a Roman Catholic Benedictine. He stated that a valid form must express the distinctive character of the order being conferred in one of three ways:

Either I. An allusion to the type, found in the ancient Testament, of the order conferred.

Or II. The mention of some spiritual power which is the distinctive privilege of the order to which the candidate is raised.

Or III. The actual mention made of the office under the name which from earliest times has become attached to it, viz., *Summus Sacerdos* or Bishop, and *Sacerdos secundi ordinis* or Priest.

It must here be noted that the words Bishops and Priests must really and truly bear the meaning attached to them by the Universal Church. A *formal denial* of the distinctive character of these two sacred offices would vitiate the *Intention*, and would render the consecration or ordination null and void.

All Eastern and Western forms fulfilled these requirements, as did the Anglican form for the diaconate. The Anglican forms for the priest-

---

[1] Frederick George Lee, *The Validity of the Holy Orders of the Church of England* (1869). Lee later came to doubt the validity of his orders, was secretly consecrated a bishop by Roman prelates near Venice in 1877, and secretly consecrated and reordained other Anglicans, before becoming a Roman Catholic in 1901; see H. R. T. Brandreth, *Dr Lee of Lambeth* (1951), pp. 118ff.

hood and episcopate, however, which consisted of the formulas at the imposition of hands and of the prayers immediately preceding these, which were morally united with them, made only vague references to the ministry and did not specify the particular orders sufficiently in any of the three ways, and no other prayers in the rites could be regarded as part of the forms.[1]

A rather different objection to the Anglican Ordinal was raised by another Roman Catholic, Canon E. E. Estcourt. He believed that its deficiency lay in its intention rather than in its forms. He came to this conclusion because he was aware, as earlier authors had not been, of an apparent decision of the Sacred Congregation of the Inquisition in 1704, reaffirmed in 1860, which seemed to allow that the words, *Accipe Spiritum Sanctum*, alone could be a valid form for the priesthood. The decree, as Estcourt understood it, declared valid the practice in Abyssinia where the ancient rites had been abandoned and candidates were ordained simply by the imposition of hands with these words. Thus he felt unable to affirm the view that "Receive the Holy Ghost" was an inadequate form for the priesthood. Instead he disputed Le Courayer's definition of the content of the form as an invocation of the Holy Spirit to obtain graces for the candidate to fulfil his ministry worthily. This definition would apply equally to the benediction of an abbot, whereas the ancient rites all treated ordination "as a supernatural gift or grace, and as the communication of a certain spiritual power", and the prayers asked for the bestowal of this gift to empower the candidate to do what he otherwise could not do. The Anglican Ordinal, on the other hand, had been framed with the deliberate intention of excluding the idea that any spiritual power was conferred, especially the power to offer sacrifice; it exhibited a Lutheran concept of ordination and its prayers asked only for sanctifying and co-operating graces and not the grace of Order. Thus there was no intention of doing what the Church did in conferring the sacrament of Order and all Anglicans who used these rites still shared in the defect of intention of its compilers by the very fact of using a rite devised with heretical intention, since the alterations made in 1662 had not remedied the defect. He concluded that *Accipe Spiritum Sanctum* was sufficient in the case of the Abyssinian ordinations because the rites of that Church, even if not used, expressed the doctrine of the Catholic Church concerning Order and the change had not been made with any heretical intention, whereas "Receive the Holy Ghost" was inadequate in the

[1] Wilfrid Raynal, *The Ordinal of King Edward VI* (1871), pp. 39-120, 161-3.

case of Anglican ordinations because the context in which it was used demonstrated an intention contrary to that of the Catholic Church.[1] This gave rise to a correspondence between Estcourt and a certain J. Jones in the magazine, *The Month*, in which Jones challenged Estcourt's interpretation of the decree on Abyssinian ordinations. He claimed that there was no suggestion that the whole rite had not been used; the decree simply ruled that the ordinations were still valid in spite of a deviation from this rite—the reciting of *Accipe Spiritum Sanctum* only and not the whole prayer at the imposition of hands on each candidate—and it did not define those words as the essential form.[2] In order to settle this uncertainty Cardinal Manning, the Archbishop of Westminster, wrote to Rome and received a reply from Cardinal Patrizi, the Vicar-general, upholding Jones' interpretation but adding that the document of 1704 was not in fact an official decree at all.[3] It was over twenty years later before further light was shed on this document and it was revealed that it was simply an opinion given by one of those consulted on the question, an opinion which was rejected.[4]

A later Roman Catholic author, Arthur Hutton, a convert from Anglicanism, although aware of this correspondence in *The Month*, was still prepared to concede that *Accipe Spiritum Sanctum*, regarded as a prayer, might be sufficient as a form if used in a Church with orthodox beliefs. He therefore followed Estcourt's line of argument: the Church of England had heretical beliefs on the Eucharistic Sacrifice and priesthood and so lacked the intention to ordain priests or bishops in the sense in which the Roman Catholic Church did. He also claimed that Anglo-Catholics ought themselves to deny the validity of ordinations in America because the alternative formula used there indicated a lack of belief in the conferring of sacramental grace in ordination.[5]

A variety of answers to these attacks was offered by Anglicans. Arthur Haddan, an ecclesiastical historian, in his book, *Apostolical Succession in the Church of England*, which became a standard work on the subject, said that the essential form of ordination was "any words that sufficed to convey the formal intention of the Church, but not necessarily every where one and the same form of words". He appar-

[1] E. E. Estcourt, *The Question of Anglican Ordinations Discussed*, esp. pp. 171–259.
[2] *The Month* xix (1873), pp. 451–60; xx (1874), pp. 97–101, 229–40, 384–5.
[3] Ibid. xxiv (1875), pp. 495–6.
[4] S. M. Brandi, *Rome et Cantorbéry* (Paris 1898), pp. 114–18.
[5] Arthur Wollaston Hutton, *The Anglican Ministry* (1879), esp. pp. 141–302.

ently did not think it need be a prayer, and he believed that the imperative formulas were sufficient as forms in the Anglical Ordinal, particularly in the context of the whole rite, since the specific order was mentioned in a prayer earlier in the services, and he saw no significant difference between naming an office and then conferring it and naming it in the act of conferring it. The form need not specify any power with respect to the Eucharist; this was not done in the early Church, and it was in any case implied in the general commission to minister the sacraments. He still believed that the Roman form for the episcopate was *Accipe Spiritum Sanctum*, which did not specify the episcopate any more than the Anglican. The intention to be considered was not that of the ministers but the formal intention of the Church, and the intention of the Church of England was clear; she mentioned the office of priesthood by name, and also the functions of absolving, preaching, and dispensing the sacraments. He argued that she had suppressed the explicit mention of the power to offer sacrifice, not because she denied the Eucharistic Sacrifice itself, but because she rejected the doctrine of sacrifice in the sense mentioned in Article 31, and in that sense only.[1]

Others, such as John Wordsworth, Bishop of Salisbury, and Charles Gore, later Bishop of Oxford, thought that the essential form of ordination was prayer for the gift of the Holy Spirit and believed that the imperative formulas in the Anglican rites constituted such a prayer,[2] obviously thinking only of the priesthood and episcopate, since if this principle were applied to the Anglican rite for the diaconate, it would have to be declared invalid. Gore also dealt with the question of intention; the Preface to the Ordinal showed that the Church of England had the general intention of doing what the Church does, which was all that was necessary. It was not essential that she should have a correct understanding of priesthood, although he believed that she did. Even if she had denied completely the Eucharistic Sacrifice, this would have affected her orthodoxy, but not her orders: "the grace of orders depends on the original intention and will of the Holy Ghost, and all that we do is to hand on the gift by a sacramental method. The method is intrusted to us; the gift is given by Him: and our insufficient

---

[1] Arthur W. Haddan, *Apostolical Succession in the Church of England* (1869), pp. 245–77.
[2] John Wordsworth, *A letter on the Succession of Bishops in the Church of England* (1892), p. 10; Charles Gore, *The Ministry of the Christian Church* (1889), p. 187, and *Roman Catholic Claims* (1889), pp. 142–54.

conception of it does in no wise impair its fulness." In his *Roman Catholic Claims*, Gore had quoted Estcourt's passage about the Abyssinian ordinations as evidence that the Ordinal had a valid form, apparently unaware of the dispute over this, and it was not until the sixth edition of this work that he appended a note on it, and commented that the validity of the Anglican form was not at all dependent upon the character of the Abyssinian document. He appeared to have had a change of mind about what constituted the content of a valid form, for he now said that all that was required was "some imperative or precatory formula which implies the intention to ordain to the particular office. This intention is in the Anglican ordinal abundantly clear, and we have both a precatory and an imperative formula both in the ordination of bishops and of priests."[1]

An anonymous article in the *Church Quarterly Review* adopted a different line of defence for the sufficiency of the imperative formulas in the Anglican rites for the priesthood and episcopate. They had not been chosen under the influence of medieval theology but simply because they were scriptural, and they indicated which order was being conferred by a typological reference to the New Testament, just as the ancient rites used a typological reference to the Old Testament; it was commonly believed at the time of the Reformation that priests were the successors of the Apostles, while bishops succeeded to the office held by Timothy and Titus. Thus they demonstrated clearly a true intention of continuing the ministry instituted by Christ.[2] This argument was later taken up by several Anglican authors, including Edward Denny, a leading Anglo-Catholic. He believed that the essential form of ordination was "appropriate prayer, of which the words have never been dogmatically fixed". These formulas were the forms in the Anglican Ordinal and by their typological reference plainly showed which order it was intended to confer, particularly when taken in the context of the rest of the rite and of the statements in the Preface. He also quoted Estcourt's passage about the Abyssinian ordinations to support the sufficiency of these forms; he was aware of the dispute about this, but he thought Estcourt's interpretation was still the correct one. He employed similar arguments to those used by Gore concerning intention: many reputable Roman Catholic theologians admitted that the only intention necessary was that of doing what the true Church did, which was undoubtedly the intention of the Church of England.

[1] Gore, *Roman Catholic Claims* (6th edn, 1897), pp. 214–15.
[2] "The Anglican Form of Ordination", *CQR* v (1878), pp. 261–90.

He also devoted considerable space in an appendix to challenging Estcourt's claim that the Ordinal exhibited a Lutheran concept of ordination.[1]

In 1894 a campaign was launched by a French Roman Catholic priest, Etienne Fernand Portal, and a leading Anglo-Catholic layman, Lord Halifax, to attempt to secure the recognition of Anglican Orders by Pope Leo XIII.[2] Portal opened the campaign by writing, under the pseudonym "F. Dalbus", a work on Anglican Orders which claimed that, if the form for the episcopate could be an imperative, then the Anglican formula seemed sufficient; it was admittedly vague and indeterminate but because of that its meaning depended on the intention of the minister using it, and therefore it was capable of being sufficient when used by a minister having the right intention. If, as many theologians thought, the form had to be a prayer, the Anglican rite for the episcopate included one prior to the imposition of hands which resembled the prayer in the Sarum rite. Thus, it was certain that this rite was adequate. On the question of intention, he concluded that, although Barlow had the general intention to do what the Church did when he consecrated Parker, he might also have had the internal intention not to do so, in view of his known opinions about ordination, and this would have rendered his action null, the conflicting intentions cancelling each other out. Since there could be no certainty what he intended, the validity of all Anglican ordinations was rendered doubtful because of this. Finally, he declared that the Anglican rite for priests was invalid because the traditional *porrectio instrumentorum* had been suppressed; the Church, having been given the power to determine the matter of Order, had declared that this was essential by the decree of Eugenius IV, and so by its suppression in the Church of England, Anglican orders were null.[3]

This pamphlet produced the result which Halifax and Portal had expected and hoped for, a storm of criticism of the arguments about the intention and the necessity of the *porrectio instrumentorum*, not only from Anglicans but also from Roman Catholics. Perhaps the most significant criticism came from Louis Duchesne, the noted French Roman Catholic ecclesiastical historian, in a review of the work. He insisted that the intention of doing what the Church did must be

[1] Edward Denny, *Anglican Orders and Jurisdiction* (1893), pp. 77–109, 195–204.
[2] See H. Hemmer, *Fernand Portal (1855–1926), Apostle of Unity* (1961), pp. 18–78; J. G. Lockhart, *Charles Lindley, Viscount Halifax* (1936) II, pp. 38–91; Hughes, *Absolutely Null and Utterly Void*, pp. 28–242.
[3] "F. Dalbus", *Les Ordinations Anglicanes* (Paris and Lyon 1894), pp. 4–15, 18–37.

presumed except where the contrary could be proved. The beliefs of individual bishops, or of the Church of England itself, made little difference provided that they still intended to make bishops and priests. He also rejected the necessity of the *porrectio instrumentorum*, which had never been declared essential by an official decision of the Church, and he allowed that Anglican ordinations could be considered valid.[1] Such an opinion by such an eminent man could not fail to attract attention.

Other Roman Catholics, however, took a different point of view. Sydney F. Smith, a Jesuit, pointed out that the prayer in the rite for the episcopate, which "Dalbus" had said was derived from the Sarum Pontifical, was not recited with the consecrator's hands outstretched but had been turned into "a mere introductory supplication". This change he regarded as sufficient to make Anglican Orders doubtful. They were rendered certainly invalid by the fact that the formulas pronounced at the imposition of hands in all three rites did not express the specific powers of the orders in the way that the prayers in the Pontificals did, and any attempt to determine their meaning from the context of the rites, from the Prayer Book, or from the beliefs of Cranmer, showed that they were intended "to exclude the sole sense which could make them fit vehicles for valid orders".[2] Another criticism of "Dalbus" came from the leading Roman Catholic canon lawyer, A. Boudinhon. He claimed that individual Churches had no power to change rites and therefore the Anglican rites were invalid because they were not those prescribed by the Church. Moreover, it was impossible to tell if someone intended not to do what the Church did if he used the rites of the Church, but, by choosing to use the Ordinal, he revealed this defect of intention clearly.[3]

In 1895 Edward Denny published a further defence of Anglican Orders, this time with the help of T. A. Lacey, another prominent Anglo-Catholic. The book was in Latin to make it easy for continental scholars to follow the arguments. It expanded Denny's earlier arguments, and it insisted, against Boudinhon, that bishops had always drawn up their own rites, and so the Church of England had the right to devise its own Ordinal. It claimed that the rite for the episcopate

[1] *Bulletin Critique* v (1894), p. 262; reproduced in A. C. Headlam, *The Doctrine of the Church and Christian Reunion* (1920), pp. 283–4.
[2] Sydney F. Smith, "M. Dalbus on Anglican Orders", *The Month* LXXXII (1894), pp. 184–204, 380–401.
[3] A. Boudinhon, *Étude Théologique sur les Ordinations Anglicanes* (Paris 1895).

expressed the order being conferred in three ways: it used in its form the words, *Accipe Spiritum Sanctum*, which through previous usage in the Church indicated this order and were commonly held to be the form in the Pontificals; the compilers of the Ordinal had added the words addressed to Timothy to indicate the particular order more clearly, and the rest of the rite also expressed it. Some scholars believed that the form must be a prayer, but this had been so only in the ancient rites; later the imposition of hands had been separated from the prayer and joined to an imperative formula, which then became the form. Nevertheless, the Anglican rite for the episcopate had retained just such a prayer, based on the one in the Pontifical. On the question of intention, the Preface to the Ordinal demonstrated that the Church of England had the general intention of conferring the same orders which had always existed in the Church. Similarly, Barlow and all other ministers had the general intention of doing what the Church did, which was all that was necessary. The rite for the priesthood was also sufficient. It retained the imposition of hands, the only essential matter; it was not necessary to mention the offering of sacrifice in the form, and the Church of England had never formally denied the doctrine of the Real Presence or of the Eucharistic Sacrifice, properly understood; there could be no doubt what order it was intended to confer, as the rite as a whole clearly indicated it, and the form used the words employed by Christ when he gave the sacerdotal power to the Apostles. In an appendix on the Abyssinian ordinations, it was accepted that the decree had not meant to say that *Accipe Spiritum Sanctum* alone was a sufficient form, but it was argued that it upheld two claims made by Anglicans, that a rite altered by the authority of some bishops could still be valid and that a form determined by the general intention of the rite could be adequate.[1]

This work impressed several continental Roman Catholic theologians. Duchesne believed the position which it defended was indisputable and Pietro Gasparri, who was later to be a member of the papal commission to investigate Anglican Orders, abandoned his unfavourable view of the question after reading the book.[2] Gasparri now believed that Anglican Orders were only doubtful on the question of intention because it was impossible to prove conclusively that some bishops had withheld their intention to confer the power to offer

---

[1] Edward Denny and T. A. Lacey, *De Hierarchia Anglicana Dissertatio Apologetica* (1895), pp. 58–141, 245–9.

[2] Viscount Halifax, *Leo XIII and Anglican Orders* (1912), pp. 195–6.

sacrifice. The essential matter of ordination was imposition of hands and the form was a prayer which invoked on the ordinand the graces necessary for his new state and which named in one way or another the particular order. The matter and form need not be simultaneous but there must be a moral union between the two. Most theologians interpreted this to mean that the two must be very close together, but Gasparri thought that it was probably sufficient that they were part of the same liturgical action, and cited as his authority for this the seventeenth-century Spanish theologian John De Lugo; nor did it matter whether the form preceded or followed the matter. Applying these principles to the Anglican Ordinal, he thought that the rite for the diaconate was probably valid. Either the collect near the beginning or the one near the end could be the form; the rite for the priesthood was also probably valid as the collect near the beginning would suffice for the form; the rite for the episcopate contained a prayer immediately before the imposition of hands which resembled part of the rite in the Roman Pontifical, but it did not name the order; it might be argued that the order was sufficiently determined by the intention of the minister and by the rest of the rite, but, on the other hand, the collect after the litany did mention the office, and this rendered the rite probably valid. He therefore believed that the practice of the Roman Church could well be modified so that Anglican ministers who were received into the Church need only be reordained conditionally.[1]

Boudinhon also modified his views. He disagreed with Denny and Lacey that the case of the Abyssinian ordinations affected the question of Anglican Orders; it was completely irrelevant to it because, although probably only *Accipe Spiritum Sanctum* and the imposition of hands were practised in the ordinations, the Sacred Congregation thought that the whole rite was still used and based its decision upon this false assumption.[2] On the other hand, he was now prepared to admit that forms other than those prescribed by the Church could be valid, provided that they were equivalent to those of the Church. From a study of the different rites approved by the Church he concluded that the probable minimum of a form was something like:

> Deus qui . . ., respice propitius super hunc famulum tuum, quem ad diaconatum (*respective*: presbyteratum *vel* episcopatum *seu* summum sacer-

---

[1] Pietro Gasparri, *De la Valeur des Ordinations Anglicanes* (Paris 1895), pp. 23–52, reprinted in *RAR* I, pp. 529–57.

[2] A. Boudinhon, "Ordinations Schismatiques Coptes et Ordinations Anglicanes", *Canoniste Contemporain* XVIII (1895), pp. 213–25, 263–81.

dotium) vocare dignatus es; da ei gratiam tuam, ut munera huius ordinis digne et utiliter adimplere valeat.

This minimal prayer existed in the Anglical Ordinal in the collects in all three rites, but they were too far from the imposition of hands to be valid forms. The prayer before the imposition of hands in the rite for the priesthood was in the right position but did not seem to have the necessary content, which made the rite doubtful, if not invalid, but the corresponding prayer in the rite for the episcopate did seem to contain the necessary minimum, and therefore this rite was valid. He did not think that the heresies of Barlow and of other Anglican ministers were sufficient to destroy the intention to do what the Church did, nor did he think that the omission of any reference to sacrifice by the compilers was enough to create a defect of intention in the rite itself.[1] Similar views on Barlow's intention were also expressed by an Irish Roman Catholic, Jeremiah Crowe.[2]

Other Roman Catholics, however, held different views. An anonymous article, later acknowledged to be written by Cardinal Segna, disagreed with Gasparri that the collects could be the forms in the Anglican rites; for a moral unity to exist matter and form, if not simultaneous, must follow one another successively, and the argument advanced by Denny and Lacey, that the rite as a whole determined the meaning of the form, was not acceptable; it was not the rite which determined the meaning of the form but the form which should determine the meaning of the rite. Nor did the scriptural quotation following the words, "Take the Holy Ghost", in the rite for the episcopate signify the order, as Denny and Lacey had also claimed; that quotation did not by itself signify the episcopal order but only through a particular interpretation of the passage of Scripture, which there was no proof that the compilers of the Ordinal shared exactly. However, the formula as amended in 1662 would probably have been sufficient if the succession had not been broken by the earlier rite.[3] Another Roman Catholic, S. Harent, added the criticism that the prayer before the imposition of hands in the rite for the priesthood did not contain, even implicitly, mention of the powers of a priest, in contrast to all other valid rites. Perhaps it could be determined by the rest of the

[1] A. Boudinhon, "De la Validité des Ordinations Anglicanes", ibid. XVIII, pp. 423–34, 531–70, 642–66.

[2] Jeremiah Crowe, "Anglican Orders and the Doctrine of Intention," *Irish Ecclesiastical Record* XVI (1895), pp. 7–17, reprinted in French in *RAR* I, pp. 783–91.

[3] "Les Ordinations Anglicanes à propos d'une brochure", *RAR* I, pp. 577–92.

rite where the word "priest" appeared, but in the Anglican Ordinal the meaning of this word was ambiguous because Cranmer had heretical beliefs about the priesthood and had eliminated all sacrificial references from the Ordinal. Its sense therefore had to be determined by the intention of the minister using the rite. There were two types of intention, the intention of doing what the Church did and the *intentio circa significationem*—the intention that the rite should have a particular meaning. The latter was applicable only in cases of ambiguity and where it was defective, as it was here, it constituted a defect of form and not of intention. The same was also true of the Anglican rite for the episcopate.[1] Another Roman Catholic, F. Tournebize, also argued that the Anglican rites did not mean to ordain true priests and bishops and so were insufficient to do so; this was revealed by the deliberate exclusion of all reference to sacrifice and the sacrificial priesthood, which were mentioned or implied in all ancient rites.[2]

A number of significant points were made by Anglicans in defence of the Ordinal. Lacey wrote an important study of primitive rites for the ordination of bishops in which he also said that many theologians believed that *Accipe Spiritum Sanctum* had replaced prayer as the form in the later rites, and this was probably the view of the compilers of the Ordinal, but he himself believed that the form was still prayer; its separation from the imposition of hands did not matter as the whole rite formed a moral unity.[3] Father F. W. Puller, a member of the Society of St John the Evangelist, who accompanied Lacey to Rome so that they might be available to supply information, if required, during the sitting of the papal commission in 1896, argued that there was no evidence either from the writings of individuals or from the official liturgies and pronouncements of the Church of England to suggest that it had ever denied the Eucharistic Sacrifice, and hence it was impossible to prove the allegation often made that Anglican bishops had the intention to exclude a necessary effect of ordination, the power to offer sacrifice, and that this cancelled out their general intention to confer the sacrament of Order.[4] F. E. Brightman, the noted liturgical

---

[1] S. Harent, "La forme sacramentelle dans les ordinations Anglicanes", *Études Religieuses, Philosophiques, Historiques et Litteraires* LXVIII (1896), pp. 177–204.

[2] F. Tournebize, "L'église Anglicane a-t-elle réellement le sacerdoce?", ibid. LXIV (1895), pp. 400–23, 574–605.

[3] T. A. Lacey, "L'Imposition des Mains dans la Consecration des Évêques", *RAR* I, pp. 193–210.

[4] F. W. Puller, "Les Ordinations Anglicanes et le Sacrifice de la Messe", *RAR* I, pp. 395–414, 433–51, 494–507.

scholar, opposed the claim made by Sydney Smith that the prayer in the consecration of a bishop ought to be morally united with the imposition of hands by the consecrator continuing to hold his hands outstretched during it. To him the Anglican order, with prayer preceding imposition of hands, seemed more logical, it was the order mentioned in the New Testament, and Smith's theory of moral continuation would not apply to a rite like that in the Exeter Pontifical where *Veni Creator* was sung after the imposition of hands and then the consecrator said the prayer with joined hands. On the question of intention Brightman adopted the popular Anglican view that the private opinions of ministers were irrelevant and that it was the official intention of the Church which mattered. The Preface to the Ordinal showed the orthodox intention of the Church of England. Yet even if her doctrine on Order or on the Eucharistic Sacrifice had been defective, it would have made no difference; she would still have conferred the full powers of the order in her general commission and not simply the limited powers she intended to confer.[1]

In March 1896 the members of a papal commission to investigate Anglican Orders were named, although the Pope himself apparently already believed that the orders were invalid because the English Reformers had not believed in the *sacerdotium* or in sacrifice.[2] There were three English members, Francis Aidan Gasquet, the Benedictine historian, Canon James Moyes, and David Fleming, a Franciscan, and three continental members, Duchesne, Gasparri, and A. M. de Augustinis, a Jesuit professor of dogmatic theology. Later two others were added, T. B. Scannell and Calasanzio de Llaveneras. The president was the Jesuit Cardinal Mazzella and he was assisted by Monsignor Raphael Merry del Val as secretary.[3] The three English members believed that a valid form must have three features, clear and explicit mention of the order conferred, prayer for grace suitable to the order, and simultaneity between the form and the imposition of hands. The imperative formulas in the Anglican rites for the priesthood and episcopate failed to meet these requirements. Moreover, the Anglican rites were not only "materially" inadequate, they were also "formally" insufficient; the meaning of the words, as could be seen from the beliefs of Cranmer and the other compilers, was not the Catholic meaning. To these defects was added the defect of intention on the part of

---

[1] F. E. Brightman, *What Objections have been made to English Orders?*, CHS VI (1896), pp. 153–8, 175–95.
[2] Hughes, *Absolutely Null and Utterly Void*, pp. 84–5.   [3] Ibid., pp. 106–16.

Parker's consecrators; they had heretical views on ordination and so did not intend to do what the Church did.[1] De Llaveneras agreed with their conclusions.[2] The views of Duchesne and Gasparri have already been given. De Augustinis believed that the form of Order was prayer and that the imperative formulas in the Anglican rites were not the whole form but were joined with the preceding prayer of which they were in a sense the conclusion. Together with the general sense of the rite this sufficiently determined the order. The only intention required was "to constitute ecclesiastical ministers by a sacred rite, and to do what has been done from the beginning of the Christian Society". This was found in the Ordinal, and the intentions of individual ministers were irrelevant. Anglican Orders were therefore valid.[3] Scannell apparently did not believe in the validity of Anglican Orders but was working for no decision at all on them.[4]

Discussion of the actual forms began at the meeting of the commission on 25 April. Duchesne said to Lacey prior to this meeting that it would be impossible to argue that the imperative formulas were valid forms and only the preceding prayers in the rites for the priesthood and episcopate could be treated as such. He himself was convinced that the prayer in the rite for the priesthood contained a petition for the ordinands, but it was slight and obscure, whereas that in the rite for the episcopate was beyond challenge.[5] Gasparri opened the debate by arguing that the collects were the forms and were morally united to the matter.[6] Little more can be gleaned about the discussion. It would appear that both Duchesne and de Augustinis accepted the words, "as well by these thy ministers", as a petition for the ordinands in the prayer in the rite for the priesthood, but the others were not convinced, and that the English members attacked the idea of the

---

[1] J. Moyes, F. A. Gasquet and D. Fleming, *Brevis Conspectus Ritualium Ordinationum in Oriente et Occidente adhibitarum quoad Formam consecratoriam cum manuum impositione conjunctam* (Rome 1896), and *Ordines Anglicani: Expositio Historica et Theologica, Cura et Studio Commissionis ab Em. o et Rev. o D. D. Herberto Cardinali Vaughan ad hoc institutae* (1896), pp. 44–55. Both these were privately printed.

[2] Hughes, p. 114.

[3] T. A. Lacey, *A Roman Diary and other documents relating to the papal inquiry into English Ordinations MDCCCXCVI* (1910), pp. 42–6.

[4] Ibid., p. 38.

[5] Ibid., p. 48. After the papal condemnation of Anglican Orders appeared, Duchesne said, "I would never have admitted the sufficiency of the rite for the diaconate; for the priesthood the more I studied the formula the less confidence I felt. As for the episcopate, I hoped that a doubt might be allowed, although there too there was a grave objection" (Lockhart, *Halifax* II, p. 83).

[6] Hughes, pp. 156–7.

moral unity of the whole rite.[1] It would also appear that the question
of who said the collect in the rite for the episcopate was also raised. The
claim had been made in a letter to the Roman Catholic newspaper, *The
Tablet*, that it was sometimes said by someone other than the consecrator and Gasparri asked Lacey if it was true. Lacey replied that he
believed that the special suffrage and collect were always said by the
consecrator, although in practice the rest of the litany was commonly
said by a priest, but he would write to the Archbishop of York for
information on the question. The Archbishop replied that it was, by
the unvarying use of both provinces, said by the Archbishop himself.[2]
At the meeting on 2 May it would appear that Duchesne, Gasparri, de
Augustinis, and Scannell all spoke in favour of the Ordinal, de Augustinis saying he "would be glad to see it used as Pontifical". At the end
of the meeting the president dictated seven questions about the form
to be answered in writing. After the replies had been read at the next
meeting on 5 May, Cardinal Mazzella abruptly terminated the work
of the commission by announcing that there would be only one more
meeting and that would be held simply to pass the *acta*. It would
appear, therefore, that the question of intention was hardly touched on
in the discussions. The final votes of the commission were apparently
Gasquet, Moyes, Fleming, and de Llaveneras for invalidity, Duchesne and
de Augustinis for validity, and Gasparri and Scannell for a doubtful
validity and hence for a conditional reordination of converts.[3]

The question was now to be submitted to a commission of cardinals.
Lacey immediately started work on a supplement to *De Hierarchia
Anglicana*, which he completed in less than a week. In this he reaffirmed
the opinion that the imperative formulas in the Ordinal were sufficient
as forms, but because it was commonly claimed that the form must be a
prayer he proceeded to expand his view that the Ordinal contained
prayers which were sufficient as forms. There were, he said, three
possible theories. The first was that the form in the rites for the priesthood and episcopate was the prayer immediately before the imposition
of hands. He cited Boudinhon to justify his claim that there need be no

[1] Lacey, *Roman Diary*, p. 100.
[2] Ibid., pp. 51–2, 63. The letter, by a certain A. G. Clarke, appeared in *The Tablet*
on 4 April 1896, not 15 February, as stated by Lacey. Clarke repeated his claim in another
letter to *The Tablet* on 30 January 1897. Lacey replied to this in a letter in *The Tablet* on
13 February 1897, in which he repeated the statement made by the Archbishop of York,
and Clarke replied with yet another letter on 20 February 1897, in which he insisted that
the Archbishop was mistaken.
[3] Hughes, pp. 158–62.

mention of the power to sacrifice, and he argued that there need not
even be mention of the order being conferred, because the rite for the
diaconate in the *Canons of Hippolytus*[1] did not name the order in its
prayer. It was sufficient that the rite as a whole made it clear what order
was intended. In the prayer in the rite for the priesthood the petition
was "by these thy ministers". If a prayer was required in the rite for the
diaconate also, it was to be sought elsewhere in the rite. The second
theory was that the form in all three rites was the collect. He referred to
Gasparri in support of the idea of a moral union between this and the
imposition of hands, and he mentioned the separation of matter and
form which existed in the Exeter Pontifical. The fact that the collect
came before the candidates had been examined and found suitable was
no proof that it could not be the form, and it was always said by the
ordaining bishop. The third theory, which he believed was new, was
that the form was not to be found in any particular prayer but in the
rite as a whole. The question of intention he divided into two: the
intention of the rite itself and the intention of those who had imposed
its use. The omission of all language about sacrifice and of the *porrectio
instrumentorum* did not mean that the Ordinal intended to institute
a ministry other than the catholic one; it merely rejected the distorted
medieval doctrine of sacrifice and omitted the *porrectio instrumentorum*
as an inessential ceremony. As for those who imposed its use, the
authors of the rite were unknown, many bishops of the time were
reconciled under Cardinal Pole without any suspicion of heresy, and
Elizabeth and those under her certainly did not intend to institute a new
and different ministry. Thus there was no proof of heretical intention.[2]

Boudinhon replied to this, reaffirming his view that the essentials
of ordination were imposition of hands and a prayer for the ordinand;
the prayer need not mention the powers being conferred, nor even
explicitly mention the order, but it must indicate this in some way, as
the rite for the diaconate in the *Canons of Hippolytus* did by reference to
Stephen. He refused to accept the claims of Gasparri and Lacey that
there was a moral union between the collects and the imposition of
hands, and he also rejected Lacey's argument that the prayer before the
imposition of hands in the rite for the priesthood contained a petition
for the ordinands. Lacey's third hypothesis, that the whole rite was the

[1] This document, first published in 1870, was then regarded as prior to the *Apostolic Tradition* and so received more attention than it really warranted. It is now agreed to be derived from the *Apostolic Tradition* and to date from about A.D. 500.

[2] T. A. Lacey, *Dissertationis Apologeticae De Hierarchia Anglicana Supplementum* (Rome 1896), pp. 19–35.

form, was also unacceptable; if not one of the prayers fulfilled the conditions for a valid form, the multiplication of accompanying ceremonies would not ensure the efficacy of the whole.[1]

Lacey's efforts did not, however, affect the decision of the cardinals. After studying the findings of the commission, they reached their verdict at a meeting under the presidency of the Pope on 16 July 1896, and the Bull *Apostolicae Curae* embodying their decision was issued in Latin and English on 18 September.[2] It declared that there were defects of both form and intention in the Anglican Ordinal. Passing over the rite for the diaconate in silence, it stated that the imperative formula at the imposition of hands in the rite for the priesthood was not sufficient as the form because it did not definitely express the order of priesthood or its grace and power. Other prayers in the rite could not provide a valid form because they were insufficient for a number of reasons, which were not stated, and particularly because "from them has been deliberately removed whatever sets forth the dignity and office of the priesthood in the Catholic rite. That form consequently cannot be considered apt or sufficient for the Sacrament which omits what it ought essentially to signify." The same was true of the formula and prayers in the rite for the episcopate. Furthermore, when the Ordinal was considered in the circumstances in which it was composed and authorized, it was clear that all reference to sacrifice and the *sacerdotium* had been deliberately struck out because of the errors of the Reformers. Any words in the Ordinal, therefore, which lent themselves to ambiguity could not possibly be understood in a Catholic sense. Nor could their meaning change in the course of time but they remained for ever "as words without the reality which Christ instituted". Thus the additions made in 1662 were in vain, and the collects, which might possibly suffice as forms in a Catholic rite, could not do so in these rites. Finally, the substitution of a new rite for that approved by the Church with the manifest intention of rejecting what the Church did and what by the institution of Christ belonged to the nature of the sacrament clearly demonstrated that "not only is the necessary intention wanting to the Sacrament, but that the intention is adverse to and destructive of the Sacrament". The Bull concluded, therefore, that "Ordinations carried out according to the Anglican rite have been and are absolutely null and utterly void".

[1] A. Boudinhon, "Nouvelles Observations sur la Question des Ordres Anglicans", *RAR* II, pp. 673–82.
[2] English text reprinted in *Anglican Orders (English)* (CHS, 1932), pp. 1–16. See also Hughes, pp. 185–98.

# 9. Roman Catholics and the Ordinal since 1896

The publication of the Papal Bull produced, as would be expected, a storm of criticism from Anglicans, much of it objecting that the examination of the Ordinal had been prejudiced from the start. Many of the Anglican critics clearly showed that they did not understand the technical requirements of the form to which the Bull referred. Thus the Bishop of Stepney, G. F. Browne, claimed that the only requirements for a valid ordination were prayer and the imposition of hands, and as the various prayers in the Ordinal said as much as the early rites of ordination he could see no reason why they should not be considered valid.[1] Many Anglicans also misunderstood what the Bull had said was necessary for a valid form. They read it as if it said that the form must "express the Sacred Order of Priesthood, *and* its grace and power, which is chiefly the power of consecrating and of offering the true body and blood of the Lord", whereas the Bull had actually said that one *or* the other was necessary. They believed, therefore, that they had shown that the Bull was wrong when they had shown that there were ancient forms which did not mention the sacrificial functions of the priesthood. This error was first made in a leader in the *Church Times* of 2 October 1896, and was repeated by very many subsequent writers, including Charles Gore in a chapter on the Bull added to the sixth edition of his *Roman Catholic Claims*.[2] It was not until a Roman Catholic Benedictine, John Chapman, pointed out this mistake in a reply to Gore's book[3] that Gore corrected it; an *erratum* slip was inserted in the eleventh edition of 1920 to amend "and" to "or", but no change was made in his subsequent argument from the ancient rites, the force of which was destroyed by this correction.

Most Anglicans accepted without question the Pope's claim that the imperative formulas were meant as the forms in the Ordinal, and many still believed that the form in the Roman Catholic rite for the

---

[1] G. F. Browne, *Anglican Orders: A Speech delivered in the large Hall of the Church House on Thursday, October 15, 1896*, CHS XVII (1896).

[2] P. 200.

[3] John Chapman, *Bishop Gore and the Catholic Claims* (1905), p. 102.

episcopate was also the words *Accipe Spiritum Sanctum*. Thus, Professor H. B. Swete, the biblical and patristic scholar, claimed that the Anglican forms were more definite than the Roman forms, since they were not simply "Receive the Holy Ghost" but had other words added to define which order was being conferred, although it was sufficient that the office was named in the rest of the rite. He defended the right of the Reformers to remove from the rites all explicit reference to sacrifice and the *sacerdotium*, since these were later additions to the ancient rites. By so doing they were not lapsing into heresy but returning to the primitive conception of the priesthood.[1] Another Anglican, F. N. Oxenham, defended the imperative formula for priests on the grounds that it was used by Christ without his mentioning any special priestly function and that the form in the *Canons of Hippolytus* did not mention any priestly powers.[2] The majority of Anglicans also presumed that the defect of intention referred to by the Bull was a defect in the official intention of the Church of England and they cited the Preface to the Ordinal as evidence that the Church of England intended to continue the orders instituted by the Apostles, which was the intention of the Catholic Church throughout history.

A few Anglicans, however, regarded prayer rather than the imperative formulas as the form. One author, H. E. Hall, said that the essentials of ordination were:

a. imposition of hands,
b. a prayer for grace to enable the ordinand to fulfil the ministry which is being imparted to him,
c. a clear understanding in the order (not necessarily explicit in the formula, but in the service) of what is being done.

These, he contended, were present in the Ordinal. He believed that the allegation of a defect of intention was based on the fact that the Ordinal omitted all reference to sacrifice, but this had only been done to correct misconceptions about sacrifice and priesthood, and the retention of the word "priest" showed that it was intended to retain the true priesthood. Yet even if the Church of England had erroneous ideas about what Christ instituted, this would not invalidate her orders,

---

[1] H. B. Swete, *On the Bull Apostolicae Curae. A Lecture delivered at the Divinity School, Cambridge on Friday, November 6, 1896* (1896), pp. 13–24. See also Vernon Staley, *Are our Clergy rightly Ordained?* (1897), pp. 13–17.

[2] F. N. Oxenham, *Some Considerations suggested by the Letter of Leo XIII on Anglican Orders* (1896), pp. 19–21.

for she still intended to perpetuate the Apostolic ministry and to celebrate the Eucharist.[1]

A more informed and detailed defence of the Ordinal was produced by F. W. Puller. He pointed out that there was no single fixed form, that it was accepted that heretical and schismatic Churches could have valid forms, and that many theologians believed that local Churches had the power to make the form imperative instead of precatory. He claimed that matter and form need only occur within the same service and did not have to be simultaneous, and that the form need not mention the powers of priesthood, nor even the order conferred, because none of the ancient rites did the former and the form for the diaconate in the *Canons of Hippolytus* did not do the latter. If the imperative formulas were regarded as the forms in the Edwardine Ordinal, they were certainly more determinate than the formulas in the Roman Pontifical, but neither were really ambiguous; in both cases the rest of the rite made it clear which order was being conferred. The Ordinal was also valid if the theory that the form must be prayer was adopted. The collects were sufficient as forms, as were also the prayers before the imposition of hands, taken in conjunction with those parts of the service which determined the purpose and object of the rite. As for intention, a defect of intention in individual bishops could not invalidate orders, for they still intended to do what the Church of England did, and she intended to continue the medieval priesthood; the striking out of sacrificial language did not mean that she repudiated the true doctrine of the Eucharistic Sacrifice.[2]

*A Treatise on the Bull Apostolicae Curae* by the committee of the Church Historical Society said that the form could determine the matter in different ways. It could mention the order by name, it could indicate it indirectly, as the form for the diaconate in the *Canons of Hippolytus* did by reference to Stephen, or it could enumerate its functions and powers. This could be done in a single prayer accompanying the imposition of hands, or in a number of prayers and blessings distributed throughout the service, the latter being the case

[1] H. E. Hall, *Anglican Orders and the Papal Bull* (1896). A similar defence of the intention was made by H. E. Jeaffreson, *A Letter on the Papal Bull Apostolicae curae* (1897), pp. 10-11, 17-22. When Hall later became a Roman Catholic he claimed that the Ordinal was invalid because the form ought to contain a clear and explicit mention of the order and be simultaneous, or in close moral connection, with the imposition of hands, and he believed that the exclusion of all reference to sacrifice indicated a defect of intention: the names "priest" and "bishop" had been retained but their meaning changed (H. E. Hall, *The Shadow of Peter* (1914), pp. 50-73).

[2] F. W. Puller, *The Bull Apostolicae Curae and the Edwardine Ordinal*, CHS XVI (1896).

in the Anglican Ordinal. It interpreted the defect of intention mentioned by the Bull as meaning a defect of intention in those who drew up the rites, and claimed that the Preface was evidence of their orthodox intention. They did not omit the *sacerdotium*, as the Bull claimed, for they had retained the name "priest" which meant just that, nor did they omit the power of consecrating and offering sacrifice, for that was included in the expressions about "ministering" and "dispensing" the sacraments. The reason that they struck out phrases which gave special prominence to sacrifice was to counter the erroneous beliefs which were current on that subject.[1]

Roman Catholics, however, were equally divided over what the Bull meant. One, A. S. Barnes, said that the form could signify the grace which it effected in only three ways: it could name the order directly, it could mention the grace and powers belonging exclusively to that order, or it could name the order indirectly. None of these was done in the Edwardine Ordinal. The rest of the rite could not be used to determine the order, since it was the function of the form to determine the meaning of the rest of the rite, nor could the collects be the form as they were too far from the imposition of hands. He believed that the defect of intention was a defect in the rite itself, not in any person or group of persons, and was shown by the removal of things, whether essential or not, which would not have been removed by any who were sound in the doctrine of Order.[2] Sydney Smith, the Jesuit, on the other hand, thought that the defect of intention referred to was in the ministers of the sacrament, who by using the Anglican rites could not possibly intend to do what the Catholic Church did. He believed that the Bull had dealt with the defect of intention on the part of the compilers of the Ordinal in the reference to the circumstances in which it was composed; the compilers had used such words as "bishop" and "priest" and had spoken in the Preface of a triple hierarchy, but their known opinions and the omission of all sacrificial language showed that none of this was meant in an orthodox sense.[3] Another Roman Catholic author, Jeremiah Crowe, thought that the Bull had declared the form invalid because of the omission of any reference to sacrifice. He also believed that the Bull meant that the

---

[1] *A Treatise on the Bull Apostolicae Curae*, CHS XIX (1896), pp. 20–42.
[2] A. S. Barnes, *The Popes and the Ordinal* (1896), pp. 29ff.
[3] Sydney F. Smith, "The Papal Bull", *Contemporary Review* LXXI (1897), pp. 37–9; see also his article, "The Condemnation of Anglican Orders", *The Month* LXXXVIII (1896), pp. 324–7.

defect of intention was a consequence of the defect of form, and would not have existed without it.[1]

Perhaps the most accurate interpretation of the Bull came in a series of nineteen articles in *The Tablet* during the first half of 1897 entitled "The Bull *Apostolicae Curae*". These are interesting not only because they were the most thorough study of the subject written at the time but also because they were written by Canon Moyes and therefore probably reflect both the views he expressed on the commission and also the reasoning underlying the condemnation. Moyes claimed that the essentials of any ordination rite were imposition of hands, prayer accompanying or closely connected with this, mention or determination of the order conferred, and petition for grace that the ordinand might worthily fulfil the functions of his order. The Anglican rites were defective because there was nothing to express or determine the order in the prayers or words which accompanied, closely preceded, or followed the imposition of hands. They differed in this way from every other ordination rite of the Church, all of which mentioned the order by name, except for the rite for the diaconate in the *Canons of Hippolytus* which determined it by reference to Stephen. The claim that the order was mentioned elsewhere in the rites did not overcome this deficiency because the purpose of the form was to determine the matter, the collects were too far from the matter to be the form, and the scriptural allusions in the formulas accompanying the imposition of hands were not sufficiently definite to refer exclusively to a particular order. He then went on to consider the meaning given to the rites by the circumstances of their origin. From the opinions of the Reformers and the changes they made in the Mass, he concluded that they did not believe in the *sacerdotium*, and, since all the parts of the Pontifical omitted from the Ordinal referred to the sacrificial character of the priesthood, it was clear that the omissions had been made so that the Catholic *sacerdotium* should no longer be signified. This substantially altered the sense and signification of the sacrament and rendered the form invalid. Thus, even if the Anglican forms had mentioned the orders by name, they would not have sufficed, for they would not have been meant in their true sense. Finally, Moyes said that the defect of intention mentioned in the Bull meant that the compilers and users of the Ordinal did not intend to use the matter and form of the Church, but

[1] Jeremiah Crowe, "The Papal Bull on Anglican Orders", *Irish Ecclesiastical Record* XVII (1896), pp. 966–71.

other matter and form in which the signification was substantially altered.

Early in 1897 the Archbishops of Canterbury and York published a reply to *Apostolicae Curae*, composed by a committee consisting of Mandell Creighton, Bishop of Peterborough, William Stubbs, Bishop of Oxford, and John Wordsworth, Bishop of Salisbury.[1] It was hailed by many Anglicans as a powerful refutation of the Bull, although it made the same error as so many others in seeming to understand the Bull to mean that the form must express both the name of the order and the power of offering sacrifice, and labouring to show that there were forms which did not do this. It also regarded the form for the episcopate in the Roman Pontifical as *Accipe Spiritum Sanctum*, although recognizing that it had been a prayer in the earlier rites, and it argued that these words were also sufficient in the Anglican Ordinal since the particular order was expressed in the scriptural phrases added to them and in the rest of the rites. Moreover, in the 1550 Ordinal the collects were part of the form and it was only when the additional phrases indicating explicitly the order being conferred were included in the imperative formulas in 1662 that they were moved to become the collects of the Communion service. Thus the forms had always been more than sufficient. All that was required for a valid form was "prayer or benediction appropriate to the ministry to be conferred". Presumably, therefore, the reply regarded the imperative formulas as a benediction. Turning to the Pope's claim that the omission of various elements from the rites was meant to change the nature of the orders conferred, the reply quoted the Preface to the Ordinal as evidence of the orthodox intentions of the Church; the omissions had only been made to remove inessential ceremonies, and the Ordinal set forth more clearly and faithfully than the Roman Pontifical the true nature of the priesthood. No separate defence was included against the charge of defective intention, presumably because it was thought that the Bull was referring to the intention of the Church of England as manifested by the omissions from the Ordinal, with which the reply had already dealt. It is noteworthy that this document claimed that the imposition of hands in the Ordinal conferred the character of Order and the *porrectio instrumentorum* jurisdiction.

Replies soon appeared to the Archbishops' letter, most of them pointing out the mistake it made over what the Bull required for a

---

[1] See *Memoirs of Archbishop Temple by Seven Friends*, ed. E. G. Sandford (1906), II, pp. 388–97. Text in *Anglican Orders (English)*, pp. 23–67.

valid form. A reply from the Roman Catholic hierarchy in England argued that the imperative formulas in the Ordinal were not definite enough and the collects were too far from the imposition of hands. They also said that the Pope, having found the forms invalid in themselves, had looked at the Ordinal as a whole in the light of those who introduced it, who clearly did not intend it in a Catholic sense. The defect of intention, however, was separate from this and was in the ministers who, by using the rites of their Church, had the intention of that Church, which had set up the rite with the express object of rejecting the Catholic priesthood.[1] Another Roman Catholic critic, Luke Rivington, questioned the Archbishops' claim that the form need only be "prayer or benediction appropriate to the ministry to be conferred". Unless it signified the order it was not appropriate. Yet even mention of the order in the Anglican form would not have sufficed, as Anglicans did not mean by "priest" one whose office consisted chiefly in consecrating the Body and Blood of Christ. He claimed that therefore the words of the Preface to the Ordinal were valueless as evidence of the orthodox intentions of the Church of England.[2]

Anglican rejoinders appeared. The committee of the Church Historical Society replied to the Roman Catholic hierarchy by saying that it was not true that the intention of the English Reformers was against the Catholic Church; their intention was to vindicate the true character of the Catholic Church by the removal of uncatholic accretions. The omissions were made, not to condemn sacrifice, but to remove errors, and therefore the Church of England intended such words as "priest" and "sacrifice" in their true catholic sense. Nor was it necessary that the prayer, imposition of hands, and the determination of the order should be very closely linked for a rite to be valid; "it would be monstrous to suggest that an Ordinal, otherwise adequate, is thus rendered nugatory in the sight of God". Moreover, the Anglican Ordinal should be treated as a single whole, not as an essential nucleus with large accretions, like the Latin rites. Nevertheless, the imperative formulas taken alone did determine the orders sufficiently.[3] In another

---

[1] *A Vindication of the Bull "Apostolicae Curae", A letter on Anglican Orders by the Cardinal Archbishop and Bishops of the Province of Westminster* (1898), pp. 34ff.

[2] Luke Rivington, *Tekel, or the Anglican Archbishops arraigned at the bar of logic and convicted of 75 flaws* (1897), pp. 5–23.

[3] *Priesthood in the English Church, A Study of the "Vindication of the Bull Apostolicae Curae"*, CHS XLI (1898), pp. 33–48.

pamphlet T. A. Lacey contributed the argument that, as the compilers of the Ordinal were unknown, it was impossible to say what they understood by the names "bishops" and "priests". It was likely that the compilers included men of unquestionable orthodoxy who understood these words in a Catholic sense. However, the compilers were in any case incapable of imposing their own meaning on the Ordinal. They were simply acting on behalf of the whole Church of England, and so it was her official intention which determined the meaning of the Ordinal. At that time the words "bishops" and "priests" had the same meaning in the Church of England as they had always had in the Catholic Church.[1]

The discovery in 1898 of the *Sacramentary of Serapion*, a fourth-century document, provided a further point of controversy in the debate. Its form for the priesthood did not name the order nor did it mention the power of offering sacrifice. It was therefore hailed by John Wordsworth, who published an English translation of the sacramentary, and by other Anglicans as an example of a valid form which did not fulfil the requirements of *Apostolicae Curae*.[2] Roman Catholics, however, denied that it constituted a real exception to the rule. John Chapman in his reply to Gore's *Roman Catholic Claims* suggested that both in this form and in the form for the priesthood in the Abyssinian rite, which was very similar, the "mystical comparison" in the form with the elders appointed to assist Moses might be thought sufficient indication of the order. Moreover, a comparison of these forms with the Coptic rite, which was also similar, suggested that part of the beginning of the prayer containing the word priesthood, retained in the Coptic rite, had accidently dropped out of the text of these two forms in the course of their history.[3]

From that date until very recently polemical works have continued to appear on both sides, but hardly any new arguments have been advanced and only few contributions seem worthy of note. The first is that made by E. C. Messenger, whose first significant work on the subject, *The Lutheran Origin of the Anglican Ordinal*, published in 1934, has already been mentioned.[4] He followed this up with a much larger work, *The Reformation, the Mass and the Priesthood*, to which reference has also been made earlier. This enormous work, running to

[1] T. A. Lacey, *The Interpretation of the English Ordinal*, CHS L (1898).
[2] John Wordsworth, *Bishop Sarapion's Prayer-Book* (1899), pp. 51–2, 73.
[3] *Bishop Gore and the Catholic Claims*, p. 102.
[4] See above, p. 20.

over 1,300 pages, has been the only attempt to present a really detailed history of the Anglican Ordinal and of the Orders controversy. Unfortunately, it abounds in errors and is written from a very partisan standpoint. Messenger is determined throughout to prove the invalidity of the Ordinal at all costs and frequently makes assertions which are not susceptible of conclusive proof. The thesis of the whole work is that the English Reformation had great affinity with the Lutheran movement on the continent, that the Ordinal was meant to establish a Lutheran ministry, and that Anglican Orders have been consistently treated as invalid by Roman Catholics from the reign of Queen Mary onwards. In his concluding theological essay Messenger stated that the most that could be said for the imperative formulas in the rites for the priesthood and episcopate in the Edwardine Ordinals was that they were ambiguous, but when their sense was determined from the rest of the rite, the Prayer Book, and elsewhere, they were unquestionably meant in a Protestant sense, and hence were insufficient. The opinions of the Reformers also showed that they had a defective intention; they intended to exclude the sacrificial functions from the ministry. Hence, in spite of the claims of the Preface to the Ordinal, Anglicans did not really intend to continue the ministry as it had been before the Reformation.

In 1944 there appeared *The Question of Anglican Orders* by the Anglican liturgical scholar, Gregory Dix, which has come to be regarded by very many Anglicans as a definitive work on the subject, in spite of the fact that it is very brief and really says nothing which had not been said earlier. The importance attached to it probably arises from the prominence of its author and from the fact that it made the arguments readily available in one small volume. Dix argued that the intention to be considered was the official intention of the Church of England and not that of Cranmer himself, whose heretical views on ordination were irrelevant. The Preface demonstrated the orthodox intention of the Church of England, and the alterations in the rites had not been made with any heretical intention; the compilers had merely selected one of the medieval theories of the matter and form and replaced the Pontifical with rites containing the imposition of hands and the imperative formulas. Nor was it necessary that the forms should have been intended in a Catholic sense by their compilers, but only that they should be capable of a Catholic interpretation. Dix also made the common mistake of believing that the Papal Bull had meant that the form must mention both the order and the powers, and demonstrated that many early rites did not fulfil this requirement.[1] This error was pointed out by Messenger in a review of Dix's book,[2] but a revised edition of the book, which appeared in 1956, included an appendix claiming that the Latin word *vel* could mean either "and" or "or", depending on its context, and that the rest of the Bull showed that it was meant in the former sense.[3]

A much longer defence of Anglican Orders, *Apostolic Succession and Anglicanism*, by an American, Felix L. Cirlot, appeared in 1946. This advanced the thesis, popular among many Anglo-Catholics, that the Church of England had never officially abandoned a Catholic position, whatever the views of a small reforming party, and it attacked the reverse conclusions reached by Messenger. On the alleged defects of form and intention Cirlot mainly reproduced at some length earlier arguments, but he did add a few new points. He pointed out that the Council of Trent had said that the power of the priesthood was double, the offering of the Eucharistic Sacrifice, which the Papal Bull had mentioned, and forgiving and retaining of sins, which it had not mentioned. As the Anglican form for the priesthood explicitly mentioned the latter power, it sufficiently determined the order, and the reference to Timothy's ordination to the episcopate in the Anglican form for the episcopate was also unmistakable. These forms were at least as definite as that in the *Sacramentary of Serapion* for the priesthood or that in the *Canons of Hippolytus* for the diaconate. As for the claim that, even if the Anglican forms had named the order they would not have had a Catholic meaning, there was nothing in the primitive rites to show what sort of priests and bishops they meant, because there was no mention of sacrifice, nor was there any reason to suppose that God would not bestow the grace of an order even if the form expressed an inadequate concept of it. Moreover, since the Roman Church had accepted as valid baptisms performed by Methodists in Oceania who disclaimed explicitly all belief in baptismal regeneration, it ought to accept as valid ordinations in the Church of England which had never officially rejected belief in the Eucharistic Sacrifice. Finally, Cirlot claimed that, although Cranmer and his party had not believed that the Eucharistic Sacrifice was implied in the Ordinal, it was nevertheless implied in it in the explicit bestowal of power to forgive and retain sins, in the bestowal of power to administer the sacraments, and in the bestowal of the order of priesthood itself. On the question of intention he

[1] Gregory Dix, *The Question of Anglican Orders* (1944).
[2] *Dublin Review* CCXVII (1945), pp. 93–7.    [3] Pp. 94–5.

drew a distinction between the views of the reforming party and the official teaching of the Church. Up to 1550 the latter was still orthodox, and therefore the intention of the Church of England was a Catholic one. Yet even the defective intention of the Reformers was only what he called a "conditional intention". They intended to do what God willed and only intended to exclude the sacrificial powers because they thought, wrongly, that they did not really exist. Therefore, their former, absolute, intention would have prevailed over their latter, conditional, intention.[1]

Two other Roman Catholic works warrant attention. The first, by Anthony A. Stephenson, a Jesuit, originally appeared as a series of articles in *The Month* in 1955 and was later published as a book. It was devoted partly to a criticism of Dix's book. After noting Dix's mistake over the requirements for a valid form, he turned to the claim that the intention of the Church of England had remained orthodox in spite of Cranmer's beliefs, and argued that the Thirty-nine Articles and the beliefs of the Reformers as a whole demonstrated that the Church of England meant by ordination something incompatible with Catholic doctrine. He also dealt with the claim made by Anglicans that the form for the priesthood in the *Sacramentary of Serapion* did not signify the order; the mention of the power to "reconcile" was to be understood as the power to offer Mass, since this expression was also found in Serapion's eucharistic rite where it referred to the reconciliation achieved by the Mass. Stephenson stressed that it was the defect of form which was decisive for invalidity. Although it was probable that the defect of intention on its own would have rendered Anglican Orders invalid, because the Reformers' intention not to confer the power to sacrifice would probably have nullified their general intention to perform a Christian rite, the mutilation of the form both made it insufficient as a form and also demonstrated the defect of intention. Dix's claim that a form could be ambiguous and need only be capable of a Catholic interpretation in order to suffice was unacceptable; a form had a definite meaning which was to be found in the circumstances in which it was produced. The Anglican form was essentially a mutilation of the Catholic rite, omitting the references to sacrifice, and it was composed by those who did not believe in sacrifice. Therefore it could not possibly confer the Catholic priesthood, because it did not mean the Catholic priesthood.[2]

[1] Felix L. Cirlot, *Apostolic Succession and Anglicanism: A Defense of Anglican Orders and Catholicity* (Lexington 1946), esp. pp. 318–91.
[2] Anthony A. Stephenson, "Anglican Orders", *The Month* XIV (1955), pp. 30–7, 78–86, 152–9; reprinted in A. A. Stephenson, *Anglican Orders* (1956), pp. 15–39. This book was

The second work, which appeared shortly after this, was also by a Jesuit, Francis Clark. He concentrated on the alleged defect of intention, and pointed out the wide divergence of beliefs on both sides as to whose intention the Bull had declared defective. He concluded that there were seven main theories which had been advanced: (*a*) there was the intention of the compilers of the Ordinal; (*b*) the internal intention of the minister in the strict theological sense; (*c*) the internal intention of the minister, not in the usual technical sense, but considered in its bearing on the validity of the form, as giving determination to otherwise ambiguous wording, what was called the *intentio circa significationem formae;* (*d*) the antecedent motive of the minister influencing his choice of matter and form; (*e*) the corporate intention of the Church of England; (*f*) the external intention of the minister, the outward purport of his actions, which had to be taken as sufficient indication of intention, irrespective of any vagaries of the inward will; and (*g*) the intention of the rite itself, considered objectively in its historical setting. Clark then examined each of these in turn and decided that there were substantial objections against any of them being the defective intention referred to by the Bull, except for (*b*) the internal intention of the minister. From a detailed study of the Bull he claimed that this was the intention in question and proceeded to defend this against two main objections. Firstly, there was the objection made much of by Felix Cirlot. If the Methodists in Oceania did not have a defective intention in baptizing, why did the Elizabethan bishops have one in ordaining? Clark said that there was a difference. The Methodists had only "concomitant heresy in the intellect", whereas the Elizabethan bishops had a positive intention to exclude certain effects of the sacrament, this being shown by the use of a mutilated rite, the significance of which was to exclude the conferring of the Catholic priesthood. Secondly, there was the objection that, even if the Elizabethan bishops had this contrary intention, they still had the general intention to do what Christ instituted, which would have prevailed over it. Clark denied this and argued on the "principle of positive exclusion" that two simultaneous contrary intentions cancelled each other out and the sacrament was rendered null. He also believed that the decisive argument against the forms had not been the fact they they did not define the order conferred—many theologians thought that an indefinite form could be valid if determined

<hr />

withdrawn in June 1960 because the author had lost confidence in his arguments and thought that they were an oversimplification of the problem; see Anthony Stephenson, "*Anglican Orders*", *The Old Palace*, No. 22 (1961), p. 31. Stephenson became an Anglican in 1966.

by the rest of the rite—but the fact that the deliberate alterations made in the rest of the Ordinal, and the circumstances surrounding its composition, showed that it was not the catholic priesthood and episcopate that the forms signified. Even the forms since 1662 were not valid because the setting in which they occurred showed that they meant something different from the ancient rites.[1]

Clark's distinction between the Methodists in Oceania and the Elizabethan bishops was criticized by Dr E. L. Mascall, the leading Anglo-Catholic theologian. He pointed out that Clark's sole ground for claiming that the Elizabethan bishops had a positive intention to exclude certain effects of the sacrament was their use of the Ordinal in place of the Pontifical. If the expression of disbelief by the Methodists was not sufficient evidence of such a positive intention, how could the use of the Ordinal be sufficient? He believed that Clark's principle could not be maintained without destroying certainty about all sacraments.[2] More recently Clark's "principle of positive exclusion" has been criticized by John Jay Hughes, who has maintained that the authorities cited by Clark do not support his argument but that, except for marriage, it is still generally agreed that where there are contrary intentions the predominant one determines the validity of the sacrament. Hughes is prepared to go further than this and argue that the whole controversy about contrary intentions is a bogus difficulty. A Protestant minister celebrating the Eucharist does not have two contrary intentions, to obey Christ's command and to exclude sacrifice from the celebration. He has only the former intention because he does not believe the Eucharistic Sacrifice exists at all, and therefore cannot by a positive act of the will exclude something which he does not believe exists. He has only a "concomitant heresy in the intellect" which can never vitiate the sacramental intention.[3]

That would seem to be the present position of the debate. The publication of the Apostolic Constitution, *Sacramentum Ordinis*, by Pope Pius XII in 1947 has only had a very indirect effect on the subject of Anglican Orders. It defined the imposition of hands and the central petitions of the original Roman ordination prayers as the essential matter and form for the diaconate, priesthood, and episcopate in the

[1] Francis Clark, *Anglican Orders and Defect of Intention* (1956).
[2] E. L. Mascall, "Intention and Form in Anglican Orders", CQR CLVIII (1957), pp. 4-20.
[3] John Jay Hughes, "Ministerial Intention in the Administration of the Sacraments", *Clergy Review* LI (1966), pp. 763-76, and *Stewards of the Lord* (1970), pp. 267-86.

present Roman Pontifical, and thus put an end to the debate on that question, but it did not go beyond this; it did not state that these had always been the form and matter in all earlier rites, nor did it deny that other matter and form could be equally sufficient.[1] It is interesting to note, however, that it thus admitted that there could be some separation between matter and form and that the forms need not make an explicit mention of the order conferred, since the central petition of the prayer in the rite for the diaconate reads:

> Emitte in eum, quaesumus, Domine, Spiritum Sanctum, quo in opus ministerii tui fideliter exsequendi septiformis gratiae tuae munere roboretur.[2]

Similarly the form for the episcopate describes the order as simply "the fullness of thy ministry" (*ministerii tui summam*). Neither of these can be said to be any more explicit than the imperative formulas in the rites for the priesthood and episcopate in the Anglican Ordinal of 1550.

The entry of the Roman Catholic Church into the ecumenical dialogue has more or less brought to an end the publication of polemic on Anglican Orders. The condemnation by Leo XIII still remains, but the new thinking generated within the Roman Church by Vatican II is likely to produce significant changes in the traditional attitudes to priesthood, sacrifice, Church, and sacraments, and this may very well affect the subject of Anglican Orders. For example, John Jay Hughes' latest book, *Stewards of the Lord*, is an attempt to show that Vatican II's understanding of the priesthood is much closer to that underlying the Anglican Ordinal than it is to that expressed in medieval and post-medieval Roman Catholic theology, and that therefore, although the Ordinal did reject the sacrificial priesthood as popularly understood, it still intended to continue the true ministry of the Church. Whilst such arguments may affect Roman Catholic attitudes to the Ordinal, they are irrelevant to most Anglicans who have always rested their defence upon the claim that a deficient meaning in a rite or a deficient intention, whether in a minister or in a Church, does not prevent the ministry instituted by Christ from being conferred. However, this does not reduce the importance of trying to reach a common understanding of the ministry, and all steps in this direction are to be welcomed.

[1] *Documents on Christian Unity, Fourth Series, 1948–57*, ed G. K. A. Bell (1958), pp. 13–16.
[2] "Send forth upon him, O Lord, we beseech thee, the Holy Ghost to strengthen him with the gift of thy sevenfold grace for his work of faithfully executing thy ministry."

## 10. Revision in the Twentieth Century

In spite of the criticisms which had been levelled against the Ordinal both by Evangelicals and by Roman Catholics during the nineteenth century, the Convocations could find hardly anything in it which they thought needed improvement when they began the work of Prayer Book revision, and at first only one change was recommended. Since 1550 the question concerning the sufficiency of Scripture in the examination of deacons had read:

> Do you unfeignedly believe all the Canonical Scriptures of the Old and New Testament?
>
> Ans. I do believe them.

The Committee of the Lower House of Canterbury proposed to substitute for this the first half of the question on the sufficiency of Scripture from the examination of priests, which seemed to imply a less fundamentalist attitude to Scripture:

> Are you persuaded that the holy Scriptures contain sufficiently all doctrine required of necessity for eternal salvation through faith in Jesus Christ?[1]

This alteration was said by Dr Henry Wace, the Dean of Canterbury and a staunch Evangelical, to be a far more important subject than any which had been raised in the House during the ten years in which he had sat in it.[2] He and several other Evangelicals were strongly opposed to any change being made as they feared that it was a weakening of belief in the full inspiration and supreme authority of Scripture, and this opposition was consistently maintained.[3] The majority, however, were insistent that some alteration was necessary, but were unable to agree on the precise wording of the new question. Thus through the years that this was debated in the Convocations there was considerable

---

[1] *Canterbury Convocation, Report 428* (1909), Resolution 128.
[2] *Chronicle of Convocation* (1912), pp. 586–7.
[3] See W. Prescott Upton, *The Proposed Revision of the Prayer Book* (1923), pp. 5–7; Arthur J. Brown, *Prayer Book Revision: what will it mean? Questions and Answers about the Composite Book* (n.d.), p. 10.

discussion and numerous alternatives were proposed.[1] At first York
Convocation wanted to retain the question as it was, but later it changed
its mind. It was finally agreed by both Convocations that the question
should read:

> Do you unfeignedly believe all the Canonical Scriptures of the Old and the
> New Testament, as given of God to convey to us in many parts and in divers
> manners the revelation of himself which is fulfilled in our Lord Jesus Christ?
>
> *Answer.* I do believe them as so given.

The doctrinal implications of this change seem to have diverted
attention from all thoughts of making any important liturgical amendments in the Ordinal, for only two other small alterations were proposed in the final report on the revision of the Prayer Book, the
substitution of the word "flock" for "fold" in the final sentence of the
second Gospel in the rite for the priesthood, and the shortening of
the litany by terminating it after the *Kyries*. Proposals were, however,
made for provisions for the Ember Days and the days fixed for ordinations. The report of the Committee on the Prayer Book at the Lambeth
Conference of 1908 had said that there was urgent need of a collect and
a special suffrage in the litany for use on the day of an ordination.[2] The
Convocations now provided a special suffrage, based on the one in the
Ordinal, for the Ember Weeks and the day of an ordination, and
directed that either of the Ember Prayers could be used after the collect
of the day in the Ember Weeks, and the second could be used on the
day of an ordination or consecration. An Epistle and Gospel, Eph.
4.7–16 and John 10.1–16, were also provided for permissive use on the
Ember Days.[3]

Nevertheless, although they had no influence on the Convocations,
proposals for changes in the Ordinal, some by eminent scholars, had
appeared both before and during the period of revision. R. C. Moberly
had suggested a clearer emphasis on the part of the Church in electing
its ministers, the restoration of the delivery of the chalice and paten,
and the mention of eucharistic offerings or sacrifice.[4] J. Wickham Legg
thought that, if any changes were to be made in the Ordinal, it should

---

[1] *Chronicle of Convocation* (1912), pp. 613–35; (1914) pp. 161–81, 191–200; (1915),
pp. 147–8, 419–28; (1917), pp. 43–4, 584–97; (1918) pp. 127–9; (1919), pp. 327–8; *Journal
of York Convocation* (1915), pp. 193–5; (1919), pp. 68–9, 278–9.

[2] *Conference of Bishops of the Anglican Communion. Holden at Lambeth Palace, July 27 to
August 5, 1908. Encyclical Letter from the Bishops, with the Resolutions and Reports* (1908),
p. 125.

[3] *Canterbury Convocation, Report 533* (1920), pp. 23, 26, 38, 66.

[4] R. C. Moberly, *Ministerial Priesthood* (1897, 2nd edn, 1969), pp. 89–90, 288–9.

be to bring the prayer and imposition of hands in the rite for the diaconate closer together, either by removing the examination to an earlier part of the rite, perhaps immediately after the litany, so letting the imposition of hands follow the collect directly, or by a more radical change, the insertion of a prayer such as that in the *Sacramentary of Serapion* immediately before the imposition of hands.[1] Walter Frere desired the restoration of the solemn ordination prayer prefaced by its bidding, salutation, and *Sursum corda* in each of the rites,[2] and A. C. Headlam, later Bishop of Gloucester, in his Bampton Lectures in 1920 criticized the tendency to make the necessary part of ordination "lie in the declaratory words spoken by the bishop in the laying on of hands and not in the prayers that accompany the rite".[3]

In 1913 there appeared an anonymous work under the title *A Prayer-Book Revised*, with a preface contributed by Charles Gore. It made a number of changes in the Ordinal. The special suffrage in the litany was abbreviated and the litany itself was shortened, ending at the *Kyries*, and was followed immediately in the rites for the diaconate and priesthood by the salutation and collect, and in the rite for the episcopate by the address and examination. The original version of "Come Holy Ghost" and the prayer, "Prevent us", etc., were omitted, and the deacons' question about the sufficiency of Scripture was altered to:

> Do you unfeignedly believe the Canonical Scriptures of the Old and the New Testament, as conveying to us the word of God, and the message of eternal life through Jesus Christ?
>
> Answer. I do believe them.

The most significant alteration, however, was the inclusion before the imposition of hands in all three rites of a bidding followed by a period of silent prayer, a collect, and an ordination prayer with the salutation, *Sursum corda*, and eucharistic preface, following the ancient Roman practice. The wording of the biddings and collects was based freely upon the early rites, the ordination prayer in the rite for the diaconate was an expansion of the final collect from that service, including a petition for the gift of the Holy Spirit, and in the other two rites it was the prayer which already preceded the imposition of hands with the eucharistic preface prefixed. In the rite for the priesthood part of the

---

[1] J. Wickham Legg, *Three Letters on the Proposed Revision of the Prayer Book* (1909), pp. 41–2.

[2] W. H. Frere, *Some Principles of Liturgical Reform* (1911), pp. 149–50; see also Procter and Frere, p. 661.

[3] Headlam, *The Doctrine of the Church and Christian Reunion*, pp. 259–60.

petition for the Holy Spirit from Bucer's original draft was also restored to this prayer:

> to pour upon these thy servants thy Holy Spirit, to teach and govern them, that faithfully and profitably they may fulfil their ministry towards them that are thy people and the sheep of the Good Shepherd.

"Come Holy Ghost", which had preceded the prayer in the rites for the priesthood and episcopate, was now inserted between the period of silent prayer and the collect. The period of silent prayer of course had already existed in the rite for the priesthood.[1] The result of all this was that the prayer of the people was now duplicated in all three rites, as each contained both the litany and later a period of silent prayer, and the rite for the episcopate had two biddings, one before each of the two acts of prayer.

The "Grey Book" produced by the Life and Liberty Movement contained no Ordinal, nor did the "Green Book", but the report of the committee of the English Church Union which produced it did comment that an ideal revision of the Ordinal would embody the transformation of the prayers before the imposition of hands in the rites for the priesthood and episcopate into solemn ordination prayers by the addition of the salutation, *Sursum corda*, and eucharistic preface. They also desired the restoration of various medieval ceremonies—the anointing of the hands of priests and the head and hands of bishops, and the clothing of deacons in dalmatics and priests in chasubles, as well as a return to the original *porrectio instrumentorum* of each rite and to the custom of new priests and bishops concelebrating the ordination Eucharist.[2] The "Orange Book", which was an attempt by Walter Frere to bring together the revision proposals which had so far been made, merely reproduced the proposals of *A Prayer-Book Revised*, and suggested that the litany "might be otherwise curtailed in scope for this special purpose" and that another version of "Come Holy Ghost" was desirable "which may more adequately represent the *Veni Creator* than Cosin's compressed version does".[3]

Nevertheless, as has already been said, none of these proposals had any influence on the revision work in the Convocations, nor did they have much effect on the deliberations of the National Assembly of the

[1] *A Prayer-Book Revised, being the Services of the Book of Common Prayer, with Sundry Alterations and Additions offered to the Reader* (1913), pp. 219–59.

[2] *English Church Union, Report of the Committee on Prayer Book Revision* (1922), pp. 11–12.

[3] *A Survey of the Proposals for the Alternative Prayer Book*, Part III, Alcuin Club Prayer Book Revision Pamphlet XIV (1924), pp. 83–91.

Church of England, where the Convocations' proposals were next submitted. A committee appointed by the Assembly merely added to these proposals the suggestion that there should be alternative Epistles and Gospels for the Ember Days—Acts 13.44-9, Acts 20.28-35, Matt. 9.35-8, and Luke 4.16-21—and it amended the answer to the deacons' question to "I do".[1] The House of Laity suggested no alterations, and the House of Clergy merely proposed two minor changes: the omission of the original version of "Come Holy Ghost" and the substitution of "unto the elected Bishop" for "unto them" in the rubric in the rite for the episcopate ordering the King's mandate to be read. A proposal to amend "Latin Tongue" in the Preface to "Humane Letters" was withdrawn after some discussion and a proposal for yet another version of the deacons' question was defeated.[2]

It was therefore left to the House of Bishops to make more far-reaching changes. They adopted all the proposals made so far by the Convocations and the Assembly, except that they preferred to amend the rubric for the reading of the King's mandate by omitting "unto them" and putting nothing at all in its place, and they made several new proposals. No doubt under the guidance of Walter Frere, now Bishop of Truro, the proposals of *A Prayer-Book Revised* were partially adopted; in the rite for the diaconate the bidding, silent prayer, *Sursum corda*, and ordination prayer were included and the final collect omitted. The collect and salutation were, however, not adopted, and the ordination prayer was slightly amended to increase the element of thanksgiving. The *Sursum corda* and eucharistic preface were added to the prayers in the rites for the priesthood and episcopate, but not the bidding, collect, or salutation, nor was the petition for the Holy Spirit restored in the prayer in the rite for the priesthood. The litany was made optional, so that the prayer of the people need not be duplicated, an improvement on *A Prayer-Book Revised*, although the bishop was still to commend the candidates to the prayers of the people in the rites for the diaconate and priesthood even when the litany did not follow, and the words he was to use were appended to this rubric. As there would otherwise have been no prayer of the people in the rite for the episcopate, when the litany was not said a period of silent prayer was to be substituted and it was to be concluded by the collect from the end of the litany. Two other small changes were also made. When deacons

[1] *Second Report of the Prayer Book Revision Committee with schedule of proposed alterations*, N.A. 60 (1922), pp. 51, 104.
[2] *Church Assembly, Minutes of Proceedings of House of Clergy*, C.A. 157C (1925), pp. 7-8.

and priests were ordained together, both collects were no longer to be said, but instead a special collect was to be used, being the one from the rite for the priesthood with the words "Order of Deacons, and of Priests" in place of "Office of Priesthood", and the rubric directing that the consecration of a bishop was to be performed on a Sunday or Holy-Day had the words "if it is convenient" substituted for "always".[1]

The bishops also included in the draft Prayer Book a rite for the Making of Deaconesses, not as part of the Ordinal but in an appendix to the Book. This rite had been adopted in 1924 by the Upper Houses of the Convocations of Canterbury and York. Deaconesses had appeared in the Church of England in the second half of the nineteenth century but at first there had been no uniform rite for their admission. In 1919 the report of a committee on the ministry of women appointed by the Archbishop of Canterbury appended a synopsis of the various rites for admitting deaconesses in use in the different English dioceses and included a suggested new one,[2] and the 1920 Lambeth Conference expressed the hope that a common rite might be drawn up which would contain provision for:

1. Prayer by the bishop and the laying on of hands.
2. A formula giving authority to execute the office of a deaconess in the Church of God.
3. The delivery of the New Testament by the bishop to the candidate.[3]

It was unfortunate that the Conference thus laid stress on two secondary elements and did not emphasize the prime importance of the association of the imposition of hands with a suitable prayer, as this led to the composition of a liturgically unsatisfactory rite in England. At the request of committees on deaconesses in their respective Convocations, the Upper Houses of Canterbury and York appointed committees to draw up a rite with these provisions in 1922. The York committee on deaconesses had also proposed that the rite should include "a formal presentation of the candidate to the Bishop and examination by him, and a formal charge by him setting forth the duties of a Deaconess", and it included in the report such a charge, drawn up by Walter Frere,

[1] National Assembly of the Church of England, Book Proposed to be annexed to the Prayer Book Measure 192–, Provisional, subject to further revision by the House of Bishops (1927), pp. 329–46.
[2] The Ministry of Women (1919), Appendix XIV.
[3] Conference of Bishops of the Anglican Communion. Holden at Lambeth Palace, July 5 to August 7, 1920. Encyclical Letter from the Bishops, with the Resolutions and Reports (1920), p. 40.

who was a member of the committee, and based on the duties assigned to deaconesses by the 1920 Lambeth Conference. It had also suggested the delivery of some symbol or instrument of her office instead of the New Testament, because the delivery of the New Testament "brought the office of a deaconess too much on a par with the office of a deacon", but the Upper House rejected this.[1]

Table 4 indicates in synopsis the rites drawn up by the two committees,[2] and also the rite finally adopted. The York committee saw the Canterbury rite before it drew up its own. The Canterbury collect at the beginning came from the Leonine Sacramentary, where it was prescribed for the anniversary of the consecration of a bishop. It read:

> Remember, O Lord, what thou hast wrought in us, and not what we deserve; and as thou hast called us to thy service, make us worthy of our calling; through Jesus Christ our Lord. Amen.

York preferred the collect from the rite for deaconesses drawn up by Thomas Deacon, the Nonjuror,[3] which they found in the report of the Archbishop's committee on the ministry of women. This, with the omission of the clause referring to Phoebe, was adopted in the final rite. The examination was identical in both rites, except for the third of the four questions, which concerned the duties of a deaconess. York preferred the wording of the charge in their earlier report on deaconesses to the Canterbury version, and after much discussion this was adopted, with a few minor changes, in the final rite. The Canterbury collect before the imposition of hands read:

> Almighty God, who has-called this thy servant to the Office and Ministry of a Deaconess in thy Church, mercifully grant unto her grace and power to perform the work which thou givest her to do, that through her service thou mayest forward thy purposes of love; through Jesus Christ our Lord. Amen.

The Canterbury rite aroused considerable criticism in the Upper House, much of it directed against the unsatisfactory collect at the beginning, and there was much discussion concerning the correct point in the Communion service for the rite to take place. It was also objected that the candidates were not required to make a declaration accepting the doctrine of the Church of England, and it was agreed to prefix the rite with a rubric requiring such a declaration to be made.[4]

[1] *York Convocation, Report 347* (1922); *Journal* (1922), pp. 113–14, 157–8.
[2] *York Convocation, Report 357* (1923); *Canterbury Convocation, Report 549* (1923).
[3] See above, pp. 107ff.
[4] *Chronicle of Convocation* (1923), pp. 158–70, 215ff.

Table 4: Synopsis of rites for Making Deaconesses

| Canterbury | York | Final Rite |
|---|---|---|
| | | Presentation and Question as to suitability |
| | | Final Inquiry of People Silent Prayer |
| Collect | Different Collect | York Collect |
| | Epistle: Phil. 2.1–11 | Epistle: 1 Cor. 12.4–11 |
| Presentation and Question as to suitability | Presentation and Question as to suitability | |
| Final Inquiry of People | Final Inquiry of People | |
| Silent Prayer | Silent Prayer | |
| Examination | Examination | Examination |
| Collect | "Let us Pray" | |
| Imposition of hands and formula: | Imposition of hands and formula: | Imposition of hands and formula: |

"Take thou authority to execute the Office of a Deaconess in the Church of God committed unto thee; in the Name of the Father, and of the Son, and of the Holy Ghost. Amen."

| Canterbury | York | Final Rite |
|---|---|---|
| Delivery of New Testament and formula: | Delivery of New Testament and formula: | Delivery of New Testament and formula: |
| "Be diligent to study the things which are written in this Book, that, as much as in thee lieth, thou mayest teach the gospel of the grace of God, and be an example of faith and of holy living." | "Meditate upon these things; give thyself wholly to them; that thy profiting may appear to all. Take heed unto thyself, and unto the doctrine; continue in them; for in doing this thou shalt both save thyself, and them that hear thee." | as Canterbury |
| Epistle: 1 Cor. 12.4–11 | | |
| Gospel: Luke 10.38–42 | Gospel: Luke 10.38–42 or Matt: 28.1–10 | Gospel: Luke 10.38–42 or Matt. 28.1–10 |
| Eucharist | Eucharist | Eucharist |
| | | Post-communion: Canterbury collect from before the imposition of hands. |
| "Prevent us", etc. | "Prevent us", etc. | "Prevent us", etc. |
| Blessing | Blessing | Blessing |

This was included in the final rite. There was also considerable discussion, when the Upper Houses sat together to draw up the final rite, on the point in the service at which the ordination should take place, and an unsuccessful attempt was made to put it outside the Communion service altogether.[1]

The Draft Book, including this rite, was submitted by the bishops to the Convocations on 7 February 1927 for their final comments. Only three small suggestions were made by the Lower Houses for changes in the Ordinal. Canterbury proposed the omission of the phrase "in the Latin tongue" from the Preface,[2] and York the use of a shortened version of the litany and the substitution of "grievous" for "horrible" in the exhortation to priests.[3] However, the inclusion of the rite for deaconesses caused considerable trouble, because it had been added to the Book without consultation with the Houses of Clergy and Laity, a proceeding contrary to the constitution of the Church Assembly. Walter Frere felt so strongly about this that he submitted a memorandum to the two Archbishops pointing out the unconstitutional character of it.[4] When, therefore, the bishops undertook the final revision, they deleted this rite from the Book. They did not accept any of the three proposals for the Ordinal made by the Lower Houses, and made only two changes of their own in the draft rites. One of these was a very minor amendment in the rubric after the Communion in the rites for deacons and priests. The other was of rather greater importance. They inserted in the prayer before the imposition of hands in the rite for the priesthood, as a brief petition for the candidates, the words "to endue them with all grace needful for their calling". It would appear that it was Dr A. Maclean, the Bishop of Moray, Ross, and Caithness, who drew attention to this defect.[5] It is very strange in view of the debate on Anglican Orders and of the proposal of *A Prayer-Book Revised*, reproduced in the "Orange Book", that nobody, even Frere himself, seems to have been aware of it previously.

Thus revised the Ordinal was passed together with the rest of the Prayer Book by the Convocations and submitted to Parliament in 1927. Unlike the other proposed changes in the Prayer Book, the alterations in the Ordinal were not to be permissive but were to be

[1] *Chronicle of Convocation* (1924), pp. 270–91.
[2] Ibid. (1927), p. 62. This was carried by 37 to 27.
[3] *Journal* (1927), p. 20, and Appendix, pp. xxii–xxiii.
[4] *Walter Howard Frere, his correspondence on liturgical revision and construction*, ed. R. C. D. Jasper, ACC XXXIX (1954), pp. 106–9.
[5] Ibid., p. 128.

adopted at all ordinations. The Ordinal was unchanged when the Book was again unsuccessfully submitted to Parliament in 1928. It has therefore never been legally approved for use in England. It has largely been ignored by critics of the 1928 Prayer Book, although F. E. Brightman did offer his comments on it as soon as it appeared. He regarded the permissible omission of the litany as "very distasteful", although he thought that some abridgement of it might be possible. Whilst admitting that the restoration of the prayer before the imposition of hands in the rite for the diaconate was admirable, he regretted the failure to restore both the biddings in the other rites and Bucer's petition for the candidates in the prayer in the rite for the priesthood, and he suggested the rendering of it which had appeared in *A Prayer-Book Revised*.[1] Further criticism could be made. The main fault of this Ordinal is that the ordination prayer and imposition of hands are still not united and emphasis continues to fall on the imperative formulas instead. It is also to be regretted that in the rite for the episcopate the prayer of the people is separated from the ordination prayer, and that it is still possible to duplicate it in the other two rites. The procedural mistake which led to the exclusion of the rite for deaconesses was also unfortunate. Although the rite is of no great merit, it deserves a place alongside the other rites. It was perhaps natural, however, that this was not recognized at the time, in view of the uncertainty which existed about the status and functions of deaconesses, and it is gratifying to observe that in 1937 the Upper House of Canterbury Convocation approved a resolution that in a future revision of the Prayer Book this rite should be published with the Ordinal.[2]

Since 1928 there have been no further official attempts to revise the Ordinal in England until the scheme for Anglican–Methodist unity was devised,[3] and none of the many unofficial attempts at revising the Prayer Book in England since then seems to have dealt with the Ordinal, except for one by Oscar Hardman in 1946, which was fairly conservative. He adopted almost all the changes proposed in 1928 and he made a number of other alterations, among them the addition of the bidding in the rites for the priesthood and episcopate, and the insertion of Bucer's petition for the candidates in the prayer in the former, following the wording of *A Prayer-Book Revised* for both. He made the litany compulsory, omitted all alternatives to the Epistles and Gospels,

[1] F. E. Brightman, "The New Prayer Book Examined", *CQR* CIV (1927), p. 251.
[2] *Chronicle of Convocation* (1937), p. 35.
[3] See below, pp. 185ff.

adopted the first part of the priests' question on the Scriptures as the deacons' question, abbreviated the exhortation to priests, and transferred most of the Preface to the beginning of the Prayer Book itself. He also restored various ceremonies to the rites, the vesting of deacons and priests with stoles, the delivery of the chalice and paten as well as the Bible to priests, and the giving of the staff to bishops.[1]

In the rest of the Anglican Communion revision of the Ordinal has been extremely conservative. In some provinces the 1662 Ordinal has been retained with only such changes as the local situation required. Elsewhere elements from the English proposals of 1928 have been adopted; several provinces have made provisions for the Ember Days and days of ordinations and consecrations similar or identical to those suggested in England, and have produced revised versions of the question on Scripture put to deacons. In addition Canada has transferred the post-communion collect in the rite for the diaconate to a position before the imposition of hands and slightly modified it, omitted the original version of "Come Holy Ghost", added to the examination of deacons a concluding prayer similar to that in the other two rites, and included in its Prayer Book a Proper Preface for use at ordinations. In America a collect for use when deacons and priests were ordained together, similar to that suggested in England, was included in the revision of the Prayer Book and Ordinal in 1928, a different version of "Come Holy Ghost" replaced the original one, and a special litany for ordinations was inserted as an alternative to the Prayer Book litany. An earlier proposal to allow the bishop to omit all but the first and last paragraphs of the long exhortation to priests was not accepted.[2] In Ireland the only changes made have been the shortening of the litany and the omission of the original version of "Come Holy Ghost".

The Episcopal Church of Scotland and the Church of India, Pakistan, Burma, and Ceylon have adopted almost all the proposals made in England, but with some interesting variations. Both have retained the litany as a compulsory element, but the former allowed any one of the three litanies in its Prayer Book to be used, the two longer ones being shortened for this purpose, and the latter permitted a special litany for ordinations to be substituted for the Prayer Book litany. Both have also altered the petitions for the candidates in the prayers before the imposition of hands in the rites for the priesthood and episcopate, one

---

[1] Oscar Hardman, *A Prayer-Book for 1949* (1946), Pt. II, pp. 179–94.
[2] *Second Report of the Joint Commission on the Book of Common Prayer appointed by the General Convention of 1913* (New York 1919), p. 201.

so that they should include explicit mention of the Holy Spirit, the other so that they should make explicit mention of the order being conferred. Scotland has adopted a shorter version of Bucer's petition, "to pour upon these thy servants thy Holy Spirit, that they may faithfully fulfil their ministry", in the rite for the priesthood and has substituted "the grace of thy Holy Spirit" for the words "such grace" in the rite for the episcopate. India preferred "endue them with all grace needful for the Office of a Priest" and "such grace for the Office of a Bishop" respectively. India also has a new formula at the imposition of hands on deacons which mentions the Holy Spirit:

> Receive the Holy Spirit for the office and work of a Deacon in the Church of God committed unto thee; In the name of the Father, and of the Son, and of the Holy Spirit. Amen.

Various other changes have been made by these two provinces. In Scotland the Eucharist begins at the collect in the rites for the diaconate and priesthood, a Proper Preface is appointed for use at ordinations and consecrations, and more recently, in 1961, the Provincial Synod has permitted the Collect, Epistle, and Gospel of the day to be substituted for those prescribed at ordinations, a return to ancient practice. In India Old Testament lessons are appointed for each rite, the examination in the rite for the episcopate includes an additional question on promoting the spread of the gospel, and various medieval ceremonies are restored with appropriate imperative formulas; the rite for the episcopate has the delivery of the pastoral staff and of the ring, and the rite for the priesthood permits the vesting with a stole and with a chasuble. The Province of South Africa has also adopted most of the provisions of the Scottish Ordinal.

A revised Ordinal was produced by the Liturgical Commission in America in 1957 as a basis for discussion. This also followed the lines of the proposals made in England. It included the prayer before the imposition of hands in the rite for the diaconate, but not the bidding, and added the salutation, *Sursum corda*, and eucharistic preface in all three rites, but did not insert the petition for the candidates in the prayer in the rite for the priesthood. Apart from minor alteration and omissions, several other interesting changes were also made. The word "Making" was omitted from the title of the Ordinal and "Ordaining" substituted for it in the title of the rite for the diaconate. A rubric was included which allowed the Preface to the Ordinal to be read before the presentation of the candidates at all ordinations, a practice which has apparently come into wide use in the Church. Since the Prayer Book litany has been so rarely used at ordinations since 1928, it was proposed that the special litany be made compulsory instead of optional, and the *Kyries* and Lord's Prayer omitted from it, since both would be said in the Communion service. The position of the litany in the rites for the diaconate and priesthood was also changed to bring it nearer to the imposition of hands, as it was in the rite for the episcopate. It was now placed after the Epistle in the former and after the Gospel in the latter. The Promise of Conformity to the Doctrine, Discipline, and Worship of the Protestant Episcopal Church was to be made publicly after the presentation in these two rites, as it already was in the rite for the episcopate, and not signed privately before the service. The alternative version of "Come Holy Ghost", inserted in 1928, was to be omitted as it was rarely used. Deacons and priests were to be vested in a stole, and it was permitted to restore the giving of the paten and chalice as well as the Bible to priests. In the rite for the episcopate the pastoral staff could also be given with the Bible, and the wording of the formula accompanying these two actions was altered so as to lay greater emphasis on other aspects of the episcopate, its priestly character, its duty of ordaining and confirming, and its office of maintaining and defending the faith. All post-communion prayers were omitted on the grounds that they were not true post-communion collects, and the first Epistle in the rite for the diaconate (1 Tim. 3.8–13), the first Gospel in the rite for the priesthood (Matt. 9.36–8), the alternative imperative formula at the imposition of hands in that rite, and the collect concluding the litany in the rite for the episcopate were all omitted.[1]

The 1928 English proposals have also had influence outside the Anglican Communion. The Ordinal in the Methodist *Book of Offices*, which appeared in 1936, included the prayer from the Anglican priests' rite with its insertion and eucharistic preface, but rather oddly, it was not preceded by the *Sursum corda*. This Ordinal differed from the earlier Methodist rite in that a long collect was now an alternative to extempore prayer, the additional questions in the examination were modified slightly, the last question was omitted and two further questions added, on building up the body of Christ and on stirring up the gift of God to testify the gospel; a new version of "Come Holy Ghost" replaced the earlier one and the collect following it was omitted, as were the prayer from the Anglican bishops' rite and the hymn before the imposition of hands. A new formula was included at

---

[1] The Standing Liturgical Commission of the Protestant Episcopal Church in the United States of America, *Prayer Book Studies, VIII, The Ordinal* (New York 1957).

the delivery of the Bible, followed by a declaration that the candidates had been ordained, and then by the formula from the giving of the Bible in the Anglican bishops' rite. Then there was a hymn, the celebration of the Lord's Supper, another hymn, the charge to the candidates, a final hymn, and the blessing.

It is perhaps inevitable that in this area of liturgical revision the greatest conservatism will be found, since a common Ordinal is one of the bonds which binds the Anglican Communion together. Indeed the report of the sub-committee on the Book of Common Prayer at the 1958 Lambeth Conference pleaded for conservatism in the revision of Ordinals, and the only amendments it suggested were the inclusion of the mention of the particular order in the prayers before the imposition of hands, and the addition after the imposition of hands of a declaration, in the manner of the Eastern Church, that the candidate was ordained to the particular ministry in the Church of God.[1] The preparatory information issued prior to the 1968 Lambeth Conference in its survey of the work of liturgical revision in the Anglican Communion gives no indication of any further attempts to revise the Ordinal,[2] and the 1968 Lambeth Conference merely concerned itself with the diaconate. It recommended that the diaconate, combining service of others with liturgical functions, be open to men and women in secular occupations and full-time church workers as well as those selected for the priesthood, that Ordinals should, where necessary, be revised to take account of this new role, that all reference to the diaconate as "an inferior office" should be removed from them and emphasis laid instead upon the continuing element of *diakonia* in the ministry of bishops and priests, and finally that those made deaconesses should be declared to be within the diaconate. This last recommendation was passed with only a very small majority (221–183).[3] Revision of the Ordinal, therefore, does not appear to rank as a very high priority in the process of liturgical revision in the Anglican Communion, and no province so far seems to have made any radical change in the traditional Anglican rites. There is one exception to this and that is the Protestant Episcopal Church in America where a new draft Ordinal appeared in 1970. Since, however, this is based upon the rites drawn up in schemes of church union, it will be considered with them,[4] for it is in this field that the revision of ordination rites has made the greatest advances.

[1] *The Lambeth Conference 1958* (1958) 2, pp. 87–90.
[2] *Lambeth Conference 1968, Preparatory Information* (1968), pp. 35–70.
[3] *Lambeth Conference 1968, Resolutions and Reports* (1968), Resolution 32, pp. 38–9.
[4] See below, pp. 189–90.

# 11. The Ordinal and Reunion
## (1) Ordination Rites

Until very recently in the movements towards unity which have taken place in the twentieth century between Anglican and non-episcopal Churches, the basic structure of the rites in the Anglican Ordinal has always been presupposed when the essentials of ordination were agreed upon and ordination rites drawn up. This is only to be expected because of the importance attached to valid ordinations by many Anglicans, but it must not be thought that the Free Churches have been entirely unconcerned about the subject. From the first they have sought to modify Anglican practice in order to make it accord with their concept of ministry and ordination. In the negotiations about union in South India it was agreed that all bishops would be elected, that the Diocesan Council would select candidates for ordination to the presbyterate and the bishop would ordain those of them whom he thought suitable after making inquiries from the congregation in which they were best known and from other persons to whom they were known, and that at least in the consecrations of the first bishops of the united Church presbyters from the non-episcopal Churches would join with the Anglican bishops in the imposition of hands. There were even attempts to give the Diocesan Council power to overrule a bishop's refusal to ordain a candidate whom he did not consider suitable.[1] Similarly in England, when a scheme of union on the lines of that adopted in South India was proposed in 1938 after a series of conferences between representatives of the Anglican and Free Churches, initiated as a result of the "Appeal to all Christian People" of the 1920 Lambeth Conference, it was agreed that in consecrations to the episcopate the presentation would be by two presbyters of the diocese who would also normally be associated in the imposition of hands, "as further symbolizing and expressing the concurrence of the Church of the diocese in the act of consecration", and that in the rite for the

[1] *Documents on Christian Unity, 1920–4*, ed. G. K. A. Bell (1924), pp. 280, 298, 307–8, 315, 319–28; *Documents on Christian Unity, Second Series*, ed. G. K. A. Bell (1930), pp. 146–148, 158–65, 185–6.

presbyterate the candidate would be presented by lay representatives of the congregation in which he was to minister and the congregation at the service would signify their assent by an answer to a question from the bishop.[1] Because of opposition this scheme proceeded no further. Similar schemes also appeared in Iran and America.[2]

Some Anglicans felt concern about the decision to allow presbyters to participate in the consecration of bishops in the South India scheme. The 1930 Lambeth Conference was willing to accept the fact that the first bishops from the non-episcopal Churches would be consecrated *per saltum* and would not have been confirmed in the particular circumstances, and it regarded the participation of presbyters in the first consecrations as a legitimate piece of symbolism, demonstrating "the full concurrence of the uniting Churches, the passing on to the Episcopate of the authority which Presbyters have hitherto exercised in their own communions to confer Ordination, and the coming together in the ministry of the united Church of the spiritual blessings previously enjoyed by the ministries of the several Churches in separation", but it preferred that it should not be adopted in subsequent consecrations lest it should tend to confusion, and, if it were adopted, it ought to be made plain that the presbyters were not taking part as consecrators.[3] On the other hand, the Free Churches were anxious that this provision should be made at all consecrations, and many wanted it to be not simply permissive but obligatory. This caused something of a deadlock in the negotiations when the Joint Committee met in 1930, which was finally broken by a proposal from Bishop Loyd of Nasik that presbyters should be allowed to join with the bishops, "provided that it always be remembered and taught that the true Consecrator is God to whom prayer is made". This satisfied the Anglicans and the provision was included in the scheme. This did not settle the matter, however. There was still pressure to make this provision obligatory, in order to signify the parity of ministers on which the Free Churches insisted. Finally, it was agreed that at all consecrations the candidate should be presented by two presbyters of the diocese who would join in the imposition of hands, unless the diocesan council concerned specifically determined that the bishops alone should do it.[4] This decision

---

[1] *Documents on Christian Unity, Third Series, 1930-48*, ed. G. K. A. Bell (1948), pp. 87–90.
[2] Ibid., pp. 169–70, 237–40.
[3] Ibid., pp. 15–17.
[4] Bell, *Documents* (2nd Series), p. 193; Bengt Sundkler, *Church of South India: The Movement towards Union 1900–1947* (1954), pp. 250–1, 264–5.

was strongly opposed by some Anglicans.[1] Later the number of presbyters was raised from two to three so that they should be equal in
number to the bishops.

There was also strong opposition to the South India scheme from
Anglo-Catholics in England on other grounds. An open letter from the
Superiors of certain religious communities to the Archbishop of Canterbury expressed the objections shared by many. They believed that the
scheme contained an "explicit and official disclaimer of the full Catholic
intention of episcopacy by those professing to continue it". Consecrations to the episcopate administered in that context would be null and
void by a defect of intention, or at the very least dubious, and, if the
Church of England accepted such consecrations as valid, grave doubts
would be cast on the intention of its own consecrations. They also
objected to the substitution of the word "presbyter" for "priest" in the
scheme, as this seemed to indicate a different concept of the ministry
"from that expressed in the Scriptural Form used in the Anglican rite
for the Ordination of Priests".[2] The Bishop of Bombay, E. J. Palmer,
tried to answer them. Under the scheme bishops would perform their
functions in accordance with the customs of the universal Church; they
would be consecrated by three bishops, and grace would be conferred
on them. Therefore the consecrations would always be performed in
the way that the historic Church had performed them and with the
intention of doing what the Church did. There was nothing wrong
with the word "presbyter"; it was the ancient word, it was still used
by the Roman Church, and it would be used with the same meaning
in the Church of South India. Whether they were called priests or
presbyters, this would not affect the powers which the ministers had.[3]
It can be seen that the main claim of the Anglo-Catholics was that a
difference in the concept of episcopacy and priesthood would affect the
validity of ordinations, a claim which had been made against Anglican
ordinations by Roman Catholics and which had then been vigorously
repudiated by most Anglo-Catholics on the grounds that an inadequate
concept of the ministry could not affect the validity of Orders.

[1] See, for example, B. J. Kidd, "Memorandum on Some Points recently raised by the
South India Scheme", *Theology* xxxi (1935), pp. 76-7.

[2] *The Unity of the Faith. An open Letter to His Grace the Lord Archbishop of Canterbury
from the Superiors of certain religious communities* (1943), pp. 7-9. See also C. D. Horsley,
*Some Problems connected with the proposed Scheme of Church Union in South India* (1942),
pp. 9-13; E. L. Mascall, *Priesthood in South India. A comparison of the proposed Basis of Union
with the reply of the English Archbishops to Pope Leo XIII*, CDCP Pamphlet No. 2 (n.d.).

[3] E. J. Palmer, *South India: The Meaning of the Scheme for Church Union* (1944), pp. 12-19,
20-1.

In spite of opposition the scheme went ahead and union was in-augurated in South India in 1947. There was some pressure to adopt Eastern ordination rites in the united Church, but both J. S. M. Hooper, the Methodist Convener of the committee responsible for drafting the rites, and Noel Hall, the Bishop of Chota Nagpur, opposed this and preferred the Anglican rites as proposed in 1928, although being willing to include other elements in them. Hall himself suggested a litany and concluding prayer and a post-communion collect might be drawn from Eastern sources, and he advocated the restoration of the giving of the pastoral staff from the 1550 Anglican rite for the episcopate. E. C. Ratcliff, the Anglican liturgical scholar, who was consulted by Bishop Hall, suggested that the giving of the staff might come after the Eucharist and so avoid the appearance of being an essential ceremony. He proposed as the accompanying formula part of verse 2 of Psalm 110: "The Lord send the rod of thy strength out of Sion".[1] The ordination services finally adopted were simply variations of the proposed 1928 English rites. The Preface was omitted and the rite for the episcopate differed from the English version in that the presentation was by pres-byters who also joined in the imposition of hands, the reading of the instrument of election and the Assent to the Basis of Union and the Con-stitution of the Church replaced the reading of the mandate for conse-cration and the Oath of Obedience, a litany adapted from the Eastern Orthodox Church replaced the Anglican one, and a period of silent prayer was included before the hymn, "Come Holy Ghost", as in the Anglican rite for the priesthood. Other differences included the substitution of the example of the appointment of Matthias for the setting apart of Paul and Barnabas in the bidding, as in the American Ordinal, the inclusion of the phrase, "to offer unto thee sacrifices of praise and thanksgiving", in the prayer before the imposition of hands, and modifications in the examination. The ceremonies around the imposition of hands were also modified. Only the first part of the Anglican formula was said during the imposition of hands and the second part was transferred to the delivery of the Bible and added to the beginning of the Anglican formula at this action. This formula too was divided in the middle, and the delivery of the pastoral staff accom-panied the second half, as it had in the 1550 Anglican rite.

[1] Letter from J. S. M. Hooper to Noel Hall, 28.12.46; Noel Hall's Memorandum "An Ordinal for the United Church of South India" (n.d.); letter from Hall to Hooper, 20.2.47; letter from E. C. Ratcliff to Hall (n.d.); letter from Hooper to all members of the committee for preparing orders of service for Inauguration and Consecration, 6.3.47 (all from the Archives of United Theological College, Bangalore).

The rites for the presbyterate and diaconate differed from the English versions in several ways. The sermon, which was to be preceded by prayer, could be either at the beginning, or after the litany, or after the Creed. The presentation was preceded by a prayer and included the reading of the authorization of the diocesan council and of the candidates' names. The litany, which was the same as that in the rite for the episcopate, was preceded by a bidding and a period of silent prayer, the bidding being composed of the words of commendation from the English rite followed, in the case of the presbyterate, by the bidding from the rite for the episcopate, this time with the setting apart of Paul and Barnabas retained in it, and, in the case of the diaconate, by a similar bidding which cited the example of the Apostles praying before they laid hands on the first deacons. The collect, which followed the litany, had inserted into it the petition, "and fill them with the power of Thy spirit", and the ceremony of the giving of the right hand of fellowship was included after the ordination. In the rite for the presbyterate the bishop's exhortation to the candidates was much abbreviated, and modifications were made in the examination; many questions were slightly altered and three more were added, on belief in the doctrine of the Church of South India and determination to preach the same, on building up the body of Christ, and on stirring up the gift of God to testify the gospel, the last two being drawn from the Methodist ordination rite. The examination in the rite for the diaconate was also slightly modified, the most significant change being the inclusion of preaching as one of the normal duties of the office. Very small alterations were made in the wording of the prayer before the imposition of hands in both rites, and changes were made in the readings; in the rite for the diaconate the alternative Epistle from 1 Timothy was omitted and in the rite for the presbyterate the Gospel was John 20.19–23 and not one of those appointed in the Anglican rite. The formula at the imposition of hands in the rite for the presbyterate was also altered, "presbyter" replacing "priest", "Spirit" replacing "Ghost", and the clause referring to the remitting and retaining of sins being omitted.[1]

Since these rites were so closely modelled on the Anglican ones, no doubts have been felt by Anglicans as to the sufficiency of matter and form, although at least one Anglo-Catholic was concerned about the

[1] *Order of Service for the Inauguration of Church Union in South India with The form of Consecrating the first new bishops and the Order of Service for the Ordination of Presbyters* (1947), pp. 8–24. *Order of Service for the Making of Deacons* (privately printed, Bangalore 1947).

omission of the clause referring to the remitting and retaining of sins, claiming that while it did not necessarily affect the validity of the ordination, it compromised the doctrinal orthodoxy of the united Church. Had it never been introduced into ordination, its absence would not have been a matter for concern, but its omission implied not merely a change of emphasis but a change in doctrine.[1] This was precisely the argument used by Roman Catholics concerning the omission from the Anglican Ordinal of the *porrectio instrumentorum* and the sacrificial language of the Pontificals, and rejected in that case by Anglicans. The writer also seemed to be unaware that the American rite permitted the omission of the whole of this formula; did that indicate a change of doctrine too?

A committee of theologians appointed by the Archbishop of Canterbury to consider the South India scheme in 1946 had been of the opinion that "the Scheme and the intentions of the Church provide adequately for the continuance and carrying on of the Episcopate as the Anglican Communion has received it", and it felt that, in view of the requirement that consecrations must be by at least three bishops and the possibility that a diocesan council could decide that only bishops were to lay on hands, "the holding of the theory that the participation of presbyters in the laying on of hands at an episcopal consecration is an essential of the rite is precluded", and the sufficiency of the ordinations could not be challenged because of this practice.[2] Others, however, were less satisfied about the sufficiency of intention because of doubts about the catholicity of faith and practice in the Church. A minority of the committee on the unity of the Church at the 1948 Lambeth Conference felt it was too early to make a judgement on this, as did a report of joint committees of the Convocations of Canterbury and York appointed to consider the validity of the ordinations in 1950, which proposed that a decision be postponed for five years.[3] The joint committees appointed five years later were unanimous in holding that the intention was sufficient, in spite of the acceptance of non-episcopally ordained ministers in the Church.[4] In

[1] B. P. Burnett, *What They Didn't Say*, CDCP Leaflet No. 12 (n.d.), p. 5.
[2] *The South India Church Scheme, being the Report of a Committee of Theologians appointed by the Archbishop of Canterbury to consider the proposed Basis of Union and Constitution of the future Church of South India* (1946), pp. 25–6.
[3] *The Lambeth Conference 1948* (1948), pt. II, pp. 47–8; *The Church of South India, being the United Report of the Joint Committees of the Convocations of Canterbury and York* (1950).
[4] *The Church of South India, being the United Report of the two Joint Committees of the Convocations* (1955), pp. 11–14.

seconding the presentation of this report to a Full Synod of the Canterbury Convocation, Canon E. W. Kemp said that, as Anglicans were accustomed to claim that the intention to continue the ministry instituted by Christ was all that was necessary in defending their orders against Roman Catholics, they could not require more in this case. The Church of South India might consider adopting a Preface like the Anglican one to state its intention clearly, but even without this the intention was clear. The substitution of "presbyter" for "priest" did not affect the validity, since the functions of the office remained the same, nor could the validity of the first consecrations be questioned because they were *per saltum* or because the candidates had not been confirmed, since the same had been true of the Scottish consecrations in 1610.[1] The Convocations agreed to accept the validity of South Indian ordinations, and several other provinces of the Anglican Communion have done the same.[2]

The Convocations' decision caused concern to many Anglo-Catholics who felt that it was a betrayal of the Catholic position of the Church of England, and so Dr E. L. Mascall, who had been a staunch opponent of the South India scheme, published a statement explaining why he could now accept and support this decision: in spite of the faults in the scheme, there could be no doubt that the ordinations were valid, since very little was required for an adequate intention in a sacrament, as Rome herself recognized, except when she was dealing with Anglican Orders, and he referred to the case of the Methodist baptisms in Oceania to illustrate this.[3] He elaborated his views in a letter to the *Church Times*: only a minister could have an intention, not the rite itself, which could only make it clear by its wording and setting what was being done. Therefore the so-called "intention of the Ordinal" need only identify what was happening, and did not have to be an accurate theological statement about the nature of ordination. This the South Indian rites did. Nor was there any such thing as the intention of the Church of South India, or of the Church of England for that matter, which was distinct from the intention of the Church Catholic. The deficiency of intention in the Oceania case was far greater than anything the Church of South India could be accused of, and it made no difference that ordination had not a dominically instituted form.[4] This

---

[1] *Chronicle of Convocation* (1955), pp. 25–9.

[2] Ibid. (1955), pp. 50–1, 87–92; *The Lambeth Conference 1958*, 2, pp. 25–8.

[3] E. L. Mascall, *The Convocations and South India* (1955), pp. 7–12. For Oceania see above, pp. 153ff.

[4] *Church Times*, 28 October 1955.

provoked a reply from the Roman Catholic, A. A. Stephenson. Following his earlier thesis that the main charge against Anglican Orders referred to a defect of form and not intention,[1] he asserted that the Oceania baptisms were valid because the form had been kept and Anglican ordinations were invalid because it had not. The Anglicans had changed the meaning of the words "priest" and "bishop" in their rites, so that neither the Anglican nor the South Indian Ordinal had the Catholic meaning and were therefore invalid; the Oceania baptisms were valid because "baptism" could have only one meaning. He disagreed with Mascall that a form need only identify what was happening; it was the precise meaning of the words which determined validity.[2]

The South Indian ordination rites became the pattern for other schemes of union. The scheme for union in Ceylon proposed an Ordinal which was simply a variation of the South Indian.[3] It differed from it, however, in that it restored the ancient order, with the rite for the episcopate coming first, followed by the presbyterate and diaconate, and it prefaced the rites with a statement of intention: "In the forms and ceremonies set forth in this Ordinal, the Church of Lanka makes provision for the continuation of the Sacred Ministry which is God's gift to His Church, and for doing what the Church does in the ordering of Bishops, Presbyters and Deacons." The main differences from the South Indian rite in the service for the episcopate were that the presentation and imposition of hands were to be by bishops alone, the formulas at the imposition of hands and the delivery of the Bible were divided as in the Anglican Ordinal, the words "from God" were inserted after "Holy Spirit" in the former, and a bidding taken from Eastern Orthodox rites was inserted before the period of silent prayer: "The grace divine, which healeth that which is infirm, and completeth that which is wanting, hath chosen N. to be bishop: wherefore let us pray for him, that the grace of the all-Holy Spirit may come upon him". A similar bidding was included in the rite for the presbyterate, and the addition of the words "from God" was also made in the imperative formula. Other differences from South India in this rite included a different final collect, the sermon being placed in its normal position in the Communion service, and an additional phrase, "to fulfil the ministry of reconciliation", being inserted in the formula at the delivery of

---

[1] See above, p. 154.
[2] A. A. Stephenson, "Oceania and Identifiability", *The Month* XIV (1955), pp. 354–64. See also Mascall's reply, "The Hunting of the Hobbit", ibid. xv (1956), pp. 87–94, and Stephenson's rejoinder, "In full Cry", ibid. xv, pp. 94–104.
[3] *Proposed Scheme of Church Union in Ceylon* (3rd edn, Madras 1955), pp. 77–105.

the Bible. An Eastern type of bidding was also introduced into the rite for the diaconate at the end of the examination, which resulted in the absurdity of two biddings in succession, since this rite already had the bidding from the 1928 English rite at this point. The Joint Committees of the Convocations of Canterbury and York in their report on the scheme in 1961 warmly approved of this Ordinal, although some had felt a difficulty about the use of the word "presbyter" instead of "priest", and thought that the arrangements for the consecration of new bishops at the inauguration of the union would ensure that the Church would have a validly consecrated episcopate.[1]

The first draft of the rite for the consecration of the new bishops in the scheme of union in North India and Pakistan, which appeared in 1955, also copied the South India rite closely. The main differences were that it came after the Prayer for the Church in the Communion service, a period of silent prayer replaced the litany, the bidding before this contained neither the example of the appointment of Matthias nor the example of the setting apart of Paul and Barnabas, the formula at the giving of the staff was slightly altered, and the final collect was omitted.[2] When work began on drawing up a rite for the presbyterate, however, it was decided to adopt features from the ordination rite of the Church of Scotland into the basic structure of the South Indian rite. Meanwhile, in South India itself work had begun on a revision of their ordination rites. C. B. Firth, one of the members of the Liturgy Committee, who undertook a preliminary survey of the services, felt that it was not possible to adapt an Eastern rite without impairing its validity in Eastern eyes, and if the imposition of hands took place during the ordination prayer, then people would be unable to see the most important part of the service. He therefore suggested that they were committed to their present services—a simplified and reformed version of the Western medieval rite—with changes only in minor details, such as a shortening of the questions and of the bishop's exhortation, and the inclusion of a more definite reference to the Holy Spirit in the rites for the presbyterate and episcopate. On the other hand, J. E. L. Newbigin, the ex-Presbyterian Bishop of Madura and Ramnad, as a result of reading the article on the Ordinal in *Liturgy and Worship*, questioned the Western medieval rite and asked whether they ought not to

---

[1] *The Church of Lanka, being the Schedule attached to the Reports of the Joint Committees of the Convocations of Canterbury and York* (1961), pp. 14–15.

[2] *Suggested Services for use at the proposed Inauguration of the Church of North India and Pakistan* (Madras 1955), pp. 15–21.

return to the primitive tradition, still observed in the reformed Churches, in which the act of ordination was a prayer and not an act preceded by prayer.[1] The first draft of a revision of the rites for the diaconate and presbyterate was very conservative, the *Sursum corda* and eucharistic preface being omitted from both, and in the latter the bishop's exhortation being omitted and the formula at the imposition of hands changed from imperative to precatory. It was also intended to shorten the services and simplify the language.[2] It was criticized, however, for not being radical enough and was subjected to further consideration.

At this time it happened that a member of the South India Liturgy Committee staying in North India was invited to join the committee drafting the rite for the presbyterate there. He returned to South India with this preliminary draft and it was accepted as the basis for the new South Indian Ordinal, it being decided to draw up services for the diaconate and episcopate on the same lines.[3] As the work of revision proceeded, several amendments suggested in South India were also adopted by the North Indian committee, with the result that the two rites for the presbyterate are very similar in structure, as can be seen from Table 5.[4] Elements drawn from the original South Indian rite are indicated by capital letters. The Scottish Ordinal was the source for the address to the candidates before the examination, some of the questions in the examination, the ordination prayer with the imposition of hands during its central petition, and the declaration that the candidates are ordained. It is customary to ordain only one candidate at a time in the Church of Scotland, so a novel expedient is employed in these rites when there are several candidates. The complete prayer is not repeated for each but instead the prayer is recited once and, when the central petition is reached, that is repeated for each ordinand while hands are laid on him. In the South Indian rite the people reply "Amen" each time this petition is read.

It must not be thought that the rites are identical in the parts they have in common. The North Indian rite is much closer to the original sources in wording whereas the South Indian has been thoroughly

[1] Circular of Synod Liturgy Committee of Church of South India, 25 August 1955.
[2] Minutes of Meeting of Church of South India Liturgy Committee on 9, 10, 12 September 1955.
[3] T. S. Garrett, *Worship in the Church of South India* (2nd edn, 1965), pp. 78–9.
[4] *Services Proposed for use at the Inauguration of the Church of North India and the Church of Pakistan and the service for the ordination of presbyters in these united Churches* (rev. edn, Madras 1957), pp. 17–24; *Church of South India, The Ordinal* (1958). See also T. S. Garrett, "The Ordinal of the Church of South India", *Scottish Journal of Theology* XII (1959), pp. 400–13.

## Table 5

| North India Rite for Presbyters (1957) | South India Rite for Presbyters (1958) |
|---|---|

EUCHARIST BEGINS

PRESENTATION BY

| | |
|---|---|
| A PRESBYTER; a layman may be associated with him.<br>NAMES OF CANDIDATES ARE READ ALOUD | "a person duly appointed" |

AUTHORIZATION OF THE DIOCESE
FOR THE ORDINATION IS READ ALOUD

FINAL INQUIRY OF THE PEOPLE

Acclamation by the people: "They are worthy"

| | |
|---|---|
| Bidding<br>SILENT PRAYER<br>LITANY WITH SPECIAL SUFFRAGE<br>or alternative prayer<br>or extempore prayer | Salutation |

COLLECT

| | |
|---|---|
| Old Testament lesson: Num. 11.16, 23–9; Isa. 61.1–6; or Ezek. 33.1–9<br>A hymn or a psalm<br>EPISTLE: EPHESIANS 4.7–13 or 1 Pet. 5.1–4 | Old Testament lesson: Ezek. 33.1–9<br><br>A hymn or Ps. 99<br>Epistle: 1 Pet. 5.1–11 |

Gospel: John 10.1–16
SERMON

| | |
|---|---|
| | Creed<br>Hymn |

Short Address

EXAMINATION AND CONCLUDING PRAYER

SILENT PRAYER

"COME HOLY GHOST"

Ordination prayer with imposition
of hands during the central petition

"Send down thy Holy Spirit upon thy servant . . ., whom we, in thy name, and in obedience to thy most blessed will, do now ordain Presbyter in thy Church, committing unto him authority to minister thy word and sacraments, to declare thy forgiveness to penitent sinners, and to shepherd thy flock."

DELIVERY OF BIBLE with formula
GIVING OF RIGHT HAND OF FELLOWSHIP

Declaration that candidates are ordained
Reply: "Amen. Thanks be to God."

| | |
|---|---|
| CREED | Doxology |

EUCHARIST CONTINUES, with petitions in the intercession
for candidates, their wives, and homes.

| | |
|---|---|
| | Proper Preface in Prayer of Consecration. |

revised. The South Indian version is the better of the two, not only because it avoids the double prayer of the people which has been a persistent feature of modern Anglican revisions and those rites derived from them, but also because being more extensively revised it has a much more polished and unified appearance. The rites for the diaconate and episcopate drawn up at the same time in South India follow the pattern set by this rite very closely, being for the most part identical but for the name of the office. This means that all three ordinations take place after the Creed, a change from the traditional Western pattern, that the hymn, "Come Holy Ghost", is introduced into the rite for the diaconate for the first time, and that the distinctive *porrectio instrumentorum* of each rite disappears, although the formulas at the giving of the Bible in each case are different and indicate the particular functions of the office, being based upon the formulas in the earlier rites but amended so as to make it clear that the ceremony does not bestow anything but is only symbolic of something already given. On the other hand, the approval of the people is restored to the rite for the episcopate. Each rite has its own proper lesson, psalm, Epistle, and Gospel,[1] questions in the examination relating to its particular functions, and its own ordination prayer, although they all follow the same basic structure, and those for the presbyterate and episcopate are closely related in wording. The central petition is the same in each case, except for the name of the office and for the omission from the other two rites of the phrase, "committing . . . flock", in the rite for the presbyterate. The rite for the episcopate further differs in that the presentation is by two presbyters, the instrument of election and appointment is read instead of the authorization of the diocese, and the ceremony of the giving of the pastoral staff from the earlier Ordinal is retained. The rite for the diaconate has no address before the examination but instead a statement of the duties of the office, and has a Proper Preface in the Eucharist different from the other two rites.

The Ordinal begins with a Preface which states the Church's understanding of ordination and ministry, and then goes on to say that according to the earliest record of ordination (Acts 6.1–6—the appointment of the Seven) there are three essential parts—election by the people, prayer, and the laying on of apostolic hands—and these form the basis of this Ordinal, the presentation of the candidates representing the last step in the process of their choice by the Church. All

[1] For the diaconate: Isa. 42.1–9; Ps. 84; 1 Tim. 3.8–13; Luke 12.35–8. For the episcopate: Ezek. 34.11–16; Ps. 119.105–12; Acts 20.28–35; John 20.19–23.

other ceremonies, "however valuable for their symbolism, are not essential elements in the rites of ordination". The North Indian rite has a similar Preface, which also includes the statement that no fewer than two presbyters are to lay their hands on the candidates with the bishop. The South Indian Ordinal is preceded by a number of directions: the ordination of deacons and presbyters should ordinarily take place at separate services, but instructions are included for use if it is thought necessary to ordain them together; when an ordination is in an Indian language, an Indian hymn for the coming of the Holy Spirit is to replace "Come Holy Ghost"; other lessons may be chosen instead of those prescribed; finally, a novel feature, the wife of a newly ordained minister is to receive Communion with her husband at the ordination.

North India also slightly modified its rite for the episcopate at the same time. The South Indian collect was adopted and the presentation, the reading of the instrument of election, and the assent of the candidate to the constitution now came between the Epistle (Acts 20.17–35) and the Gospel (John 21.15–17). Before the examination the presiding bishop presented the candidate to the people, who declared their assent to the consecration with the words, "Amen, Thanks be to God". A central petition similar to that adopted in South India was inserted into the ordination prayer and the imposition of hands took place then and not afterwards, the formula originally accompanying it being omitted. The declaration, the petitions in the intercession, and the Proper Preface from the rite for the presbyterate were suitable modified and included. In 1960 the rite was revised and the whole ceremony came after the Creed. The South India Ordinal has also undergone one further revision in 1962 and a number of small changes were made. The phrase "with all thy people" was inserted into the ordination prayer in the rites for the presbyterate and episcopate in a reference to the function of offering spiritual sacrifices, presumably to emphasize the priesthood of all believers; the number of presbyters presenting a candidate for the episcopate and laying hands on him was raised from two to three so that they were numerically equal to the bishops; and a small alteration was made in the wording at the delivery of the pastoral staff. The main change, however, was in the final inquiry in all three rites. This no longer asked for objections but, because ill-disposed persons had actually raised objections at one episcopal consecration,[1] the people were simply asked to declare their assent. Directions were included that notice of ordinations was to be given in the church in which the service

[1] Garrett, *Worship in the Church of South India*, p. 77.

was to be held and in the churches in which the candidates were best known and objections made beforehand in writing; the congregations were also to be asked to pray for the candidates.

The South India Ordinal has received wide approval. Professor E. C. Ratcliff commended the rites as resembling the simplicity of the primitive rites and suggested that they might provide a model for any province of the Anglican Communion desiring to revise its Ordinal. He did not think that the participation of presbyters in the imposition of hands at an episcopal consecration was sufficient to nullify the act, as the Ordinal nowhere suggested that they might entirely replace the bishops, nor did it, directly or indirectly, assign to them the function of consecrating, and the Preface explicitly stated that only three bishops were needed for a valid consecration. The practice, he suggested, might be seen as a symbol of the essential unity of character between episcopal and presbyteral ministries.[1]

The South India Ordinal has become a model for the ordination rites in all recent reunion schemes. The scheme of union in Nigeria adopted an Ordinal based very closely upon it, but introducing a number of verbal improvements and a new ordination prayer for deacons. It also added a presentation of a chalice and paten as well as the Bible in the rite for presbyters. This was done without any intention of imitating Roman Catholic practice; the proposer of the idea was unaware of its existence in that Church.[2] The South India Ordinal was also the model on which the proposed Anglican–Methodist Ordinal in England was based. From the beginning of this movement towards unity the drawing up of a common Ordinal was recommended in order to remove ground for suspicion and criticism of Methodist practice and belief in ordination, and draft rites were included in the interim report of the Unity Commission in 1967. A Preface was included, very different from that in the Anglican Ordinal and showing some resemblance to that in the South Indian Ordinal. It made no claims as to the origin of the threefold ministry, merely saying that it had come down from early times. It also stated what was to be done when deacons and presbyters were ordained at the same time. The use of the term presbyter was defended in an introduction to the draft Ordinal in the report; it was ancient, it had wide ecumenical usage, and the word "priest"

[1] E. C. Ratcliff, "The Ordinal of the Church of South India", *Theology* LXIII (1960), pp. 7-15.
[2] T. S. Garrett, "Products of Nigeria's Liturgy Committee", *Studia Liturgica* v (1966), p. 183.

had overtones which made it unacceptable to many Protestants. The words, "also called priests", were, however, retained in the title of "The Ordination of Presbyters", legislation was to be introduced which would state that no change in doctrine was intended, and the draft Canons C.1–4 of the Church of England were attached to the Ordinal as a statement of Anglican discipline and belief in ordination, since they revised and expanded the Preface to the Anglican Ordinal. The rites differed from the South India Ordinal in that the whole of the ordination, including the presentation, took place after the Creed. The collect, which was the same in all three rites, was a version of the collect in the primitive Roman rite for the episcopate. The readings also differed from those appointed in the South India rite.[1] The reading of the candidates' names was substituted for the reading of the authorization in the rites for the diaconate and presbyterate. The rest of the rites followed the pattern of the South India rites, with minor modifications in wording, much alteration in the examination, and the inclusion of a fixed bidding before the period of silent prayer, that in the rite for the episcopate being the bidding from the Anglican rite for the episcopate. Two alternative versions of *Veni Creator* were included, and the central petitions in the ordination prayers differed very slightly from those in South India.[2] In the rite for the episcopate this petition was said by all the bishops, and presbyters were not to be involved in the imposition of hands. The ceremony of the giving of the right hand of fellowship, the declaration, doxology, petitions in the intercession, and Proper Prefaces of the South India rite were not adopted, but a new post-communion collect, identical for all three rites, was included. In addition, a shortened and revised version of the exhortation to priests from the Anglican Ordinal was included before the examination in the rite for presbyters, and there was no delivery of the pastoral staff in the rite for bishops. Rubrics directed that it was desirable that the newly ordained presbyters should concelebrate with the bishop, and that a newly consecrated bishop was to concelebrate with the presiding bishop. An appendix contained a hymn for use at ordinations, taken from the Methodist Ordinal.[3]

[1] For the diaconate: Rom. 12.1–12 and Mark 10.35–45; for the presbyterate: Rom. 12.1–12 and John 20.19–29; for the episcopate: 2 Tim. 4.1–5 and John 21.15–17. No Old Testament lessons or proper psalms were appointed.

[2] "Send down thy Holy Spirit upon thy servant N. whom thou hast called to serve thee as a Deacon in thy Church." "Send thy Holy Spirit upon thy servant N. whom thou hast called to be a Presbyter in thy Church." "Pour forth thy Holy Spirit upon thy servant N. whom thou hast chosen to be a Bishop and Chief Pastor in thy Church."

[3] *Towards Reconciliation, the Interim Statement of the Anglican–Methodist Unity Commission* (1967), pp. 51–75.

In the final report which appeared the following year the Ordinal was considerably revised in the light of comments which had been made about it. The Preface was expanded to include a fuller statement on the ministry. The acclamation of the people was revised so as to make it clearer in what sense the candidates were declared to be worthy, and language closer to the South India rites was used. A further question on evangelism was included in the examination because of criticism that the earlier examination was too domestic in character. A collect, identical in all three rites, was inserted before the hymn to sum up the silent prayers of the people, following the ancient Roman practice. Minor changes in wording were made in many parts of the rites, particularly in the ordination prayers, and a more explicit reference to the celebration of the Eucharist was made in the prayers in the rites for presbyters and bishops, in the light of comments made by Roman Catholic scholars. The central petition in all three prayers was revised: "Send down thy Holy Spirit upon thy servant N. for the office and work of a Deacon in thy Church/ for the office and work of a Presbyter in thy Church/ for the office of a Bishop and Chief Pastor in thy Church". The rubrics now directed that newly ordained deacons were to assist, with any other deacons present, in the preparation of the bread and wine and in distributing it to the people at the Eucharist, and at the consecration of a bishop all bishops present were to concelebrate. A change was also made in the formula at the giving of the Bible in the rite for presbyters, so as to include a reminder of the commission to the Apostles in John 20.21–3, since this was no longer said at the imposition of hands. A Latin version of the Preface, for the benefit of scholars whose mother tongue was not English, and a commentary were included with the Ordinal. The commentary sought to justify the position of the rites in the Eucharist, and the absence of different collects for each rite and of a different *porrectio instrumentorum* for each order, on the grounds of simplicity. It was felt that this factor outweighed symbolism, which had been reduced to a minimum in order that the central features might stand out more clearly.[1]

This Ordinal has met with praise and approval both within and outside the Anglican Communion, both as a liturgical composition and as a statement of the doctrine of the ministry. One Roman Catholic, in expressing his approval, suggested that it might be used by Roman Catholics in England as a step to further the cause of unity. He had,

---

[1] *Anglican–Methodist Unity, 1. The Ordinal* (1968).

however, a few minor criticisms, especially of the rite for the diaconate which saw the office principally in its liturgical and sacramental functions and not in its ministry of service; this had been the cause of its decline in the West.[1] The Ordinal has not altogether escaped criticism from Anglicans, however. The use of the term presbyter has met with much opposition, because it has seemed to some Anglo-Catholics to imply a change in the doctrine of the priesthood. For the same reason the omission of the imperative commission to remit and retain sins was also criticized. It was argued that the phrase in the new ordination prayer, "to declare to the penitent the absolution and remission of their sins", did not have the same meaning, and the omission of the formula would be taken by many to have some significance with regard to the doctrine of the Church of England.[2] Canon Lindsay Dewar argued that the new Ordinal, when used in the Methodist Church, would be invalid through a defect of intention, although it would be valid when used by Anglicans. This would be the case because the Methodist Deed of Union rejected the sort of priesthood in which Anglicans believed and therefore Methodists did not intend to ordain men to the true priesthood. He also criticized the Preface for being ambiguous and so allowing the Ordinal to be interpreted in this way.[3] The historian, Professor Margaret Deanesly, also claimed that the omission of the clause requiring episcopal ordination in the Preface of the Anglican Ordinal demonstrated a change in intention, but she rather marred her argument by her assumption that the clause had been present in the Elizabethan Ordinal.[4] To this Dr G. G. Willis, the Anglican scholar, added a number of liturgical criticisms of the new rites. In addition to objecting to the word "presbyter" and the absence of the imperative commission to forgive sins, he disliked the retention of features which were of comparatively late introduction, such as the examination and the exhortation to the candidates for the presbyterate, while more primitive elements, such as the litany and the practice of a newly ordained deacon reading the Gospel, were omitted. The later hymn, "Come Holy Ghost", was not only retained but added to the rite for the diaconate. He would also have preferred that the *porrectio instrumentorum* should have been abolished entirely or that something distinctive of the func-

[1] "More about Anglican Orders", *Herder Correspondence* v (1968), pp. 122–3.
[2] *The Unity of the Faith* (1967), pp. 9–12; F. H. Mountney, "*No Priest, No Church*" (1968), esp. pp. 35–47.
[3] Lindsay Dewar, *The New Ordinal: Valid or Invalid?* (n.p., n.d.).
[4] Margaret Deanesly and G. G. Willis, *Anglican–Methodist Unity: Some considerations historical and liturgical* (1968), pp. 11ff.

tions of the particular order should have been given. He disliked the collect, since it had no obvious connection with ordination, except to those who knew its origin, and also the post-communion prayer, because the phrase in it, "whom thou hast made thy Ministers this day", was really applicable only to deacons and not to the other orders.[1]

Attempts were made to answer some of these criticisms. Canon E. W. Kemp, chairman of the committee which drew up the Ordinal, argued that no change in doctrine was intended, that members of the Oxford Movement had been happy to call themselves presbyters, that the word was used in the Roman Catholic Church, and in the Episcopal Church of Scotland, and that the Ordinal itself, which would be the official interpretation of the beliefs of the Methodist and Anglican Churches, clearly stated a doctrine of ministry and priesthood which was sound and catholic, and the welcome given to it by Roman Catholic theologians was additional evidence of its soundness.[2] Dr R. C. Mortimer, Bishop of Exeter, also denied Lindsay Dewar's claim that the Methodist doctrine of ordination was radically different from the Anglican, and Prebendary G. B. Timms followed this up by pointing out that the Deed of Union was as much an embarrassment to many Methodists as the Thirty-nine Articles were to Anglicans, and that the commission to forgive sins, to which Dewar and others clung, had now been entirely omitted from the new Roman Catholic Ordinal, and the power was not even mentioned in the ordination prayer, as it was in this rite.[3] Such defences of an adequate intention in the Methodists, however, were really not required, as in the Anglican Orders controversy almost every Anglican had argued that it was not necessary to have an accurate understanding or interpretation of priesthood for a valid ordination. It was not really possible, therefore, to raise this objection against Methodist ordinations.

It is impossible to close this chapter without some reference to the draft Ordinal produced by the Episcopal Church in America in 1970.[4] Although not intended for a united Church, it is derived from the South India rites, and therefore is logically to be considered here. It follows the basic structure of the South India rites, but with many minor,

---

[1] Ibid., pp. 72–87.
[2] E. W. Kemp, *The Anglican–Methodist Unity Scheme* (n.p., n.d.), pp. 7–9; *The Anglican–Methodist Unity Conference 1968, Report of Proceedings* (1968), pp. 10–12.
[3] *Chronicle of Convocation* (1969), pp. 147–55.
[4] *The Ordination of Bishops, Priests, and Deacons, Prayer Book Studies 20* (New York 1970).

and sometimes adventurous, modifications. It is an improvement on other modern Ordinals in clarity of layout, in the use of more modern language, and in the restoration of the ancient order of the rites, placing that for the episcopate first. It is marred, however, by the fact that it retains the fault of the double prayer of the people, a litany before the ministry of the Word, and a period of silent prayer between the hymn and the ordination prayer in all three rites. It is arranged for one ordinand, although provision is made for occasions when there are several, and in the rite for the episcopate priests do not join in the imposition of hands and the central petition in the ordination prayer is said by all the bishops, as it is in the Anglican–Methodist rite. There is no use of the term "presbyter", no Preface, and it is accompanied by an excellent introduction. Other points worthy of note are that the prayer for bishops is a free translation of the prayer from the *Apostolic Tradition* and not a version of the South India prayer, the giving of the *Pax* is allotted a prominent place, as it had in the early rites, and, because the rites are intended for experimental use, considerable freedom is allowed in various parts, especially in the choice of readings and in the giving of instruments of office. It is in many ways superior to the Anglican–Methodist Ordinal and represents an important advance in the revision of ordination rites.

# 12. The Ordinal and Reunion
## (2) Unification Rites

Any suggestion of their accepting episcopal ordination as a method of unification has been consistently rejected by Free Church ministers, and yet it has quite frequently been suggested by Anglicans, usually under the proposal that each Church should do to the ministers of the other Churches what it would do if those ministers were seeking admission to its ministry. This proposal was first made by the Lambeth Conference of 1920 and has been repeated at intervals since.[1] The Free Churches have seen it as a denial of their former ordination, in spite of the claim made by the Lambeth Conference of 1920 that it was not a repudiation of their past ministry by either side: "We shall be publicly and formally seeking additional recognition of a new call to wider service in a reunited Church, and imploring for ourselves God's grace and strength to fulfil the same." Similarly, suggestions that Free Church ministers should undergo conditional episcopal ordination have also been rejected by them as casting doubts on their former ordinations.[2]

One solution to the problem has been that adopted ultimately in South India—to dispense entirely with any sort of unification rite and to accept Free Church and Anglican ministries as equal, but to limit this by a pledge that no former Free Church minister would be forced upon a congregation which refused to accept him as sufficiently ordained. At the same time new bishops have been consecrated within the historic succession and all ordinations within the united Church will be episcopal so that it is hoped that eventually the pledge will be rendered unnecessary as all ministers will be episcopally ordained. This method has its attractions. It is similar to the growth towards episcopal ordination initiated in Scotland in 1610, and it avoids the

---

[1] Bell, *Documents on Christian Unity, 1920–4*, pp. 4–5; F. De Witt Batty, *The Australian Proposals for Intercommunion* (1948), pp. 23–36; *The Plan of Church Union in North India and Pakistan, a memorandum by the Theological Committee of the Church Union* (1957), pp. 7–10; E. L. Mascall, "Unity and Unification: A Constructive Proposal", *Theology* LXV (1962), pp. 12–15.

[2] Bell, *Documents* (2nd Series), pp. 83–6.

ambiguity inherent in most other methods of unification. On the other hand, it also has drawbacks. Although the scheme claims to recognize the equality of episcopal and non-episcopal ministries, the operation of the pledge in some areas is a denial of this and a retention of two classes of ministers—those who are acceptable to all and those who are not. From the first many Anglo-Catholics felt that the scheme, in recognizing the equality of all ministries, was sacrificing vital Catholic principles,[1] and the report of the committee on the Unity of the Church at the 1948 Lambeth Conference felt obliged to express doubts about the South India method and suggest that "the unification of the ministry in a form satisfactory to all the bodies concerned, at the inauguration of the union or as soon as possible thereafter, is likely to be a prerequisite to success in all future proposals designed to secure the reunion of the Churches". This was endorsed by the Lower House of the Canterbury Convocation in 1955.[2] Thus at least since then Anglicans have been more or less committed to demanding some rite to secure unification at the outset of a reunion scheme rather than a "growth into unity" method.

It has become clear, therefore, in most negotiations towards unity that some new method or rite is needed, something which is not explicitly an ordination rite, for that would be rejected by the Free Churches, and yet something which will suffice as the equivalent of episcopal ordination, if it is to be acceptable to many Anglicans. At first some sort of commissioning of Free Church ministers or mutual commissioning by Anglicans and Free Church ministers was proposed. A mutual commissioning was suggested early in the South India negotiations. It was to consist of a declaration read by all ministers that it was not a repudiation of past ministries but the recognition of a new call, and an imposition of hands accompanied by a prayer, which was to be the same for both groups. In spite of the declaration that it was not reordination, the prayer proposed was clearly an ordination prayer:

We pray Thee, O God, to anoint with Thy Holy Spirit these Thy servants that they may faithfully perform the work of a presbyter in Thy Church, and especially in those parts of it which are now entering into closer fellowship in accordance with the prayer of Thy Son that they all may be one. May the grace of Him who in sending forth His Apostles said, "As the Father

[1] *The Proposed Scheme of Union in South India, An Opinion by Charles Gore and others* (1929), pp. 5–6; *South India Reunion Scheme, A Statement of the Catholic Advisory Council* (n.p., n.d.); J. C. Williams, *A Voice from India*, CDCP Pamphlet No. 3 (n.d.), pp. 1–6.
[2] *The Lambeth Conference 1948*, pt. II, p. 63; *Chronicle of Convocation* (1955), pp. 383–6.

hath sent me even so send I you", be ever present with them, and may the gift of love now and ever illumine their lives, and may they faithfully preach Thy Word and dispense Thy Sacraments in the larger sphere now opened to them by our union in Thee.[1]

Strangely enough the South India United Church found this satisfactory, and it was on the Anglican side that doubts were expressed about its sufficiency. Bishop Palmer saw the service as a camouflage of the truth and would have preferred some ceremony "which will express the addition to every minister of anything that the members of the other uniting church think to be lacking in his ministry". Anglicans in England were also concerned. Professor C. H. Turner of Oxford was opposed to the use of the same prayer by both groups with each interpreting it in a different sense and using it with a different intention, and he wanted distinct rites for each group which would be "sufficient from its own point of view, to convey whatever seems to it lacking in the previous commission or ordination already possessed by the other". Archbishop Lang of York felt that a mutual commission did not seem to recognize the Anglican belief that the non-episcopal ministry had any defect.[2]

Because of such opposition the idea was abandoned in South India, but rites of commissioning were proposed elsewhere. The Anglican delegates to a Joint Conference with representatives of the Free Churches in England in 1925 suggested that Free Church ministers might be made acceptable to Anglicans by a solemn authorization accompanied by the imposition of hands from a bishop, prefaced by explanatory words, prayer, and the invocation of the Holy Spirit, and expressed by a formula such as:

Take thou Authority, now committed unto thee by the imposition of our hands, for the office and work of a Priest (or Presbyter). And be thou a faithful dispenser of the Word of God, and of his Holy Sacraments; in the name of the Father, and of the Son, and of the Holy Ghost. Amen.

Those who put forward this suggestion, however, admitted that it was open to many serious objections: there would be doubt whether what was conferred was the authority of order or only of jurisdiction; there would be the ambiguity of it being understood in a wider sense by those who spoke the formula, and in a more restricted sense by those over whom it was spoken; and there was the possibility that its suffici-

[1] Bell, *Documents* (1st Series), pp. 311-15.     [2] Sundkler, pp. 149-54.

ency might be questioned by other episcopal Churches. The proposal, therefore, went no further.[1] Later, however, the idea was taken up in other parts of the world and similar rites of commissioning, consisting of an imposition of hands and an imperative formula, appeared in reunion schemes in Australia, Iran, North India, and the United States of America.[2] The idea was also proposed again by Anglicans in South India in 1944, and the Archbishop of Canterbury, William Temple, wrote to the Metropolitan of Calcutta and expressed his opinion that the adoption of this method in India would make the scheme easier for Anglicans to accept. The other Churches in India were divided over the question, however, some fearing that it was really a reordination of the non-episcopal ministries and nothing more, and in the end the proposal was dropped, to the bitter disappointment of many Anglicans.[3]

Underlying almost all of these proposals was the idea of "supplemental ordination", based on the theory that through the division and disunity of the Church all ministries had been rendered imperfect and limited in authority, and that this defect could be overcome by each Church bestowing on the others that element which it lacked. This theory was first advanced by A. C. Headlam, although he thought that reunion itself would remedy the defect and that no special rite was needed.[4] The idea of "supplemental ordination" was developed by the Anglican theologian, O. C. Quick, in 1927,[5] and it achieved considerable popularity in the reunion discussions of the 1940s.[6] Strong support for it came from an English Anglo-Catholic, Dr Gerald Broomfield, in a pamphlet, *Anglican and Free Church Ministries*, to which the Archbishop of Canterbury contributed a foreword. Broomfield believed that the 1920 Lambeth Conference had intended that supplemental ordination should be adopted in its proposal for mutual commissioning, and he thought that each Church should use its normal ordination rite, but should indicate the special character of the ceremony by prefacing the imposition of hands by some such formula as: "Seeing that thou

[1] Bell, *Documents* (2nd series), pp. 82–3.

[2] Bell, *Documents* (3rd series), pp. 167, 209–11, 241; Batty, pp. 37–56; C. C. Richardson, *The Sacrament of Reunion* (New York 1940), pp. 1–4; H. R. T. Brandreth, *An American Plan for Unity*, CDCP Pamphlet No. 10 (n.d.); *Round-Table Conference on Church Union, Proposed Basis of Negotiation* (Allahabad 1947), pp. 4–5.

[3] Sundkler, pp. 306–15; *The Church and Union, Papers by Members of the South India United Church* (Madras 1944), pp. 23–4, 33; E. W. Thompson, *The Church Catholic and Free* (1944), pp. 79–86.

[4] Headlam, *Doctrine of the Church and Christian Reunion*, pp. 265, 291.

[5] O. C. Quick, *The Christian Sacraments* (1927), pp. 140–60.

[6] See, for example, Richardson, *The Sacrament of Reunion*, pp. 25–31.

hast been ordained to the ministry in the . . . Church, and dost desire to exercise thy ministry in union with the . . . Church, we do now, on behalf of this latter Church confer ordination upon thee according to its customary rites and ceremonies".[1] The Lower House of the Canterbury Convocation suggested that the Archbishop of Canterbury should commend Broomfield's proposals for adoption in South India when he wrote to the Metropolitan of Calcutta.[2]

Broomfield's concept of supplemental ordination differed, however, from that held by the majority, who had adopted the position that there was only one ministry in the Church, which was limited in each denomination by the fact of disunity. Broomfield, on the other hand, seemed to assume that there were different ministries ordained to different functions and with different powers, which could be united by supplemental ordination into a new ministry embodying all the previous ministries. This probably accounts for his use of the normal ordination rite rather than a special ceremony; there was no repetition of ordination but each ordination was a different rite conferring different powers. The same idea can be seen to underlie a scheme of union drawn up in 1946 between the Anglican Church and the United Church of Canada. Each would confer ordination on the other by its own rite of ordination, and the scheme stated that "the essential proposition, on which all the rest of this report depends, is that the two types of ministry are different. If that is conceded, then the grace of each may be conveyed to the other, without reservation."[3] A similar proposal was made by an Anglo-Catholic, H. R. T. Brandreth, to replace the American scheme for union. Although he criticized the theory of supplemental ordination held by many, he thought that Anglicans could ordain Presbyterians, and vice versa, because "whatever may be conveyed through the ordination rites of the various groups, it is certainly not the same ministry or commission". The Presbyterians, for example, would receive from the Anglicans the priesthood, which they did not have or claim to have.[4] This distinction between different ministries had first been put forward by Roman Catholic controversialists who had argued that Anglican ordination might make men ministers but it did not confer the Catholic priesthood, and it had then been denied by Anglicans—there might be

---

[1] Gerald Broomfield, *Anglican and Free Church Ministries, unification through reciprocal supplementary ordination* (1944).
[2] *Chronicle of Convocation* (1944), pp. 62–4.
[3] Bell, *Documents* (3rd series), pp. 181–202.
[4] Brandreth, *An American Plan for Unity*.

different concepts but they were of the same ministry—but now it was to be used frequently by Anglo-Catholics to claim that the Free Church and Anglican ministries were of different types.

The theory of supplemental ordination met with strong criticism. The report of the Committee on the Unity of the Church at the 1948 Lambeth Conference included an appendix on the subject which stated the views for and against the theory, and suggested that further study was necessary. The theory implied that the grace of ordination had been received on a previous occasion. What then was the something which was being added? The apostolic commission could not be quantitively conceived, and so on a traditional view of ordination it was difficult to attach a theological meaning to such a rite. "A man either has received the commission of Christ, or he has not. The Church can only recognize the fact, not 'supplement' it, since the efficacy of ordination comes from Him, and not merely from the Church's administration."[1]

Such criticism caused the idea of supplemental ordination to be dropped. The Canadian proposals for exchange of ordination were abandoned completely,[2] and the rites of unification in the various schemes underwent a significant change. The emphasis fell rather on asking God to supply whatever deficiencies might be lacking in any of the ministries than on each Church claiming to supply something to the others, and in almost every rite since 1948 prayer has assumed at least an equal place to an imperative commission. The only real exception to this is the rite proposed in an alternative to the official Anglican–Methodist scheme by C. O. Buchanan, E. L. Mascall, J. I. Packer, and the Bishop of Willesden, which seems to be a return to an ambiguous formula in preference to an ambiguous prayer. The bishop is to stretch out his hands towards each minister and say:

I A. B., bishop of —— in the united Church, do recognize and accept you as a presbyter in the Church of God, now to serve within the presbyterate of this diocese in the threefold ministry of this Church. I now commit to you authority to exercise your ministry within this Church wherever you may be called and licensed. May God use your ministry to his great glory.[3]

The "authority" which the formula claims to convey is not explicitly

---

[1] *The Lambeth Conference 1948*, pt. II, pp. 64–6. See also J. E. L. Newbigin, *The Reunion of the Church. A Defence of the South India Scheme* (1948), pp. 111–14.

[2] Bell, *Documents* (4th series), p. 151.

[3] C. O. Buchanan, E. L. Mascall, J. I. Packer, and the Bishop of Willesden, *Growing into Union: Proposals for forming a united Church of England* (1970), pp. 121–2.

defined, and the absence of a tactual imposition of hands may allay the fears of Free Churchmen but the extension of hands over the minister is suggestive of the medieval practice of ordination.

The scheme of union inaugurated in North India and Pakistan in 1970 and the scheme proposed for Ceylon reflect this change in emphasis in their rites of unification. The rites in the two schemes are almost identical, since in the course of their composition and revision there has been close co-operation, and it is therefore necessary only to describe the North India and Pakistan rite and indicate the points at which the proposed Ceylon rite makes any significant divergence.[1] The rite contained four main elements, a Preface, a declaration by those taking part, a prayer, and the imposition of hands accompanied by an imperative formula. The Preface stated that it was the intention to bring about a unification of the ministry and to continue the threefold ministry of bishop, presbyter, and deacon; that it was acknowledged that all the ministries of the uniting Churches had been used by the Holy Spirit but that all were limited by the fact of separation; that it was intended by prayer and the imposition of hands to seek from God "whatever of the fullness of Christ's grace, commission and authority each may need for the performance of his proper office in the Church of North India/ Pakistan"; and that it was believed that God would thereby transcend any differences between ministers of different traditions. The Ceylon Preface was somewhat briefer. The declaration stated that the ministers were prepared to commit themselves to God to receive "such grace, commission and authority" as they might need. The prayer began in the same way as the prayer before the imposition of hands in the Anglican rite for the priesthood, with minor variations, but when the central petition was reached, it continued:

We humbly beseech Thee through Thy Son, our great High Priest, to gather us into one fellowship. Continue, we pray Thee, Thy blessings already given, and upon all Thy servants, called this day to a fresh dedication

[1] *Proposed Scheme of Church Union in Ceylon, section on Faith and Order* (Tellippalai 1947), pp. 12–17; *Proposed Scheme of Church Union in Ceylon* (3rd edn, Madras 1955), pp. 20–7, (3rd edn, as amended 1963, Madras 1964), pp. 20–7; *Plan of Church Union in North India and Pakistan as revised in August 1953* (Madras 1954), pp. 12–16, 46–7; (4th edn, Madras 1965), pp. 49–55; *Suggested Services for use at the proposed Inauguration of the Church of North India and Pakistan*, pp. 6–10, 12–15; *Services proposed for use at the Inauguration of the Church of North India and the Church of Pakistan and the service for the ordination of presbyters in these united Churches*, pp. 7–9. See also T. D. Sully, *A United Ministry for a united Church* (Calcutta 1967), and James Kellock, *Breakthrough for Church Union in North India and Pakistan* (Madras 1965).

to Thy service, pour out Thy Holy Spirit to endue each according to his need with grace and authority for the exercise of his ministry whether as bishop or presbyter in the Church Universal and according to the order of the Church of North India/Pakistan: that therein we may faithfully proclaim the Gospel of Thy Kingdom, minister the Word of Thy truth, and administer the Sacraments which Thou hast ordained; so that at the coming of our Lord and Saviour Jesus Christ, we may each receive the reward of a good and faithful steward; through the same Thy son Jesus Christ, our Lord, who liveth and reigneth with Thee in the unity of the same Holy Spirit, world without end. Amen.

The Ceylon prayer was almost identical, except that it preferred to begin with the *Sursum corda* and eucharistic preface as in the proposed English 1928 Ordinal and it adopted the word "Renew" instead of "Continue". Earlier drafts of the Ceylon rite preferred the word "Confirm". The formula at the imposition of hands in the North India and Pakistan rite read:

Forasmuch as you were called and ordained in your several Churches to the ministry of the Church of God, and are now called to the ministry of the Church of God within the Church of North India/Pakistan, may you receive from God the power of the Holy Spirit to continue in you His gifts, and in accordance with His will to bestow on you grace, commission and authority for the ministry of a presbyter (bishop) of the Church of God and according to the order of this Church; and take authority to preach the Word of God, to fulfil the ministry of reconciliation and to minister Christ's Sacraments in the Church of North India/Pakistan; and see that thou do all these things in brotherly partnership with God's fellow-workers whom in this union of Churches He has made your own.

Ceylon, however, adopted a slightly different formula:

Forasmuch as you were called and ordained Minister/Priest/Presbyter in the Church of God within the . . . Church, and are now called to minister within this Church of Lanka as Presbyter in the Church of God: Receive from God the Grace of the Holy Spirit.

Take thou authority to exercise the office of Presbyter in the Church of Lanka, to preach and teach the Word, to fulfil the ministry of reconciliation and to minister Christ's Sacraments in the congregations whereunto you shall be duly appointed. Amen.

Earlier editions of the scheme contained a slightly longer version.

The procedure at the imposition of hands varied in each successive edition of the North India and Pakistan scheme. At first three representatives of one Church were to lay their hands on the ministers of all the other Churches, and then representatives of all the others were to do the same until everyone had received the imposition of hands from ministers of every other Church. Later the number of representatives was reduced to two, and later still the whole procedure was changed; one representative from each Church was to lay hands on three ministers, one a bishop, and these three were to lay hands on all the others, including those who had laid hands on them. Finally, it was decided to included four ministers from outside North India and Pakistan, two bishops in the historic episcopate and two ministers from non-episcopal Churches, in the initial imposition of hands, to make it clearer that continuity with the historic episcopate was not something supplied only by the former Anglican bishops. The Ceylon scheme chose a different method. All the new bishops of the united Church would be commissioned to exercise their ministry by ministers of all the uniting Churches, and then they would receive all the ministers into the united Church by the rite of unification. The commissioning consisted of the reading of a Preface and the imposition of hands with a formula acknowledging those commissioned as "possessed of the fullness of the ministry of this Church in which are joined together our divers ministries".

Because the Methodists involved in the negotiations for unity in North India and Pakistan also had bishops, it was originally proposed that the scheme should include a rite in which the wider authority of the united Church would be conferred upon both Anglican and Methodist bishops. At first this was called the "unification of the episcopate" and followed the unification of the ministries. Presbyters from non-episcopal Churches were also to join in the imposition of hands, "thus signifying the complete acceptance of the existing Bishops as Bishops of the united Church". Later, however, it preceded the unification of the ministries, its title became "the bringing together of the episcopates", and presbyters did not participate. The rite itself was almost identical with the unification of the ministries, and this troubled the Committee on Church Unity at the 1958 Lambeth conference when it considered the scheme. It disliked the bishops being involved in two very similar ceremonies and would have preferred that the unification of the episcopate should have been completed in a single action, with ministers from all the Churches joining in the imposition of hands. The committee also recommended that in both the Ceylon and North India/Pakistan rites of unification the specific order involved should be named in the prayer, although recognizing that the Anglican Ordinal on which the rites were based did not do this, and that in both the prayers and formulas the universal Church should be mentioned before the particular Church, instead of after it. Neither of these was done at this time. With these two clarifications it felt that the rites would be satisfactory.[1] The clarifications were accepted in both schemes, but the Negotiating Committee in North India would not accept the change in the bringing together of the episcopates. In contrast to the Lambeth Conference, they saw this not as part of the unification of the ministry itself, but simply as a preliminary act so that all the bishops might without question be involved in the unification of the ministry, and a note to this effect was then included in the rite.[2] Later, however, in response to further criticism of the complexity of the scheme and of the bringing together of the episcopates, this rite was entirely omitted from the scheme, and other minor changes were made in the wording of the rite of unification to try to remove any trace of the theory of supplemental ordination.

The 1948 Lambeth Conference felt that the Ceylon rite was satisfactory, as did a committee of theologians appointed by the Archbishop of Canterbury in 1951,[3] but both rites have been criticized by others. Stephen Neill, who had been involved in the scheme in South India, objected to the element of subterfuge and dishonesty which he saw in the Ceylon scheme; it was all very well to say that it was left to God to decide what was conveyed by the rite of unification, but other Churches could not avoid making a judgement on it.[4] The Church Union disliked the use of the same words over Anglicans and non-Anglicans with different meanings in the North India scheme; it was immoral, since the purpose of words was to express meaning and not to conceal it.[5] J. E. L. Newbigin criticized the rite of unification in both schemes. Although the term, "supplemental ordination", had been dropped, he believed that the rites proposed amounted to the same thing, and he put forward what came to be called the "Newbigin dilemma" in later discussion; either the rites were the equivalent of episcopal ordination, in which case Anglicans who underwent them

[1] *The Lambeth Conference 1958*, 2, pp. 36–40.

[2] S. F. Bayne, Jr, *Ceylon, North India, Pakistan: A Study in Ecumenical Decision* (1960), pp. 204–11, 219.

[3] *The Lambeth Conference 1948*, pp. 57–9; *The Scheme for Church Union in Ceylon, being the Report of a Committee of Theologians appointed by the Archbishop of Canterbury* (1951).

[4] S. C. Neill, *Christian Partnership* (1952), pp. 103–5.

[5] *The Plan of Church Union in North India and Pakistan, a memorandum by the Theological Committee of the Church Union*, p. 7.

were committing the sin of being reordained, or they were not, in which case Anglicans could not recognize former non-episcopal ministers who underwent them as sufficient to minister in Anglican Churches. The rites were essentially ambiguous and therefore undesirable.[1] Canon T. D. Sully, one of the Anglican delegation in the North India negotiations, tried to answer this by arguing that these rites differed from supplemental ordination in that they came after union and not before it; they were acts of the united Church seeking what they needed from God, not of the separated Churches claiming to bestow something on each other.[2]

When, however, the Convocations of Canterbury and York were asked in 1961 to consider whether they would enter full communion with united Churches thus constituted in Ceylon and North India, the Newbigin dilemma was strongly felt by many, and both the Joint Committee reports on the schemes and the Convocations themselves were divided. Some thought that the rites were entirely new ceremonies necessitated by a unique situation which could not be equated with ordination or anything else; others thought they were sufficient to convey episcopal ordination to those who lacked it, while others denied this because the rites were ambiguous and did not explicitly claim to be ordinations. Many felt that the Newbigin dilemma was unanswerable; the same rite could not do two things, ordain some and commission others, because this confused its intention, and they refused to accept the view that the rites were only doing one thing, asking God for what was needed in each case, or the theory put forward by Dr Mortimer, Bishop of Exeter, that it was no more profane for Anglicans to undergo such a rite, believing that they needed nothing, than it was for Jesus to submit to the baptism of John, or the idea that there was a parallel for this rite in the consecration of a bishop, where a priest who became a bishop received only episcopal consecration but a layman consecrated *per saltum* by the same rite received both the priesthood and episcopate. Some thought that either one or both schemes involved the theory that all orders were defective in a divided Christendom, which the Archbishop of Canterbury maintained was quite inconsistent with the Anglican position in defence of their orders against Roman Catholics, and the explicit statement that the rite was not reordination, included in the Preface to the North India rite at that time, came in for much criticism.

[1] Newbigin, *The Reunion of the Church* (2nd edn, 1960), pp. xx–xxvii.
[2] T. D. Sully, "Uniting the Ministries", *CQR* CLXII (1961), pp. 210–23. See also Kellock, pp. 124–34.

Some also expressed concern about the lack of an adequate intention to receive Holy Orders in those not episcopally ordained and were not satisfied that the intention to receive what, if anything, God knew them to need was sufficient.

The results of these protracted debates were somewhat chaotic. The Upper Houses of Canterbury and York were in favour of recognizing both Ceylon and North India and Pakistan as part of the Church universal, possessing the apostolic ministry and holding the catholic faith, and of entering full communion with them; the Lower House of Canterbury agreed to communion with Ceylon only when the resolution was amended by the addition of the words, "provided that ambiguities in the rite of unification are removed so as to make it clear that episcopal ordination is being conferred on those who have not already received it", but later, by a very small majority, it agreed to enter communion with North India and Pakistan without any such proviso, in spite of the greater complexity of the scheme at that time. The Lower House of York, on the other hand, agreed that Ceylon would be a part of the Church universal, possessing the apostolic ministry, but refused to enter into full communion with it, and defeated both resolutions in the case of North India and Pakistan.[1] The 1968 Lambeth Conference, however, recommended entering full communion with both Churches.[2]

These rites have become the model for recent schemes of union. On the recommendation of the 1958 Lambeth Conference, the scheme for union in Nigeria abandoned the South India method and incorporated a rite of unification based on that in the Ceylon scheme, and a similar rite was also adopted in the scheme of union in Ghana.[3] The rite of unification proposed in the Anglican–Methodist reunion scheme in England was also a development of the rite in the Ceylon and North India schemes. The first version, suggested in the report of the conversations between the two Churches in 1963, began with a declaration of intention to be made by all taking part; the reality and spiritual effec-

---

[1] *The Church of Lanka, being the Schedule attached to the Reports of the Joint Committees of the Convocations of Canterbury and York*, esp. pp. 14–19, 24–8, 32–5; *The Churches of North India and Pakistan, being the Schedule attached to the Reports of the Joint Committees of the Convocations of Canterbury and York* (1961); *Chronicle of Convocation* (1961), pp. 177–208, 229–42, 264–85, 289–312, 501–35, 545–95; (1962), pp. 3–52, 126–63; *York Journal of Convocation* (1961), pp. 64–133; (1962), pp. 23–43, 86–105.

[2] *Lambeth Conference 1968*, Resolutions 49 and 50.

[3] *The Lambeth Conference 1958*, 1, p. 38; T. S. Garrett and R. M. C. Jeffery, *Unity in Nigeria* (1965), pp. 51–4; *Proposed Basis of Union prepared by the Ghana Church Union Committee* (Accra 1963), pp. 17–19; *Interim Proposals for the Service of Inauguration of the Union and Unification of the Ministry* (Accra 1965).

tiveness of neither ministry was being questioned, but all were submitting themselves to God for the renewal of gifts already received and to enable each to enter that which had been given to the other. The Methodist ministers knelt before four Anglican priests and a bishop who stretched out their right hands towards them while the bishop recited a prayer composed of the first part of the ordination prayer for presbyters from the South India Ordinal and of the central petition and conclusion of the prayer from the Ceylon rite of unification, with the central petition amended to read: "Renew thy blessings already given, and upon these thy servants do thou pour out thy Holy Spirit, to endue each according to his need with grace for the office of priest in the Church of God". The bishop then laid hands on each in silence and afterwards he pronounced an imperative commission, receiving them into the ministry of the Church of England and giving them authority to minister. The procedure for the Anglican bishops and priests was similar. A different prayer was used, based on one from the Methodist ordination rite, but the central petition was very similar: "renew thy blessings already given and pour out thy Holy Spirit upon them for the work of a minister in thy Church". The presiding minister alone read the prayer and laid hands on the Anglicans; no other ministers were associated with him. The imperative commission concluding the ceremony gave the Anglicans authority to minister in the Methodist Church.[1] A later revision of the rite introduced a declaration to be subscribed by all taking part which stated that the minister submitted himself wholly to God to receive "such further grace, commission, and authority as he may now wish to give me", and the central petitions of the prayers were altered; both omitted the phrase, "renew thy blessings already given", and asked for the Holy Spirit to endue each according to his need with grace for the office and work. Notes were appended to state that "priest" was used in the prayer over the Methodists, and "minister" in the prayer over the Anglicans, as being the language of the respective Ordinals and service-books.[2]

In the final report of the Unity Commission the rite was extensively revised in the hope of meeting criticism which had been made. The declaration to be subscribed by those taking part now stated that the grace and authority which each was prepared to receive from God was "for my ministry as a Presbyter/Bishop in his Church". This was done

---

[1] *Conversations between the Church of England and the Methodist Church, a report* (1963), pp. 37–47.
[2] *Towards Reconciliation*, pp. 28ff.

to try to make the intention clearer. The two actions, instead of coming separately within the reception of each Church by the other, now came successively, following the reconciliation of the Churches. They began with the reading of a brief preface, a prayer said by all the ministers, and the hymn, "Come Holy Ghost". The prayer thanked God for the past ministry and for calling them together, and asked that he would renew his blessings and transcend the differences of their calling by bestowing on them what they needed. The prayers over the two groups which followed, that over the Anglicans now coming first, differed considerably from the earlier versions. The prayer over the Anglican bishops was loosely based on the ordination prayer for bishops in the new Ordinal and that over the Methodist ministers on the ordination prayer for presbyters from the new Ordinal. At later local unifications of the ministries, where Anglican priests were also to be involved, the prayer over them was similar, although not identical, to that over the Methodists. In each case the central petition was very similar, although the slight differences in phrasing were significant; the prayer over Anglican priests now asked for the Holy Spirit *in* the office of presbyter, that over the Methodist ministers continued to ask for the Holy Spirit *for* the office, and the prayer over the Anglican bishops restored the request for the renewal of blessings, omitted in the earlier revision.[1] The imposition of hands on the Anglicans was now performed by the President of the Methodist Conference and other ministers, and the stretching out of hands during the prayer over the Methodists was omitted. The formula following each imposition of hands was now exactly the same, apart from the naming of the particular Church. It simply welcomed the ministers of the one Church into the other and no longer claimed to bestow authority on them.[2]

Criticism of the rite came from both Methodists and Anglicans. Four of the Methodists engaged in the original conversations objected to it because it was capable of being interpreted as an ordination of Metho-

[1] Over Anglican bishops: "Renew, we beseech thee, the blessings already granted to these thy servants whom thou didst call to be Bishops in thy Church, and pour out upon each of them thy Holy Spirit for a fresh dedication to thy service in the coming together of the Methodist Church and the Church of England." Over Methodist ministers: "We pray thee to send upon each of these thy servants according to his need thy Holy Spirit for the office and work of a presbyter in thy universal Church and in the coming together of the Methodist Church and the Church of England." Over Anglican priests: "Send thy Holy Spirit upon them, each according to his need, that in the office of Presbyter in thy Church, in the coming together of the Methodist Church and the Church of England, they may serve thee acceptably."

[2] *Anglican–Methodist Unity*, 2. *The Scheme* (1968), pp. 146ff.

dists, because of the imposition of hands on Anglicans by Methodists, which they regarded as superfluous, and because of the implications of the retention of the word "priest" in the rite.[1] Strong opposition to the rite came from many Evangelicals, who believed that the Methodists were already adequately ordained and that this rite, with its implication of ordination, was unnecessary. They would have preferred the South India method.[2] Others, however, were content with the rite.[3] Many Anglo-Catholics who had opposed the Ceylon and North India rites were at first willing to support this scheme because it provided two separate prayers and not one common form. The Church Union felt in 1963 that the matter and form were sufficient to bestow the priesthood on the Methodists, and that the Methodist intention to enter into the Anglican spiritual heritage and continuity of commission was probably sufficient, but felt it would be intolerable to use the rite until greater harmony of interpretation was reached.[4] As time went on, however, Anglo-Catholic opposition to the rite increased, not on the ground that its matter and form were insufficient in themselves but on the ground of an ambiguity of meaning. They wanted it made explicit that Methodists were receiving episcopal ordination.[5] Dr E. L. Mascall, who had welcomed the rite in 1963 as an improvement on the North India and Ceylon rites, rejected it in 1968: "My personal opinion is that the Service of Reconciliation would in fact produce a validly ordained ministry, but I have the gravest reservations on the ground of plain morality."[6] Archbishop Fisher regarded the service as a "pious sub-

---

[1] *Conversations*, pp. 59–61.

[2] R. T. Beckwith, *Priesthood and Sacraments* (1964), pp. 106–10; *All in each place: Towards reunion in England*, ed. J. I. Packer (1965); C. O. Buchanan, "The Service of Reconciliation", in *The Church of England and the Methodist Church*, ed. J. I. Packer (1963), pp. 36–42. Cf. the reply to this by Gordon Rupp, *Consideration Re-considered* (1964), pp. 37–42.

[3] See, for example, *The Anglican–Methodist Conversations, an Evangelical Approach*, ed. Peter Morgan (1964), pp. 22–31.

[4] The Church Union, *Anglicans and Methodists, Is This the Way? Notes on the report on Conversations between the Church of England and the Methodist Church* (n.d.), and *A Statement on the Report on Conversations between the Church of England and the Methodist Church* (n.d.).

[5] F. Bertram Jones, *I am Church of England* (1964), p. 4; *The Unity of the Faith* (1967), pp. 9–10; E. Garth Moore, "No. The Scheme for Anglican–Methodist Reunion", *Theology* LXXI (1968), pp. 482–92; Graham Leonard, Bishop of Willesden, "*to every man's conscience ...*" comments on the report of the Anglican Methodist Unity Commission (n.p., n.d.), esp. pp. 20–1.

[6] E. L. Mascall, "The Anglican–Methodist Scheme (2), reasons for rejection", *C.R.* (Quarterly Review of the Community of the Resurrection), No. 263 (Christmas 1968), pp. 22–6. Cf. his letter to the *Church Times*, 29 March 1963.

terfuge", because of contradictory conceptions of what happened in it.[1] There were also doubts whether the Methodist intention to be receptive to all that God had to give them constituted a sufficient intention for them to receive the priesthood by this rite.[2]

Attempts were made to answer the charge of ambiguity. The report of the Joint Committees of the Canterbury and York Convocations appointed in 1965 to consider the reactions of the dioceses to the scheme argued that in a rite of unification, as in ordination itself and in the manner of God's presence in the Eucharist, there would always have to be room for theological diversity of opinion because of human limitations. Nevertheless, the prayer over the Methodists was not ambiguous; it was "explicit and can be made with the same certainty of an effectual response as a similar solemn prayer at an ordination service". The only ambiguity was what action God would take in response.[3] Similarly, the interim report of the Unity Commission in 1967 claimed that the petition in the prayers contained no ambiguity:

> the end desired is made quite plain, and the issue is deliberately placed in God's hands with the conviction that he will, by such action as he thinks fit, bring about the desired end, as the prayer has stated it. . . . We pray that what the one ministry has received from God will be given to, and received by, the other.[4]

The final report argued that the rite was not a subterfuge; there was deliberate ambiguity and a freedom of interpretation was permitted, but the limits of this, and the reasons for it, were made explicit in advance. Nor could the Methodist intention be held insufficient, since Anglicans had never demanded a particular view of priesthood from its ordination candidates.[5] Dr Ramsey, the Archbishop of Canterbury, said that it was wrong to ask what the rite was to be called—ordination or not—and that the real question should be: "What was God asked to do in the rite, was he able to do it, and what would be the result for the recipients?"[6] The opponents refused to be convinced by these claims, however, nor did they find that the amendments made to the rite in the

[1] G. Fisher, *Covenant and Reconciliation* (1967), pp. 9–13.

[2] Willis and Deanesly, *Anglican–Methodist Unity*, pp. 94–7; *Chronicle of Convocation* (1965), *passim*.

[3] *Relations between the Church of England and the Methodist Church, being the Schedule attached to the Report of the Joint Committees of the Convocations of Canterbury and York* (1965).

[4] *Towards Reconciliation*, p. 28.

[5] *The Scheme*, pp. 127ff.

[6] *Chronicle of Convocation* (1969), p. 1.

various revisions of the scheme made it any easier to accept, and when the scheme was put to the vote in 1969, largely because of difficulties over this rite it failed to receive the required support in the Church of England to enable it to go ahead, although the Methodists were prepared to accept it.

The Anglican–Methodist rite has one important difference from the North India and Ceylon rites. It is set within a "two-stage" scheme —the integration of the ministries preceding the organic union of the Churches—and because of this retains something of the idea that each Church has something to give to the other. The rites in the other schemes, on the other hand, are actions performed within the new united Churches where representative ministers seek for those who desire to be its ministers what they need from God, and all, whatever their previous ordination, are treated equally. In a sense, therefore, the Anglican–Methodist scheme is a step backwards from that. The ghost of "supplemental ordination" has not entirely been laid.

Apart from this one important difference, however, the difficulties felt about current rites of unification are common to them all, and fall into four main categories. There is, first of all, the objection that those not previously episcopally ordained lack an adequate intention to receive ordination by such rites. It is difficult for Anglicans to raise this objection and be consistent with their own practice and defence of their orders. They have never demanded a particular "internal intention" in those whom they have ordained, and in controversy with Roman Catholics have almost always rejected the need for such an intention, maintaining that the outward participation in the rite must be taken as sufficient intention. To demand more might cast doubts on the validity of some of their past ordinations. Secondly, there is the objection that the rites themselves are not sufficient to convey ordination. Hardly anyone has argued that the matter and form are insufficient, but many have claimed that the rites are inadequate because of a defect in their intention or meaning; they do not explicitly state that they are ordinations. This again is difficult for Anglicans to maintain consistently, as it is similar to the Roman Catholic argument that the Anglican Ordinal does not intend or mean to confer the same sort of priesthood and episcopate as the Catholic Church has, and Anglicans have nearly always rejected the necessity for this and insisted that a defect in concept does not invalidate orders. It is true that the two cases are not absolutely identical, but they have much in common. The ultimate question which must be faced is this: Is a rite which calls itself an ordination but has little resemblance to a primitive ordination rite any better than one which does not explicitly use that name but which closely resembles the early rites in structure and intends to produce the effect of ordination, if that is required? And how is the latter different from a conditional ordination, apart from the name? The third class of objections is of a moral nature. They claim that it is immoral to express uncertainty and agnosticism in the rites, when the participants themselves have no such doubts as to the sufficiency of their ordination. Such a criticism assumes that it is certain either that only bishops can ordain or that all ordinations are valid, depending upon the critic's own ecclesiastical allegiance. Many participants, however, are really agnostic and so for them this is the only way of honesty and integrity.

The fourth class of objections is perhaps the most significant of all. Several critics have pointed out that there will not even be full communion between the various united Churches formed by this method, let alone between them and other Churches, since the requirement that any minister wishing to serve in such a Church must be "unified" means that there will not be mutual recognition and acceptance of ministries, which is an essential feature of full communion. Thus it is strictly impossible for Anglicans to resolve to enter full communion with any Church formed in this way, in spite of the fact that such resolutions have been made. Moreover, if a minister has to be "unified" again and again each time a new union takes place between his Church and another, the meaning of the whole idea is brought into question: just what is the rite doing?[1] The result of such practice can only be to suggest that ordination is simply to the ministry of a particular denomination and not to the ministry of the universal Church. For that reason alone the concept of unification seems to need further study before it is assumed to be the only way to unity, for it may in practice lead merely to greater disunity.

[1] R. C. D. Jasper, *Arthur Cayley Headlam, Life and Letters of a Bishop* (1960), p. 239; C. O. Buchanan, "Dilemmas of Unification", in *All in each place;* Michael Hollis, *The Significance of South India* (1966), p. 67; *Growing into Union*, Appendix 5, pp. 193–207.

# Conclusion

If there is one point which stands out clearly from this survey of the history of the Anglican Ordinal, it is the unsatisfactory nature of that rite. Cranmer's attempts to construct simple ordination rites to replace the complex ceremonies of the Middle Ages were in part successful; they restored the imposition of hands to its central position and gave greater emphasis to the prayer of the people, but in other ways they left much to be desired, particularly in the absence of an ordination prayer in close association with the imposition of hands in the rites for the priesthood and diaconate. The attempts made in the twentieth century to rectify this have not been altogether successful because they have only tried to insert material into the rites and have not been bold enough to try to restore the original simultaneity of prayer and the imposition of hands. It has been left, therefore, to the Church of South India to furnish the Anglican Communion with rites which follow the primitive pattern, and it seems likely that through the Anglican–Methodist rite and the American draft revision this will become the foundation of all future revisions in Anglican provinces.

In spite of the importance attached by many Anglicans to the imperative formulas at the imposition of hands in the Anglican rites, particularly that in the rite for the priesthood, their continued use can really no longer be defended. They have no place in the primitive pattern of ordination, and they serve only to detract from the ordination prayers and induce erroneous ideas about ordination; they suggest, for example, that the grace of Order is something that can be bestowed by command rather than sought in prayer. Their presence has also caused some Anglicans and others to perpetuate the medieval theory that the form of ordination need not be prayer. This theory rests upon the hypothesis that the Church has power to alter forms from precative to imperative, a hypothesis which has no evidence to support it and which is contrary to the claim made in the Preface to the Ordinal that the essentials of ordination are prayer and the imposition of hands. The hypothesis arose in medieval theology when it was thought that the forms in the Pontificals were imperative formulas and it became necessary to justify this, but it commands little support today among Roman Catholics. It is, however, strongly defended by John Jay Hughes who regards the argument in the papal commission of 1896 that the form must be prayer as "a red herring introduced into the discussion unnecessarily", and as an assertion "made merely for controversial purposes", and treats the claim that the form was the collect in the rites as "a needless complication of the argument" and as interpreting the Ordinal "according to principles foreign to its structure".[1] It can be doubted whether those who champion this hypothesis would do so if it did not appear to them that the Anglican rites would be invalid unless the imperative formulas could be the forms. If the hypothesis is rejected, however, the Anglican rites are not necessarily invalid, but their validity depends upon two factors which it is perhaps impossible to assess: In the first place, how far can prayer and imposition of hands be separated? And secondly, what is the necessary content of the form? Is the petition in the Anglican collects, "replenish them so with the truth of thy doctrine, and adorn them with innocency of life", sufficient as an ordination prayer? It may never be possible to make a clear decision on this because of the wide variety of rites accepted by the Church as valid and because of the absence of agreed criteria, but, even if it is thought that the Anglican rites do contain the minimum sufficient for a valid form, it should be realized that they are far from the ideal of the primitive rites, and that they should have been questioned by Roman Catholics is not surprising.

On the other hand, the new pattern of ordination rites set by South India is not entirely without fault. Firstly, the practice of imposing hands on the candidate only during the central petition may be questioned. It has no primitive precedent, it smacks of the medieval "moment of consecration" idea, and breaks the unity of the prayer. Indeed, to the undiscerning it may seem to be three separate prayers instead of one. To continue the imposition of hands throughout would help to emphasize that it is in response to the whole prayer that God bestows his gift and not through the recitation of particular words. Where only one candidate is usually ordained at a time, as, for example, in America, it is not as difficult to make this alteration as it is where several candidates are involved, but in the latter case it could perhaps be considered whether there is not some better method of dealing with them than that adopted in South India. Secondly, the prayer of the people has not altogether been restored to its due prominence. The

[1] Hughes, *Absolutely Null and Utterly Void*, p. 157, and *Stewards of the Lord*, pp. 232–4.

Anglican Orders controversy has tended to centre attention on the ordination prayer and to reduce the prayer of the people to a mere preliminary, whereas the prayer of the people, either spoken or in silence, is one of the central elements in ordination, as the early rites show, and a rite which does not give due weight to this is impoverished. The ordination prayer proper is the culmination of the prayer of the people, and the two ought to be closely linked. This the South India and Anglican–Methodist rites do, but the North India and American rites permit the duplication of the prayer of the people, the effect of which is to obscure its importance. The structure of the primitive Roman rites—bidding, silent prayer or litany, concluding collect, and ordination prayer—has much to commend it in stressing the prayer of the people. Linked with this subject is the question of the hymn, "Come Holy Ghost". Anglicans tend to use this hymn excessively; it finds its way into many rites other than ordination, and it has now been introduced into the rite for the diaconate, for which there is no ancient precedent. As an alternative to the litany in the prayer of the people it is unexceptionable, but to make it compulsory in all ordination rites raises it to the status of an essential element, which it most certainly is not. Finally, the *porrectio instrumentorum* needs careful consideration. Its original purpose was to express the particular functions of the order being conferred, and the tendency in modern rites to give a Bible to candidates for all orders defeats this object. On the other hand, the tendency in some Anglican provinces to multiply the ceremonies does not help as it serves only to increase the complexity of the rites and to remove the emphasis from the prayers, which was the main fault of the medieval rites. Perhaps it would be better to omit this ceremony entirely unless it can be restricted to the giving of something really indicative of the order.

Apart from these criticisms, the new pattern is to be welcomed, and the boldness of the American revision in attempting to deal with the language as well as the structure of the rites is to be commended. With certain alterations this Ordinal would seem to be the best of all the modern rites for providing the foundation of a new Anglican Ordinal to replace Cranmer's much-loved but liturgically unsatisfactory rite.

# Select Bibliography

The literature on ordination and orders is vast, and therefore this list is restricted to those aspects of the history of the Anglican Ordinal which are described in this work. For a more complete bibliography of other aspects of the Anglican Orders controversy see Hughes, *Absolutely Null and Utterly Void*, pp. 309–42.

## 1. UNPUBLISHED SOURCES

Henry VIII's annotations on the seventeen questions and answers, in British Museum Cotton Ms. Cleo. E.V, fols. 36–44.

Thomas Cranmer, "Commonplace Book", British Museum Royal Ms. 7. B. XI.

—— *De Sacramentis*, Lambeth Palace Library Ms. 1107, fols. 84–93.

Thomas Cooper, "Defence of Ceremonies", in "the Seconde Parte of a Register", Dr Williams's Library, Morrice Ms. B. II, fols. 236–7.

A copy of the Book of Common Prayer with Ms. alterations by Samuel Clarke in the British Museum.

Archives of the United Theological College, Bangalore, South India.

Minutes and Circulars of the Church of South India Synod Liturgy Committee.

## 2. LITURGICAL TEXTS

*The Treatise on the Apostolic Tradition of St Hippolytus of Rome*, ed. Gregory Dix, revised H. Chadwick. 1968.

John Wordsworth, *Bishop Sarapion's Prayer-Book*. 1899.

M. Andrieu, *Les Ordines Romani du haut Moyen age*. Vols. III and IV. Louvain 1951 and 1956.

H. B. Porter, Jr, *The Ordination Prayers of the Ancient Western Churches*. ACC XLIX. 1967.

W. Maskell, *Monumenta Ritualia Ecclesiae Anglicanae*. 3 vols. 2nd edn, 1882.

*The Pontifical of Magdalen College*, ed. H. A. Wilson. HBS XXXIX. 1910.

*Luther's Works*. Vol. LIII. Philadelphia 1965.

A. L. Richter, *Die Evangelischen Kirchenordnungen des sechszehnten Jahrhunderts*. 2 vols. Weimar 1846.

John a Lasco, *Forma ac Ratio tota ecclesiastici ministerii, in peregrinorum, potissimum vero Germanorum, ecclesia: instituta Londini in Anglia per Edvardum Sextum*. n.p., n.d.

F. E. Brightman, *The English Rite*. 2 vols. 2nd edn, 1921.

*Liturgical Services in the Reign of Queen Elizabeth*, ed. W. K. Clay. PS, 1847.

*The Liturgy of Compromise*, ed. G. W. Sprott. 1905.

W. D. Maxwell, *The Liturgical Portions of the Genevan Service Book*. 1931.

*Reliquiae Liturgicae*, ed. Peter Hall. 5 vols. 1847.

*Fragmenta Liturgica*, ed. Peter Hall. 7 vols. 1848.

*The Book of Common Order of the Church of Scotland*, ed. G. W. Sprott. 1901.

*Scottish Liturgies of the Reign of James VI*, ed. G. W. Sprott. 2nd edn, 1901.

*The Manner of the Coronation of King Charles the First of England*, ed. Charles Wordsworth. HBS II. 1892.

*The Durham Book*, ed. G. J. Cuming. 1961.

William McGarvey, *Liturgiae Americanae*. Philadelphia 1895.

*The Book of Common Prayer according to the use of the Church of Ireland*. Dublin 1878.

*The Book of Common Prayer with additions and deviations approved in 1927*. 1927.

*The Book of Common Prayer with additions and deviations approved in 1928*. 1928.

*The Scottish Book of Common Prayer*. 1929.

*The Book of Common Prayer according to the Use of the Church of Ireland*. 1926.

*The Book of Common Prayer ... according to the use of the Protestant Episcopal Church in the United States of America*. New York 1928.

*The Book of Common Prayer according to the use of the Church of England in the Dominion of Canada*. 1922.

*The Book of Common Prayer according to the use of the Anglican Church of Canada*. 1959.

*A Book of Common Prayer ... for use in the Church of the Province of South Africa*. 1954.

*The Book of Common Prayer of the Church of India, Pakistan, Burma, and Ceylon*. 1960.

*A Supplement to the Book of Common Prayer of the Church of India, Pakistan, Burma, and Ceylon*. 1960.

*Order of Administration of the Lord's Supper and Baptism; the forms of Solemnization of Matrimony, and of the Burial of the Dead; together with the Ordination Service: As used by the Wesleyan Methodists*. 1848.

*The Book of Public Prayers and Services for the use of the people called Methodists*. 1883.

*The Book of Offices, being the Orders of Service authorized for use in the Methodist Church*. 1936.

*Order of Service for the Inauguration of Church Union in South India with The form of Consecrating the first new bishops and the Order of Service for the Ordination of Presbyters*. 1947.

*Order of Service for the Making of Deacons*. Privately printed, Bangalore 1947.

*Church of South India, The Ordinal*. 1958; 2nd edn, 1962.

*Suggested Services for use at the proposed Inauguration of the Church of North India and Pakistan.* Madras 1955.

*Services Proposed for use at the Inauguration of the Church of North India and the Church of Pakistan and the service for the ordination of presbyters in these united Churches.* Rev. edn, Madras 1957; 2nd rev. edn, Madras 1960.


### 3. OTHER OFFICIAL PUBLICATIONS AND REPORTS

*Journals of the House of Lords.*

*Journals of the House of Commons.*

*Acts of the Privy Council,* ed. J. R. Dasent. New Series, 1890–.

Westminster Assembly, *Propositions Concerning Church-government and ordination of ministers.* 1647.

*Parliamentary Paper* 283. 1854.

*Report of the Clerical Subscription Commission.* 1865.

Convocation of Canterbury, *Chronicle* and Reports.

Convocation of York, *Journal* and Reports.

*The Church of South India, being the United Report of the Joint Committee of the Convocations of Canterbury and York.* 1950.

*The Church of South India, being the United Report of the two Joint Committees of the Convocations.* 1955.

*The Church of Lanka, being the Schedule attached to the Reports of the Joint Committees of the Convocations of Canterbury and York.* 1961.

*The Churches of North India and Pakistan, being the Schedule attached to the Reports of the Joint Committees of the Convocations of Canterbury and York.* 1961.

*Relations between the Church of England and the Methodist Church, being the Schedule attached to the Report of the Joint Committees of the Convocations of Canterbury and York.* 1965.

National Assembly of the Church of England, *Second Report of the Prayer Book Revision Committee with schedule of proposed alterations,* N.A. 60. 1922.

—— *Minutes of Proceedings of House of Clergy,* C.A. 157C. 1925.

—— *Book proposed to be annexed to the Prayer Book Measure 192–, Provisional, subject to further revision by the House of Bishops.* 1927.

*Conference of Bishops of the Anglican Communion. Holden at Lambeth Palace, July 27 to August 5, 1908. Encyclical letter from the Bishops, with the Resolutions and Reports.* 1908.

*Conference of Bishops of the Anglican Communion. Holden at Lambeth Palace, July 5 to August 7, 1920. Encyclical Letter from the Bishops with the Resolutions and Reports.* 1920.

*The Lambeth Conference 1948.* 1948.

*The Lambeth Conference 1958.* 1958.

*Lambeth Conference 1968, Preparatory Information.* 1968.

*Lambeth Conference 1968, Resolutions and Reports.* 1968.

*The Ministry of Women, the report of a committee appointed by the Archbishop of Canterbury.* 1919.

*The South India Church Scheme, being the Report of a Committee of Theologians appointed by the Archbishop of Canterbury to consider the proposed Basis of Union and Constitution of the future Church of South India.* 1946.

*The Scheme for Church Union in Ceylon, being the Report of a Committee of Theologians appointed by the Archbishop of Canterbury.* 1951.

General Synod of the Church of Ireland, *Report of Master Brooke's Committee.* Dublin 1871.

—— *Revision Committee, Report of Progress.* Dublin 1872.

*Second Report of the Joint Commission on the Book of Common Prayer appointed by the General Convention of 1913.* New York 1919.

The Standing Liturgical Commission of the Protestant Episcopal Church in the United States of America, *Prayer Book Studies, VIII, The Ordinal.* New York 1957.

—— *20, The Ordination of Bishops, Priests, and Deacons.* New York 1970.

*Proposed Scheme of Church Union in Ceylon, section on Faith and Order.* Tellippalai 1947.

*Proposed Scheme of Church Union in Ceylon.* 3rd edn, Madras 1955; 3rd edn as amended 1963, Madras 1964.

*Round-Table Conference on Church Union, Proposed Basis of Negotiation.* Allahabad 1947.

*Plan of Church Union in North India and Pakistan as revised in August 1953.* Madras 1954; 4th edn, Madras 1965.

*Proposed Basis of Union prepared by the Ghana Church Union Committee.* Accra 1963.

*Interim Proposals for the Service of Inauguration of the Union and Unification of the Ministry.* Accra 1965.

*Conversations between the Church of England and the Methodist Church: an Interim Statement.* 1958.

*Conversations between the Church of England and the Methodist Church, a report.* 1963.

*Towards Reconciliation, the Interim Statement of the Anglican–Methodist Unity Commission.* 1967.

*Anglican–Methodist Unity, 1. The Ordinal.* 1968.

*Anglican–Methodist Unity, 2. The Scheme.* 1968.

*The Anglican–Methodist Unity Conference 1968, Report of Proceedings.* 1968.

Catholic Advisory Council, *South India Reunion Scheme, A Statement.* n.p., n.d.

Church Historical Society, *A Treatise on the Bull Apostolicae Curae.* CHS XIX. 1896.

—— *Priesthood in the English Church, A Study of the "Vindication of the Bull Apostolicae Curae".* CHS XLI. 1898.

—— *Anglican Orders (English).* 1932.

English Church Union, *Report of the Committee on Prayer Book Revision*. 1922.
—— *The Plan of Church Union in North India and Pakistan, a memorandum by the Theological Committee*.
—— *Anglicans and Methodists, Is This the Way? Notes on the report on Conversations between the Church of England and the Methodist Church*. n.d.
—— *A Statement on the Report on Conversations between the Church of England and the Methodist Church*. n.d.
*Amendments in the Book of Common Prayer prepared by the Committee of the Liturgical Amendment Society (Ireland)*. 1861.
Prayer-Book Revision Society, *Auricular Confession and Priestly Absolution. Lord Ebury's Prayer-Book Amendment Bill, with letters containing reasons and authorities in support of it*. 1880.
*The Church and Union, Papers by Members of the South India United Church*. Madras 1944.
*A Survey of the Proposals for the Alternative Prayer Book, Part III*. Alcuin Club Prayer Book Revision Pamphlet xiv. 1924.
*A Vindication of the Bull "Apostolicae Curae", A Letter on Anglican Orders by the Cardinal Archbishop and Bishops of the Province of Westminster*. 1898.

## 4. BOOKS AND PAMPHLETS

*An abridgment of that booke which the Ministers of the Lincoln Diocess delivered to his Majestie upon the first of December last*. 1605.
*Acts and Proceedings of the General Assemblies of the Kirk of Scotland from the Year MDLX*. 3 vols. 1839–45.
J. L. Ainslie, *The Doctrines of Ministerial Order in the Reformed Churches of the Sixteenth and Seventeenth Centuries*. 1940.
Lancelot Andrewes, *Works*. 11 vols. LACT, 1841–54.
Thomas Aquinas, *Summa Theologica*.
W. J. Armitage, *The Story of the Canadian Revision of the Prayer Book*. 1922.
A. S. Barnes, *The Popes and the Ordinal*. 1896.
—— *Bishop Barlow and Anglican Orders, a study of the original documents*. 1922.
F. De Witt Batty, *The Australian Proposals for Intercommunion*. 1948.
Richard Baxter, *A Petition for Peace with the Reformation of the Liturgy. As it was presented to the Right Reverend Bishops by the Divines appointed by his Majesties Commission to treat with them about the Alteration of it*. 1661.
—— *A Treatise of Episcopacy*. 1681.
S. F. Bayne, Jr, *Ceylon, North India, Pakistan: A Study in Ecumenical Decision*. 1960.
R. T. Beckwith, *Priesthood and Sacraments*. 1964.
G. K. A. Bell, ed., *Documents on Christian Unity, 1920–4*. 1924.
—— *Documents on Christian Unity, Second Series*. 1930.
—— *Documents on Christian Unity, Third Series, 1930–48*. 1948.
—— *Documents on Christian Unity, Fourth Series, 1948–57*. 1958.

Christopher Benson, *Discourses upon the Powers of the Clergy, Prayers for the Dead, and the Lord's Supper, preached at the Temple Church.* 1841.

Joseph Berington, *The Memoirs of Gregorio Panzani.* 1793.

N. Bernard, *The Judgement of the Late Arch-Bishop of Armagh and Primate of Ireland of the Extent of Christs death, and satisfaction, etc., Of the Sabbath, and observation of the Lord's Day, Of the Ordination in other reformed Churches.* 1657.

—— *Clavi Trabales.* 1661.

George Biller, *A Few Suggestions On Prayer Book Reform.* 1878.

Thomas Bilson, *The Perpetual government of Christes Church.* 1593.

Richard Bingham, *Liturgiae Recusae Exemplar. The Prayer Book as it might be.* 1863.

Thomas Birch, *The Life of Dr John Tillotson.* 1752.

—— ed., *A Collection of the State Papers of John Thurloe.* 7 vols. 1742.

Edmund Bonner, *A Profitable and necessarye doctryne.* 1555.

A. Boudinhon, *Étude Théologique sur les Ordinations Anglicanes.* Paris 1895.

*Writings of John Bradford,* ed. A. Townsend. 2 vols. PS, 1848, 1853.

John Bramhall, *Works.* 5 vols. LACT, 1842–5.

S. M. Brandi, *Rome et Cantorbéry.* Paris 1898.

H. R. T. Brandreth, *An American Plan for Unity.* CDCP Pamphlet No. 10. n.d.

—— *Dr Lee of Lambeth.* 1951.

Thomas Brett, *The Divine Right of Episcopacy, and the Necessity of an Episcopal Commission for Preaching God's Word, and for the valid Ministration of the Christian Sacraments, Proved from the Scriptures, and the Doctrine and Practice of the Primitive Church.* 1718.

John Bridges, *A Defence of the government established in the Church of England for Ecclesiastical matters.* 1587.

*A Brieff discours off the troubles begonne at Franckford in Germany Anno Domini 1554.* 1846 edn.

F. E. Brightman, *What Objections have been made to English Orders?*, CHS VI. 1896.

V. J. K. Brook, *A Life of Archbishop Parker.* 1962.

P. Brooks, *Thomas Cranmer's Doctrine of the Eucharist.* 1965.

Gerald Broomfield, *Anglican and Free Church Ministries, unification through reciprocal supplementary ordination.* 1944.

Richard Broughton, *The Iudgement of the Apostles, and of those of the first age, in all points of doctrine questioned betweene the Catholikes and Protestants of England as they are set downe in the 39 Articles of their Religion.* Douai 1632.

Arthur J. Brown, *Prayer Book Revision: What will it mean? Questions and Answers about the Composite Book.* n.d.

A. T. Browne, *Concio ad clerum Habita coram Academia Cantabrigiensi Junii 11° Anno 1687, Pro Gradu Baccalaur in S. Theologia, Ubi Vindicatur Vera et Valida Cleri Anglicani, Ineunte Reformatione, Ordinatio.* 1688.

G. F. Browne, *Anglican Orders: A Speech delivered in the large Hall of the Church House on Thursday, October 15, 1896*. CHS XVII. 1896.

Henry Broxap, *A Biography of Thomas Deacon*. 1911.

Martin Bucer, *Scripta Anglicana*. Basle 1577.

C. O. Buchanan, E. L. Mascall, J. I. Packer, and the Bishop of Willesden, *Growing into Union: Proposals for forming a united Church of England*. 1970.

Gilbert Burnet, *A Vindication of the Ordinations of the Church of England*. 1677.

—— *An Exposition of the Thirty-Nine Articles of the Church of England*. 1699.

—— *History of My Own Time*. 2 vols. 1724, 1734.

—— *History of the Reformation of the Church of England*. 2 vols. 1841.

B. P. Burnett, *What they Didn't Say*. CDCP Leaflet No. 12. n.d.

E. Burton, ed., *A Short Instruction into Christian Religion being a Catechism set forth by Archbishop Cranmer in MDXLVIII together with the same in Latin translated from the German by Justus Jonas in MDXXXIX*. 1829.

Edward Cardwell, *Documentary Annals of the Reformed Church of England*. 2 vols. 1839.

—— *Synodalia*. 2 vols. 1842.

—— *A History of Conferences and other proceedings connected with the revision of the Book of Common Prayer*. 3rd edn, 1849.

*The Second Replie of Thomas Cartwright agaynst Maister Doctor Whitgiftes second answer touching the Churche Discipline*. 1575.

Anthony Champney, *A Treatise of the vocation of bishops and other ecclesiasticall ministers*. Douai 1616.

John Chapman, *Bishop Gore and the Catholic Claims*. 1905.

Felix L. Cirlot, *Apostolic Succession and Anglicanism: a Defense of Anglican Orders and Catholicity*. Lexington 1946.

Francis Clark, *Anglican Orders and Defect of Intention*. 1956.

C. S. Cobb, ed., *The Rationale of Ceremonial 1540–1543*. ACC XVIII. 1910.

Patrick Collinson, *The Elizabethan Puritan Movement*. 1967.

Thomas Comber, *A discourse upon the Form and Manner of Making, Ordaining and Consecrating Bishops, Priests and Deacons According to the Order of the Church of England*. 1699.

*Comprehension or Secularization? by a Presbyter of the Province of Canterbury*. 1872.

[John Constable], *Remarks upon F. le Courayer's Book in Defence of the English Ordinations by Clerophilus Alethes*. n.p., n.d.

*The copies of certaine letters which have passed betweene Spaine and England in matter of Religion. Concerning the generall Motives to the Romane obedience. Betweene Master James Wadesworth, a late Pensioner of the Holy Inquisition in Sivill, and W. Bedell a Minister of the Gospell of Jesus Christ in Suffolke*. 1624.

John Cosin, *Works*. 5 vols. LACT, 1843–55.

"Miles Coverdale", *The Exeter Diocesan Synod Reviewed*. 1851.

*The Works of Thomas Cranmer*, ed. John Edmund Cox. 2 vols. PS, 1844, 1846.

[Hugh Paulin de Cressy], *An Epistle Apologetical of S. C. To a Person of Honour Touching his Vindication of Dr Stillingfleet.* 1674.

Zachary Crofton, *A Serious Review of Presbyters Reordination by Bishops.* 1661.

G. J. Cuming, *A History of Anglican Liturgy.* 1969.

Christopher Davenport, *Deus, Natura, Gratia.* Lyon 1634.

—— *An Enchiridion of Faith.* 2nd edn, Douai 1655.

Horton Davies, *The Worship of the English Puritans.* 1948.

C. H. Davis, *Moderate Revision of the Prayer-Book, on the orthodox principles of its preface, advocated and illustrated in a Conciliatory Spirit, to promote the union of sound Protestant–Catholic Churchmen holding no extreme opinions.* 1853.

—— *Liturgical Revision Illustrated and Vindicated on Orthodox Principles.* 1859.

—— *Hints and Suggestions on a Revision of the Liturgy by Philecclesia.* n.d.

Margaret Deanesly and G. G. Willis, *Anglican–Methodist Unity: Some considerations historical and liturgical.* 1968.

*A Defence of the Ordinations and Ministry of the Church of England.* 1688.

Edward Denny, *Anglican Orders and Jurisdiction.* 1893.

—— *The English Church and the Ministry of the Reformed Churches.* CHS LVII. 1900.

Edward Denny and T. A. Lacey, *De Hierarchia Anglicana Dissertatio Apologetica.* 1895.

H. Denzinger, *Enchiridion Symbolorum Definitionum et Declarationum de rebus fidei et morum.* 33rd edn, Barcinone 1965.

Lindsay Dewar, *The New Ordinal: Valid or Invalid?* n.p., n.d.

*Directions propounded and Humbly Presented to the High Court of Parliament, Concerning the Booke of Common Prayer, and Episcopall Government.* 1642.

Gregory Dix, *The Question of Anglican Orders.* 1944; 2nd edn, 1956.

L. Duchesne, *Christian Worship, its origin and evolution.* 1903.

*Encheridion Christianae Institutionis.* Cologne 1537.

D. Erasmus, *Paraphrase upon the newe testamente.* 2 vols. 1548.

E. E. Estcourt, *The Question of Anglican Ordinations Discussed.* 1873.

G. Every, *The High-Church Party 1688–1718.* 1956.

Henry Fern, *Certain Considerations of present Concernment touching this reformed Church of England with a particular Examination of Anthony Champny (Doctor of Sorbon) his exceptions against the Lawful Calling and Ordination of the Protestant Bishops and Pastors of this Church.* 1653.

G[iles] F[irmin], *Presbyterial Ordination Vindicated in a Brief and Sober Discourse concerning Episcopacy.* 1660.

W. K. Firminger, *The Alterations in the Ordinal of 1662: Why were they made?* CHS XXXI. 1898.

G. Fisher, *Covenant and Reconciliation.* 1967.

John C. Fisher, *Liturgical Purity our Rightful Inheritance.* 1857.

Henry Fitzsimon, *Britannomachia Ministrorum in plerisque fidei fundamentis et articulis dissidentium.* Douai 1614.

W. R. Foster, *Bishop and Presbytery. The Church of Scotland 1661–1688*. CHS, 1958.

John Foxe, *Acts and Monuments*. 8 vols. 1841.

W. H. Frere, *The Marian Reaction in its relation to the English Clergy*. CHS XVIII. 1896.

—— *Some Principles of Liturgical Reform*. 1911.

—— *Correspondence on liturgical revision and construction*, ed. R. C. D. Jasper. ACC XXXIX. 1954.

W. H. Frere and C. E. Douglas, ed., *Puritan Manifestoes*. 1907.

William Fulke, *A briefe confutation of a Popish Discourse*. 1581.

—— *Defence of the sincere and true translations of the Holy Scriptures into the English Tongue*, ed. C. H. Hartshorne. PS, 1843.

—— *Answers to Stapleton, Martiall, and Sanders*, ed. Richard Gibbings. PS, 1848.

*A full and plaine declaration of Ecclesiasticall Discipline owt off the word off God*. 1574.

S. R. Gardiner, *The Constitutional Documents of the Puritan Revolution 1628–1660*. 1889.

T. S. Garrett, *Worship in the Church of South India*. 2nd edn, 1965.

T. S. Garrett and R. M. C. Jeffery, *Unity in Nigeria*. 1965.

Pietro Gasparri, *De la Valeur des Ordinations Anglicanes*. Paris 1895. Reprinted in *RAR* I, pp. 481–93, 529–57.

John Gauden, *Considerations touching the Liturgy of the Church of England*. 1661.

Philip Gell, *The Difficulties of an Honest and Conscientious Use of the Book of Common Prayer considered as a loud and reasonable call for the only remedy, Revision*. 1860.

James Gordon, *History of Scots Affairs*. 3 vols. 1841.

Charles Gore, *The Ministry of the Christian Church*. 1889.

—— *Roman Catholic Claims*. 1889; 6th edn, 1897; 11th edn, 1920.

Charles Gore and Others, *The Proposed Scheme of Union in South India, An Opinion*, 1929.

G. C. Gorham, *Gleanings of a few Scattered Ears*. 1857.

C. Green, *A Letter to C. N. Wodehouse*. 1843.

Arthur W. Haddan, *Apostolical Succession in the Church of England*. 1869.

Viscount Halifax, *Leo XIII and Anglican Orders*. 1912.

H. E. Hall, *Anglican Orders and the Papal Bull*. 1896.

—— *The Shadow of Peter*. 1914.

Joseph Hall, *Works*. 10 vols. 1808.

Oscar Hardman, *A Prayer-Book for 1949*. 1946.

Jean Hardouin, *La Dissertation du P. Le Courayer, Sur la Succession des évêques Anglois, et sur la validité de leurs ordinations, réfutée*. 2 vols. Paris 1725.

—— *La défense des Ordinations Anglicanes refutée*. 2 vols. Paris 1727.

A. C. Headlam, *The Doctrine of the Church and Christian Reunion*. 1920.

A. G. Hebert, *Unity in the truth: an examination of the "Outline of a reunion scheme for the Church of England and the Evangelical Free Churches in England"*. n.d.

H. Hemmer, *Fernand Portal (1855–1926), Apostle of Unity*. 1961.

Thomas Heskyns, *The Parliament of Chryste*. Antwerp 1566.

Lewes Hewes, *Certaine Grievances*. 1641.

Peter Heylyn, *Aerius Redivivus, or The History of the Presbyterians*. 1670.

Michael Hollis, *The Significance of South India*. 1966.

Christopher Holywood, *De Investiganda vera ac visibili Christi ecclesia*. Antwerp 1604.

Richard Hooker, *Of the Laws of Ecclesiastical Polity*. 1597.

*Early Writings of John Hooper*, ed. Samuel Carr. PS, 1843.

C. Hopf, *Martin Bucer and the English Reformation*. 1946.

C. D. Horsley, *Some Problems connected with the proposed Scheme of Church Union in South India*. 1942.

John Jay Hughes, *Absolutely Null and Utterly Void*. 1968.

—— *Stewards of the Lord*. 1970.

J. Hull and W. W. Hull, *Observations on a Petition for the Revision of the Liturgy*. 1840.

W. W. Hull, *An Enquiry concerning the Means and Expedience of proposing and Making any changes in the Canons, Articles, or Liturgy, or in any of the Laws affecting the Interests of the Church of England*. 1828.

John Humfrey, *The Question of Reordination, whether, and how, a Minister Ordained by the Presbytery, may take Ordination also by the Bishop?* 1661.

—— *A second discourse about reordination*. 1662.

Arthur Wollaston Hutton, *The Anglican Ministry*. 1879.

Thomas Hutton, *The Second and Last Part of Reasons for Refusall of Subscription to the Booke of Common Prayer ... With an Answere to both at severall times returned them in publike conference, and in divers Sermons upon occasion preached in the Cathedral Church of Exeter*. 1606.

Edward Hyde, *State Papers collected by Edward, Earl of Clarendon*. 3 vols. 1767–86.

—— *The Life of Edward, Earl of Clarendon written by himself*. 2 vols. 1857.

J. Jackman, *Success no Rule*. 1718.

—— *Presbyterian Ordination presumptuous*, 1719.

R. C. D. Jasper, *Prayer Book Revision in England 1800–1900*. 1954.

—— *Arthur Cayley Headlam, Life and Letters of a Bishop*. 1960.

H. E. Jeaffreson, *A Letter on the Papal Bull Apostolicae Curae*. 1897.

Claude Jenkins, *Bishop Barlow's Consecration and Archbishop Parker's Register, with some new documents*. 1935. Reprinted from the *Journal of Theological Studies* (October 1922).

*The Works of John Jewel*, ed. John Ayre. 4 vols. PS, 1845–50.

F. Bertram Jones, *I am Church of England*. 1964.

Matthew Kellison, *A Reply to Sotcliffe's Answer to the Survey of the new Religion*. Rheims 1608.

—— *Examen reformationis novae praesertim Calvinianae in quo synagoga et doctrina Calvini, sicut et reliquorum huius temporis novatorum tota fere ex suis principiis refutatur*. Douai 1616.

James Kellock, *Breakthrough for Church Union in North India and Pakistan.* Madras 1965.

E. W. Kemp, *The Anglican–Methodist Unity Scheme.* n.p., n.d.

B. J. Kidd, ed., *Documents Illustrative of the Continental Reformation.* 1911.

John Glen King, *The Rites and Ceremonies of the Greek Church in Russia.* 1772.

Peter King, *An Enquiry into the Constitution, Discipline, Unity and Worship of the Primitive Church.* 1691.

K. E. Kirk, ed., *The Apostolic Ministry.* 1946.

John Knox, *History of the Reformation in Scotland,* ed. W. C. Dickinson. 2 vols. 1949.

T. A. Lacey, *Dissertationis Apologeticae De Hierarchia Anglicana Supplementum.* Rome 1896.

—— *The Interpretation of the English Ordinal.* CHS L. 1898.

—— *A Roman Diary and other documents relating to the papal enquiry into English Ordinations MDCCCXCVI.* 1910.

George G. Lawrence, *A Few Thoughts on the Revision of the Liturgy.* 1859.

A. B. Lawson, *John Wesley and the Christian Ministry.* 1963.

P. F. Le Courayer, *Dissertation sur la Validité des Ordinations des Anglois, et sur la succession des Évêques de l'Église Anglicane.* 2 vols. Brussels 1723.

—— *Défense de la Dissertation sur la validité des Ordinations des Anglois.* 2 vols in 4. Brussels 1726.

—— *Supplément aux deux Ouvrages fait pour la Défense de la validité des ordinations Anglicanes.* Amsterdam 1732.

Frederick George Lee, *The Validity of the Holy Orders of the Church of England.* 1869.

J. Wickham Legg, *Three Letters on the Proposed Revision of the Prayer Book.* 1909.

—— *English Church Life from the Restoration to the Tractarian Movement.* 1914.

—— ed., *Cranmer's Liturgical Projects.* HBS L. 1915.

Graham Leonard, *"to every man's conscience . . ." comments on the report of the Anglican–Methodist Unity Commission.* n.p., n.d.

Michel Le Quien, *Nullité des Ordinations Anglicanes.* 2 vols. Paris 1725.

—— *La Nullité des Ordinations Anglicanes demontrée de nouveau contre la Défense du R. P. Courayer.* Paris 1730.

[John Lewgar], *Erastus Senior, Scholastically Demonstrating this Conclusion, that (admitting their Lambeth Records for true) those called Bishops here in England are no Bishops, either in Order, or Jurisdiction, or so much as Legal.* n.p., 1662.

Richard Littlehales, *A Review of the Liturgy and Articles of the Church of England.* 1813.

Charles Lloyd, ed., *Formularies of Faith put forth by authority during the reign of Henry VIII.* 1825.

J. G. Lockhart, *Charles Lindley, Viscount Halifax.* 2 vols. 1936.

W. Mcmillan, *The Worship of the Scottish Reformed Church, 1550–1638.* 1931.

E. L. Mascall, *Priesthood in South India. A Comparison of the proposed Basis of Union with the reply of the English Archbishops to Pope Leo XIII.* CDCP Pamphlet No. 2, n.d.

—— *The Convocations and South India.* 1955.

A. J. Mason, *The Church of England and Episcopacy.* 1914.

Francis Mason, *Of the Consecration of the Bishops in the Church of England.* 1613.

—— *Vindiciae Ecclesiae Anglicanae.* 1625.

E. C. Messenger, *The Lutheran Origin of the Anglican Ordinal.* 1934.

—— *The Reformation, the Mass and the Priesthood.* 2 vols. 1936–7.

Luke Milbourne, *A Short Defence of the Orders of the Church of England, as by law Established: Against some scatter'd Objections of Mr Webster of Linne, By a Presbyter of the Diocess of Norwich.* 1688.

—— *A Legacy to the Church of England, Vindicating her Orders from the Objections of Papists and Dissenters, Fully explaining the Nature of Schism, and cautioning the Laity against the Delusion of Imposters.* 2 vols. 1722.

R. C. Moberly, *Ministerial Priesthood.* 1897; 2nd edn reprinted with introduction by A. T. Hanson, 1969.

Peter Morgan, ed., *The Anglican–Methodist Conversations, an Evangelical Approach.* 1964.

Jean Morin, *Commentarius de Sacris Ordinibus.* Paris 1655.

F. H. Mountney, "*No Priest, No Church*". 1968.

J. Moyes, F. A. Gasquet, and D. Fleming, *Brevis Conspectus Ritualium Ordinationum in Oriente et Occidente adhibitarum quoad Formam consecratoriam cum manuum impositione conjunctam.* Rome 1896, privately printed.

—— *Ordines Anglicani: Expositio Historica et Theologica, Cura et Studio Commissionis ab Em.o et Rev.o D. D. Herberto Cardinali Vaughan ad hoc institutae.* 1896, privately printed.

J. E. Neale, *Elizabeth I and her Parliaments 1559–1581.* 1953.

S. C. Neill, *Christian Partnership.* 1952.

*A New Form of Common-Prayer, with the Offices thereto belonging, to which are prefixed Reasons for the Proposed Alterations, by a Clergyman of the Church of England.* 1753.

J. E. L. Newbigin, *The Reunion of the Church. A Defence of the South India Scheme.* 1948; 2nd edn, 1960.

William Nicholls, *A Supplement to the Commentary on the Book of Common Prayer.* 1711.

Sylvester Norris, *The Guide of Faith, Or, A Third Part of the Antidote against the Pestiferous writings of all English Sectaries.* n.p. 1621.

*Original Letters relating to the Ecclesiastical Affairs of Scotland, chiefly written by, or addressed to His Majesty King James the Sixth after his accession to the English Throne.* 2 vols. 1851.

James Owen, *A Plea for Scripture Ordination.* 1694.

—— *Tutamen Evangelicum.* 1697.

—— *The Validity of the Dissenting Ministry.* 1716.

F. N. Oxenham, *Some Considerations suggested by the Letter of Leo XIII on Anglican Orders*. 1896.

J. I. Packer, ed., *The Church of England and the Methodist Church*. 1963.

—— *All in each place: Towards reunion in England*. 1965.

E. J. Palmer, *South India: The Meaning of the Scheme for Church Union*. 1944.

[Robert Parsons], *A Brief Discours contayning certayne Reasons why Catholiques refuse to goe to Church*. Douai 1580.

*A Parte of a Register, contayninge sundrie memorable matters, written by divers godly and learned in our time, which stande for and desire the reformation of our Churche, in discipline and ceremonies, according to the pure worde of God, and the lawe of our lande*. 1593.

A. E. Peaston, *The Prayer Book Reform Movement in the Eighteenth Century*. 1940.

—— *The Prayer Book Revisions of the Victorian Evangelicals*. Dublin 1963.

—— *The Prayer Book Tradition in the Free Churches*. 1964.

Albert Peel, ed., *The Seconde Parte of a Register*. 2 vols. 1915.

James Peirce, *Presbyterian Ordination prov'd regular*. 1716.

—— *A Defence of the Dissenting Ministry and Presbyterian Ordination*. 1717.

*The Works of James Pilkington*, ed. James Scholefield. PS, 1842.

F. Portal, *Les Ordinations Anglicanes*, by "F. Dalbus". Paris and Lyon 1894.

*A Prayer-Book Revised, being the Services of the Book of Common Prayer, with Sundry Alterations and Additions offered to the Reader*. 1913.

J. R. Pretyman, *Thoughts on the Revision of the Prayer-Book, and of the Terms of Clerical Conformity*. 1855.

Humphrey Prideaux, *The Validity of the Orders of the Church of England*. 1688.

J. H. Primus, *The Vestments Controversy*. Kampen 1960.

F. Procter and W. H. Frere, *A New History of the Book of Common Prayer*. 1901.

W. Prynne, *Hidden Workes of Darkness brought to publicke Life, or a necessary Introduction to the History of the Archbishop of Canterburies Traill*. 1645.

F. W. Puller, *The Bull Apostolicae Curae and the Edwardine Ordinal*. CHS XVI. 1896.

*Queries Recommended to the Consideration of the Public with regard to the Thirty-Nine Articles*. 1772.

O. C. Quick, *The Christian Sacraments*. 1927.

Wilfrid Raynal, *The Ordinal of King Edward VI*. 1871.

*Reasons shewing the Necessity of Reformation of the Public Doctrine, Worship, Rites and Ceremonies, Church Government and Discipline, by Divers Ministers of sundry Counties*. 2nd edn, 1660.

Charles Parsons Reichel, *Shall we alter the Ordinal? A Paper originally submitted to the Revision Committee of the Church of Ireland*. Dublin 1872.

C. C. Richardson, *The Sacrament of Reunion*. New York 1940.

*The Works of Nicholas Ridley*, ed. Henry Christmas. PS, 1841.

Luke Rivington, *Tekel, or the Anglican Archbishops arraigned at the bar of logic and convicted of 75 flaws*. 1897.

Hastings Robinson, ed., *Original Letters relative to the English Reformation.* 2 vols. PS, 1846–7.

Gordon Rupp, *Consideration Reconsidered.* 1964.

John Rushworth, *Historical Collections.* 4 vols in 7. 1659–1701.

Nicholas Sanders, *De origine ac progressu schismatis Anglicani.* Ingolstadt 1586.

E. G. Sandford, ed., *Memoirs of Archbishop Temple by Seven Friends.* 2 vols. 1906.

William A. Shaw, *A History of the English Church during the Civil Wars and under the Commonwealth 1640–1660.* 2 vols. 1900.

Massey Hamilton Shepherd, Jr, *The Oxford American Prayer Book Commentary.* New York 1950.

F. J. Shirley, *Elizabeth's First Archbishop.* 1948.

Richard Travers Smith, *We ought not to alter the Ordinal.* Dublin 1872.

C. H. Smyth, *Cranmer and the Reformation under Edward VI.* 1926.

Thomas Sparke, *A Brotherly Perswasion to Unitie and Uniformitie in Iudgment and Practise touching the received and present Ecclesiastical government, and the authorised rites and ceremonies of the Church of England.* 1607.

John Spottiswoode, *History of the Church of Scotland.* 3 vols. 1851.

Vernon Staley, *Are our Clergy rightly Ordained?* 1897.

Thomas Stapleton, *A Fortresse of the Faith first planted amonge us englishmen, and continued hitherto in the universall Church of Christ.* Antwerp 1565.

—— *A Counterblast to M. Hornes vayne blaste against M. Fakenham.* Louvain 1567.

Edward Stillingfleet, *Irenicum. A weaponsalve for the Churches Wounds.* 1661.

John Strype, *Memorials of Thomas Cranmer.* 2 vols. 1812.

—— *The History of the Life and Acts of Edmund Grindal.* 1821.

—— *The Life and Acts of John Whitgift.* 3 vols. 1822.

—— *Annals of the Reformation.* 4 vols in 7. 1824.

T. D. Sully, *A United Ministry for a United Church.* Calcutta 1967.

Bengt Sundkler, *Church of South India: The Movement towards Union 1900–1947.* 1954.

*A Survey of the Booke of Common Prayer.* 1606.

Matthew Sutcliffe, *A Treatise of Ecclesiasticall Discipline.* 1591.

H. B. Swete, *On the Bull Apostolicae Curae. A Lecture delivered at the Divinity School, Cambridge, on Friday, November 6, 1896.* 1896.

Matthew Sylvester, *Reliquiae Baxterianae.* 1696.

Norman Sykes, *Old Priest and New Presbyter.* 1956.

—— *William Wake, Archbishop of Canterbury 1657–1737.* 2 vols. 1957.

[Peter Talbot], *A Treatise of the Nature of Catholick Faith and Heresie, by N. N.* Rouen 1657.

[——] *The Nullity of the Prelatique Clergy, and Church of England Further discovered in answer to the plaine prevarication, or vaine presumption of D. John Bramhall in his Booke, intituled The Consecration and Succession of Protestant Bishops justified, etc. by N. N.* Antwerp 1659.

John Thomas, *An Answer to James Owen's arguments for Ordination by Presbyters without Bishops.* 1711.

E. W. Thompson, *The Church Catholic and Free.* 1944.

Herbert Thorndike, *Theological Works.* 6 vols in 10. LACT, 1844–56.

*Tracts for the Times.* 6 vols. 1833–41.

*Doctrinal Treatises and Introductions to Different Portions of the Holy Scriptures by William Tyndale*, ed. Henry Walter. PS, 1848.

John Udall, *A Demonstration of the trueth of that Discipline which Christ hath prescribed in his worde for the government of his Church, in all times and places, untill the end of the world.* 1588.

*The Unity of the Faith. An Open Letter to His Grace the Lord Archbishop of Canterbury from the Superiors of certain religious communities.* 1943.

*The Unity of the Faith.* 1967.

W. Prescott Upton, *The Proposed Revision of the Prayer Book.* 1923.

James Ussher, *Works*, ed. C. R. Elrington. 17 vols. Dublin 1864.

Thomas Ward, *The Controversy of Ordination truly stated: As far as it concerns the Church of England by Law Established.* 1719.

E. Wells, *The invalidity of Presbyterian Ordination.* 1707.

William Whiston, *Primitive Christianity Reviv'd.* 5 vols. 1711–12.

J. C. Whitebrook, *The Consecration of Matthew Parker.* 1945.

*The Works of John Whitgift*, ed. John Ayre. 3 vols. PS, 1851–3.

Daniel Williams, *The Succession of Protestant Bishops Asserted; or, the Regularity of the Ordinations of the Church of England Justify'd.* 1721.

J. C. Williams, *A Voice from India.* CDCP Pamphlet No. 3. n.d.

G. G. Willis, *Essays in Early Roman Liturgy.* ACC XLVI. 1964.

C. N. Wodehouse, *A Petition to the House of Lords for Ecclesiastical Improvements, with Explanations.* 1832.

John Wordsworth, *A letter on the Succession of Bishops in the Church of England.* 1892.

## 5. ARTICLES, AND CHAPTERS IN COMPOSITE WORKS

"The Anglican Form of Ordination", *CQR* v (1878), pp. 261–90.

B. Botte, "Holy Orders in the Ordination Prayers", in *The Sacrament of Holy Orders, Some Papers and Discussions concerning Holy Orders at a Session of the Centre de Pastorale Liturgique, 1955* (1962), pp. 5–29.

A. Boudinhon, "Ordinations Schismatiques Coptes et Ordinations Anglicanes", *Canoniste Contemporain* XVIII (1895), pp. 213–25, 263–81.

—— "De la validité des Ordinations Anglicanes", ibid. XVIII, pp. 423–34, 531–70, 641–66.

—— "Nouvelles Observations sur la Question des Ordres Anglicans", *RAR* II, pp. 625–32, 673–82, 770–91.

F. E. Brightman, "The New Prayer Book Examined", *CQR* CIV (1927), pp. 219–52.

Jeremiah Crowe, "Anglican Orders and the Doctrine of Intention", *Irish Ecclesiastical Record* XVI (1895), pp. 7–17, reprinted in French in *RAR* I, pp. 783–91.

— "The Papal Bull on Anglican Orders", ibid. XVII (1896), pp. 961–71.

L. N. Crumb, "Presbyteral Ordination and the See of Rome", *CQR* CLXIV (1963), pp. 19–31.

J. G. Davis, "Deacons, Deaconesses, and the Minor Orders", *Journal of Ecclesiastical History* XIV (1963), pp. 7–15.

Gordon Donaldson, "Scottish Ordinations in the Restoration Period", *Scottish Historical Review* XXXIII (1954), pp. 169–75.

L. Duchesne, Review of Portal, *Les Ordinations Anglicanes*, in *Bulletin Critique* V (1894), p. 262.

C. W. Dugmore, "The First Ten Years, 1549–59", in *The English Prayer Book, 1549–1662* (1963), pp. 6–30.

W. K. Firminger, "The Ordinal", in *Liturgy and Worship*, ed. W. K. Lowther Clarke and Charles Harris (1932), pp. 626–82.

W. H. Frere, "Early Forms of Ordination", in *Essays on the Early History of the Church and the Ministry*, ed. H. B. Swete (1918), pp. 263–312.

S. R. Gardiner, "A Scheme of Toleration propounded at Uxbridge in 1645", *English Historical Review* II (1887), pp. 340–2.

T. S. Garrett, "The Ordinal of the Church of South India", *Scottish Journal of Theology* XII (1959), pp. 400–13.

— "Products of Nigeria's Liturgy Committee", *Studia Liturgica* V (1966), p. 183.

S. Harent, "La forme sacramentelle dans les ordinations Anglicanes", *Études Religieuses, Philosophiques, Historiques et Litteraires* LXVIII (1896), pp. 177–204.

John Jay Hughes, "Ministerial Intention in the Administration of the Sacraments", *Clergy Review* LI (1966), pp. 763–76.

B. J. Kidd, "Memorandum on Some Points recently raised by the South India Scheme", *Theology* XXXI (1935), pp. 72–9.

T. A. Lacey, "L'imposition des Mains dans la Consecration des Évêques", *RAR* I, pp. 193–210.

E. L. Mascall, "The Hunting of the Hobbit", *The Month* XV (1956), pp. 87–94.

— "Intention and Form in Anglican Orders", *CQR* CLVIII (1957), pp. 4–20.

— "Unity and Unification: A Constructive Proposal", *Theology* LXV (1962), pp. 12–15.

— "The Anglican–Methodist Scheme (2), reasons for rejection", *C.R.* (Quarterly Review of the Community of the Resurrection), No. 263 (Christmas 1968), pp. 22–6.

E. C. Messenger, Review of Dix, *The Question of Anglican Orders*, in *Dublin Review* CCXVII (1945), pp. 93–7.

E. Garth Moore, "No. The Scheme for Anglican–Methodist Reunion", *Theology* LXXI (1968), pp. 482–92.

"More about Anglican Orders", *Herder Correspondence* v (1968), pp. 122–3.

J. Moyes, "The Bull *Apostolicae Curae*", 19 articles in *The Tablet*, February–July 1897.

F. W. Puller, "Les Ordinations Anglicanes et le Sacrifice de la Messe", *RAR* I, pp. 395–414, 433–51, 494–507.

E. C. Ratcliff, "The Ordinal of the Church of South India", *Theology* LXIII (1960), pp. 7–15.

[Cardinal Segna], "Les Ordinations Anglicanes à propos d'une brochure", *RAR* I, pp. 577–92.

Duncan Shaw, "The Inauguration of Ministers in Scotland, 1560–1620", *Records of the Scottish Church History Society* XVI (1966), pp. 35–62.

Sydney F. Smith, "M. Dalbus on Anglican Orders", *The Month* LXXXII (1894), pp. 184–204, 380–401, 543–70.

—— "The Condemnation of Anglican Orders", ibid. LXXXVIII (1896), pp. 305–29.

—— "The Papal Bull", *Contemporary Review* LXXI (1897), pp. 30–40.

Anthony A. Stephenson, "Anglican Orders", *The Month* XIV (1955), pp. 30–7, 78–86, 152–9.

—— "Oceania and Identifiability", ibid. XIV, pp. 354–64.

—— "In full cry", ibid. XV (1956), pp. 94–104.

—— "*Anglican Orders*", *The Old Palace*, No. 22 (1961), p. 31.

T. D. Sully, "Uniting the Ministries", *CQR* CLXII (1961), pp. 210–23.

Roger Thomas, "Comprehension and Indulgence", in *From Uniformity to Unity 1662–1962*, ed. Geoffrey F. Nuttall and Owen Chadwick (1962), pp. 189–253.

F. Tournebize, "L'Église Anglicane a-t-elle réellement le sacerdoce?", *Études Religieuses, Philosophiques, Historiques et Litteraires* LXIV (1895), pp. 400–23, 574–605.

## 6. NEWSPAPERS

*Church Times.*
*The Tablet.*
*The Times.*

# Index

THE ALCUIN CLUB—of which Dr Walter Howard Frere was for many years the President—exists for the object of promoting liturgical studies in general, and in particular a knowledge of the history and use of the Book of Common Prayer. Since its foundation in 1897 it has published over one hundred and twenty books and pamphlets. The annual subscription is £2 and members of the Club are entitled to the publications of the current year *gratis*. Subscriptions, applications for membership and for the list of publications, should be sent to the Assistant Secretary.

*President*
The Right Reverend H. E. Ashdown, D.D., Bishop of Newcastle.

*Committee*
The Venerable G. B. Timms, M.A. (Chairman)
St Andrew's Vicarage, St Andrew Street, London EC4A 3AB
The Reverend Canon R. C. D. Jasper, D.D. (Editorial Secretary)
1 Little Cloister, Westminster Abbey, London SW1.
The Reverend J. T. A. Gunstone, M.A. (Honorary Secretary)
The Reverend Canon G. J. Cuming, D.D.
The Reverend Canon J. D. C. Fisher, M.A., B.D.
The Reverend Canon P. C. Moore, D.PHIL.
The Reverend C. E. Pocknee, A.K.C., D.TH., F.S.A.
The Reverend H. B. Porter, PH.D.

*Assistant Secretary and Treasurer*
c/o St Andrew's Vicarage, St Andrew Street, London EC4A 3AB
(01-353 3544).